Freud/Tiffany

With over 90 archival photographs and nine original, wide-ranging essays, *Freud/Tiffany* brings to life the fascinating intersection of psychoanalysis and education. Out of the cultural and political ferment of interwar Vienna emerged the Hietzing School, founded in the 1920s by Anna Freud, the youngest daughter of Sigmund Freud, and Dorothy Tiffany Burlingham, the youngest daughter of the great American artist Louis Comfort Tiffany.

Anna Freud's story unfolds over three decades from her adolescence through the 1940s, as she and Dorothy Tiffany Burlingham leverage their hands-on research with children into educational innovations at the Hietzing School and beyond. The Viennese psychoanalysts of the 1920s demonstrated a unique sensitivity to marginalised populations and to the impact of war, its threats and its aftermath, especially on the lives of children. The book features never-before-seen historical photographs, including four of Sigmund Freud, as well as unpublished archival material and original paintings. Drawings, manuscripts and memoirs make vivid the founders' vision of the Hietzing School's origins, its day-to-day experience and its enduring significance for our understanding of education and the developing mind.

Marking the first publication of many of the historic materials originally showcased in 2017 at a major Freud Museum London exhibition, the international scholarship behind *Freud/Tiffany* demonstrates that the Hietzing School remains the seedbed for a surprising range of modern theory and practice in child and adolescent mental health, from Erik Erikson's lifespan model of 'identity' to the legal concept of 'the best interests of the child.' The Freud and Tiffany legacies are now brought together as never before in this lively book, and the Hietzing School is restored to its rightful place in the history of so many ideas with which we are still working today. The book is essential for any reader interested in the cultural legacy of interwar Vienna.

Elizabeth Ann Danto is emeritus professor at Hunter College – City University of New York, and an independent curator who writes and lectures internationally on the history of psychoanalysis as a system of thought and a marker of urban culture. She is the author of *Historical Research* (Oxford University Press, 2008) and her book *Freud's Free Clinics – Psychoanalysis and Social Justice, 1918–1938* (Columbia University Press, 2005) received the Gradiva Book Award and the Goethe Prize.

Alexandra Steiner-Strauss is a historian of Viennese art and culture; former curator, Theatermuseum Vienna and lecturer at the Kunsthistorisches Museum; co-author of *Gustav Klimt und Wien* (2012), *Trägt die Sprache schon Gesang in sich. Richard Strauss und die Oper* (2014), and *Anna Freud in Wien* (2016).

The History of Psychoanalysis Series
Professor Brett Kahr and Professor Peter L. Rudnytsky (Series editors)

Other titles in the series:

Freud/Tiffany
Anna Freud, Dorothy Tiffany Burlingham and the 'Best Possible School'
Elizabeth Ann Danto, editor
Alexandra Steiner-Strauss, research editor

Freud at Work
On the History of Psychoanalytic Theory and Practice, with an Analysis of Freud's Patient Record Books
Ulrike May

What is this Professor Freud Like? A Diary of an Analysis with Historical Comments
Edited by Anna Koellreuter

Corresponding Lives
Mabel Dodge Luhan, A. A. Brill, and the Psychoanalytic Adventure in America
Patricia R. Everett

A Forgotten Freudian
The Passion of Karl Stern
Daniel Burston

The Skin-Ego
A New Translation by Naomi Segal
Didier Anzieu

For further information about this series please visit https://www.routledge.com/The-History-of-Psychoanalysis-Series/book-series/KARNHIPSY

Freud/Tiffany

Anna Freud, Dorothy Tiffany Burlingham and the 'Best Possible School' 1920s Vienna and beyond

An illustrated book of memoir and history

Edited by Elizabeth Ann Danto with Research Editor Alexandra Steiner-Strauss

Routledge
Taylor & Francis Group
LONDON AND NEW YORK

First published 2019
by Routledge
2 Park Square, Milton Park, Abingdon, Oxon OX14 4RN

and by Routledge
711 Third Avenue, New York, NY 10017

Routledge is an imprint of the Taylor & Francis Group, an informa business

British Library Cataloguing-in-Publication Data
A catalogue record for this book is available from the British Library

Library of Congress Cataloguing-in-Publication Data
Names: Danto, Elizabeth Ann, editor. | Steiner-Strauss, Alexandra, editor.
Title: Freud/Tiffany: Anna Freud, Dorothy Tiffany Burlingham and the "best possible school" / edited by Elizabeth Ann Danto with research editor Alexandra Steiner-Strauss.
Description: New York: Routledge, 2018.
Identifiers: LCCN 2018023504 (print) | LCCN 2018047892 (ebook) | ISBN 9780429439889 (Master eBook) | ISBN 9781138342026 (hardback) | ISBN 9781138342088 (pbk.) | ISBN 9780429439889 (ebk)
Subjects: LCSH: Hietzing School—History. | Freud, Anna, 1895–1982. | Burlingham, Dorothy T. | Private schools—Austria—Vienna—History—20th century. | Vienna (Austria)—Social conditions—20th century. | Psychoanalysis—Austria—Vienna—History—20th century.
Classification: LCC LC53.A9 (ebook) | LCC LC53.A9 F74 2018 (print) | DDC 371.0209436/13—dc23
LC record available at https://lccn.loc.gov/2018023504

ISBN: 978-1-138-34202-6 (hbk)
ISBN: 978-1-138-34208-8 (pbk)
ISBN: 978-0-429-43988-9 (ebk)

Typeset in Times New Roman
by codeMantra

Contents

Acknowledgments

For their financial and intellectual support, without which this collection would not have been possible, we gratefully acknowledge the generous partnership of the following individuals and organisations:

The Anna Freud Foundation; the Zukunftsfonds der Republik Österreich; the Botstiber Institute for Austrian-American Studies; Carol Seigel (director), Karolina Urbaniak, Sophie Leighton, Bryony Davies, and the curators, specialists and staff at the Freud Museum London; Monika Pessler (director), Simone Faxa, Daniela Finzi and the staff at the Sigmund Freud Museum Vienna; the Anna Freud National Centre for Children and Families (London); the archivists and staff of the Manuscript Reading Room and of the Prints and Photographs Division at the US Library of Congress, Washington DC; the archives of the British Institute of Psychoanalysis; Ralph Engelman and Thomas Engelman; the Collection of Michael J. Burlingham (New York); the Collection of Daniel Benveniste (Bellevue, WA); the Estate of August Aichhorn (Vienna); Jackie Jones and the Ernest Jones Rehabilitation Fund collection; Michael Simonson, Leo Baeck Institute (New York); the Museum of the City of New York; Anna Meadmore, Royal Ballet School (London); Olga Umansky, Hanns Sachs Library and Archives, Boston Psychoanalytic Society and Institute; Kathleen Schmeling and Elizabeth Clemens, Walter P. Reuther Library, Archives of Labor and Urban Affairs, Wayne State University; Miriam Cady and the Philadelphia Museum of Art; Nick Midgley, Anna Freud National Centre for Children and Families (London); Victor Ross (London); and Marisa Shaari, Oskar Diethelm Library, DeWitt Wallace Institute for the History of Psychiatry, Weill Cornell Medical College (New York).

For their kind permission to reproduce images and to quote previously published or unpublished materials in their collections, we thank:

The Freud Museum London; the Sigmund Freud Museum Vienna; the Anna Freud National Centre for Children and Families; the archives of the British Institute of Psychoanalysis; Ralph Engelman and Thomas Engelman; Michael J. Burlingham; Daniel Benveniste; Thomas Aichhorn; Jackie Jones; Ruth Bernstein Hoch; the Royal Ballet School, London; the

Hanns Sachs Library and Archives and the Boston Psychoanalytic Society and Institute; the Museum of the City of New York; the Leo Baeck Institute; the Philadelphia Museum of Art; the Metropolitan Museum of Art, New York; the Siegfried Altmann Papers, Leo Baeck Institute, New York; the Oskar Diethelm Library, DeWitt Wallace Institute for the History of Psychiatry, Weill Cornell Medical College; the Association for Child Psychoanalysis and Taylor & Francis Ltd on behalf of the Association for Child Psychoanalysis.

All works of art are reproduced with the kind permission of the owners. Every attempt has been made to trace the photographers, artists and the copyright holders of works reproduced, and we regret any unwitting infringement.

The Freud/Tiffany authors

Thomas Aichhorn (Vienna) is a psychoanalyst; author and lecturer specializing in the "general seduction theory" of Jean Laplanche, the history of psychoanalysis, the psychoanalysis of adolescence and the life and work of August Aichhorn; editor of *The letters of Anna Freud – August Aichhorn, 1921–1949* (Brandes & Apsel 2012).

Michael John Burlingham (New York) is a writer, editor, and photographer based in New York City. He is the copy chief of *Barron's* financial newsweekly and the author of *The Last Tiffany: A Biography of Dorothy Tiffany Burlingham* (Atheneum, 1989).

Elizabeth Ann Danto (New York and Vienna) is professor emeritus of social welfare, Hunter College/City University of New York; writer in history of psychoanalysis, urban public welfare and labor studies; author of *Historical Research* (Oxford University Press 2009); and recipient of the Gradiva Award (USA) and the Goethe Prize (Canada) for *Freud's Free Clinics – Psychoanalysis & Social Justice, 1918–1938* (Columbia University Press 2005).

Florian Houssier (Paris) is a psychoanalyst; professor of clinical psychology and psychopathology at the Sorbonne, Paris 13; president of the Collège International de L'adolescence (CILA); author of *Anna Freud et son école, créativité et controversies* (Campagne Première 2010) and *Freud Adolescent* (Campagne Première 2018); co-author of *Éduquer l'adolescent? Pour une pédagogie psychanalytique* (éditions Champ social, 2007).

Hélène Keable (New York) is an adult, adolescent and child psychoanalyst; faculty – Training and Supervising Analyst in New York Psychoanalytic Society and Institute; senior psychiatrist at Columbia University Irving Medical Center Student Health Service Mental Health and Columbia University Counselling and Psychological Services; and co-author of *Ethical Practice in Child and Adolescent Analysis and Psychotherapy: Protecting Safety in a Therapeutic Environment* (Jason Aronson, 2011).

Michael Molnar (London) is a historian of photography, researcher and former director of the Freud Museum London. His books include *The Diary of Sigmund Freud, 1929–1939: A Record of the Final Decade* (Scribner 1992) and *Looking Through Freud's Photos* (Karnac Books, 2015).

Inge-Martine Pretorius (London) is a psychotherapist, clinical leader of the Parent-Toddler Service at the Anna Freud Centre and Curator of the Archives; lecturer at University College London; co-editor with Marie Zaphiriou Woods, of *Parents and toddlers in groups: a psychoanalytic developmental approach.* (Routledge 2011).

Carol Seigel (London) is the Director of the Freud Museum.

Alexandra Steiner-Strauss (Vienna) is a historian of Viennese art and culture; former curator, Theater Museum Vienna; author of *Trägt die Sprache schon Gesang in sich. Richard Strauss und die Oper* (2014), co-author of *Gustav Klimt und Wien* (2012) and *Anna Freud in Wien* (2016).

Nellie L. Thompson (New York) is a psychoanalyst, historian and curator of Archives and Special Collections at the New York Psychoanalytic Society and Institute, a member of the board of the Sigmund Freud Archives, editor of *Play, Gender, Therapy: Selected Papers of Eleanor Galenson* (Karnac Books, 2015), and co-editor with Peter Loewenberg of *100 Years of the IPA: The Centenary History of the International Psychoanalytical Association, 1910–2010* (Karnac Books, 2011).

Paul Werner (New York and Vienna) is an art historian and cultural critic, author of *Museum Inc. – Inside the Global Artworld* (2005), editor of *WOID. An online journal of Visual Language* and the *Red Vienna Reader.*

Foreword

The collection of wide ranging, probing essays in this book explores the fascinating worlds of psychoanalysis and education, using as their historical starting point the Hietzing School founded by Anna Freud and Dorothy Tiffany Burlingham in the intense cultural and political ferment of interwar Vienna.

The germination of this work was the research and scholarship behind the innovative exhibition *The Best Possible School: Anna Freud, Dorothy Tiffany Burlingham and the Hietzing School in 1920s Vienna*, held at the Freud Museum London in Spring 2017.

The Freud Museum London at 20 Maresfield Gardens was the final home of both Sigmund Freud, the founder of psychoanalysis, and Sigmund Freud's daughter Anna, pioneer of child analysis. Anna lived at Maresfield Gardens for over forty years until her death in 1982. This was also the home of Dorothy Tiffany Burlingham, and the two women pursued their groundbreaking work with children throughout their lives.

At the wish of Anna Freud, 20 Maresfield Gardens opened as a museum after her death. The Museum has become both a popular London historic house and a renowned international center for exhibitions, research, education and innovative public programs. The Museum's aim is to preserve the legacy of Sigmund and Anna Freud, and to be a center for learning and discussion on psychoanalysis today.

Curated by Elizabeth Ann Danto, *The Best Possible School* exemplified that mission. Imaginatively designed, the exhibition featured historical photographs and vintage memorabilia from private collections, as well as key archival material from the Museum's own holdings. Four remarkable photographs of Sigmund Freud were on view for the first time, along with numerous period photographs, manuscripts, paintings and objects. Together these told the story of Anna Freud and Dorothy Tiffany Burlingham, their vision of the Hietzing School, the day-to-day experience of its teachers and pupils and its significance for modern education and child psychology.

The exhibition was inaugurated with an international symposium, held over a May weekend in 2017. This brought together the contributors to this book from around the world in a stimulating weekend of presentations and dialogue which united historical and psychoanalytic insights with personal memoir. With its innovative research and scholarship, the combined exhibit and symposium advanced the Museum's goal of broadening knowledge and awareness of the history of psychoanalysis.

With its lively writing and ample illustrations, this benchmark volume expands this knowledge far beyond the initial academic discourse. The essays range from Vienna to London to the United States, and all examine pioneering work done in the field of education, child psychology and psychoanalysis, as well as the more poignant personal stories of the men, women and children involved. Close analysis of never-before-seen photographs and texts, and of the psychoanalytic and pedagogical pioneers, offers new insights to the 21st-century viewer and reader.

This project of researching the Hietzing School, culminating in the work contained in this book, has been both a product of rigorous research and a labor of love by Professor Elizabeth Ann Danto. She, Alexandra Steiner-Strauss and their fellow authors are to be congratulated for this sparkling, scholarly and thought-provoking series of contributions to the story of education and child analysis in 1920s Vienna and beyond.

Carol Seigel
Director, Freud Museum London

April 2018

Series Editor's Foreword

Since 2011, I have had the privilege of serving as a Trustee of the Freud Museum London in Swiss Cottage, and in this capacity, I have had many opportunities to speak to some of the tens of thousands of visitors who make a pilgrimage to this marvellous historical building every year.

When tourists arrive at the museum, some of them, quite dazed by the special atmosphere, will often brim with excitement, "Oh, my God, what a joy to be in Freud's house" or "Freud's home is absolutely amazing." And whenever they do deploy the phrase "Freud's house," they mean, of course, the home of *Sigmund* Freud. No one ever refers to the Freud Museum in the first instance as the home of *Anna* Freud, even though she lived on Maresfield Gardens for more than forty-three years, whereas her father inhabited the home for less than twelve months. Indeed, every single poster advertising the Freud Museum London boasts an image of the aged father of psychoanalysis, with balding pate and greying beard. Our publicity and design teams have never dared to foreground Freud's daughter on the London Underground, as few people, apart from mental health clinicians and historians, would recognise the late Miss Freud.

Although numerous adept historians have written very accomplished, full-length biographies of Anna Freud (e.g., Peters, 1979; Dyer, 1983; Young-Bruehl, 1988), most people still regard this remarkable woman, first, as the daughter of Sigmund Freud, and second, as one of the founders of child psychoanalysis, along with Hermine von Hug-Hellmuth and Melanie Klein. While the quietly spoken and highly modest Miss Freud might have endorsed this characterisation, such a summation does not recognise the pioneering project that she undertook with her friends and colleagues in Vienna in the 1920s, long before she became codified as the daughter of Freud and the mother of child analysis.

In 1927, Anna Freud and her much-cherished colleague Dorothy Trimble Tiffany Burlingham, along with Eva Rosenfeld and others, inaugurated a unique school, known as the Hietzinger Schule, located on the Wattmanngasse in Vienna, designed to provide compassionate, psychologically orientated pedagogy to young children. Whereas many educational institutions at this time emphasised rote learning and harsh discipline, this psychoanalytically inspired school offered its pupils a more liberal and more humane experience, which encouraged play and a delight in learning.

Although the Hietzinger Schule project could hardly be regarded as a secret – all of the Viennese psychoanalysts knew about it – this forward-thinking project has, over time, become marginalised, if not completely forgotten, in many narratives about the early history of child psychology and psychoanalysis.

Happily, Professor Elizabeth Ann Danto and Alexandra Steiner-Strauss, two highly erudite historical scholars, have undertaken a great deal of important primary archival research and have reconstructed the work of the Hietzinger Schule, as engineered by Miss Freud and Mrs. Burlingham and their enlightened colleagues. Elizabeth Danto (2005) will be well known to fellow historians of psychoanalysis for her landmark book *Freud's Free Clinics: Psychoanalysis and Social Justice, 1918–1938*, in which she explored the visionary *Ambulatorium* of Vienna and the *Poliklinik* of Berlin, designed to provide psychoanalysis to those who could not afford private fees. Alexandra Steiner-Strauss, an art historian and cultural historian of note, has, in recent years, embarked upon an examination of Anna Freud's life in Vienna (Johler, Sommer, and Steiner, 2016). In a collaboration which, in many ways, has mirrored the creativity of Miss Freud and Mrs. Burlingham, these two researchers have not only worked tirelessly to produce a superb exhibition and conference and catalogue (Danto and Steiner, 2017) about the Hietzinger Schule, co-sponsored by the Freud Museum London, but they have now also edited a superb text full of stellar contributions by some of the world's leading historical experts.

This edited book, richly illustrated with many hitherto unknown photographs (including several of Sigmund Freud himself), represents a significant contribution to the history of psychoanalysis by bringing the Hietzinger Schule back to life. In the chapters that follow, written by distinguished colleagues from Austria, France, the United Kingdom, and the United States of America, readers will enjoy learning about the lives of both Anna Freud and Dorothy Burlingham and their contemporaries, as well as about the details of the day-to-day operation of the school and its legacy. These competent historians not only provide rich descriptions of the life of the school and of the nature of psychoanalytical pedagogy and its legacy, but they also contextualise the work brilliantly within Viennese social and cultural history. The contributors include noted academics and clinical practitioners, and as a special treat, we have the pleasure of essays written by none other than Michael Burlingham, the grandson of Dorothy Burlingham, and also by Thomas Aichhorn, the grandson of August Aichhorn, one of the progenitors of psychoanalytical child and adolescent psychotherapy and also forensic psychotherapy. These family-based chapters provide a touching authenticity to this excellent collection.

In the post-Anschluss years, psychoanalysis in London and New York quickly developed a reputation for its insularity, often confined to the tiny consulting rooms of Hampstead or the Upper East Side. But back in the 1920s, Anna Freud and Dorothy Burlingham took the gems of Freudian psychoanalysis into the community and helped to develop early intervention by exposing young, impressionable children to the fruits of depth psychology, rather than waiting until they became entrenched neurotic adults. In this respect, both Miss Freud and Mrs. Burlingham long anticipated the notion of preventative mental health by reaching young people *prior* to any breakdowns, rather than subsequent to the development of psychological illness and distress.

I congratulate the editors and the contributors of this fine volume. This book not only offers a fuller examination of the early contributions of Anna Freud and, also, Dorothy Burlingham, but also portrays Miss Freud as a woman with her own mind and in her own right and not solely as Freud's daughter or as the mother of five-times-weekly child psychoanalysis. Danto and Steiner-Strauss have reframed Anna Freud as a social innovator and as a person who inspired those practitioners who, quite boldly, left the consulting rooms and took to the streets in creative and enhancing manners. I cannot recommend this volume warmly enough.

Professor Brett Kahr
Series Co-Editor, "History of Psychoanalysis Series"

London, 2019

References

Danto, Elizabeth Ann (2005). *Freud's Free Clinics: Psychoanalysis and Social Justice, 1918–1938*. New York: Columbia University Press.

Danto, Elizabeth Ann, and Steiner, Alexandra (Eds.). (2017). *Freud/Tiffany and the Best Possible School: Anna Freud, Dorothy Tiffany Burlingham and the Hietzing School in 1920s Vienna. Freud Museum London. May 10 through July 17, 2017. Exhibition Catalogue with Added Essays and History*. London: Freud Museum London, and Vienna: ZukunftsFonds der Republik Österreich.

Dyer, Raymond (1983). *Her Father's Daughter: The Work of Anna Freud*. New York: Jason Aronson.

Johler, Birgit; Sommer, Monika, and Steiner, Alexandra (2016). *Anna Freud in Wien: Ein Rundgang zu Orten der Psychoanalyse*. Vienna: Verlag Turia und Kant.

Peters, Uwe Henrik (1979). *Anna Freud: Ein Leben für das Kind*. München: Kindler Verlag.

Young-Bruehl, Elisabeth (1988). *Anna Freud: A Biography*. New York: Summit Books/Simon and Schuster.

Introduction

ERBAUT VON DER GEMEINDE WIEN.../Built by the Community of Vienna

Elizabeth Ann Danto

In 1927, the most dramatic event in Vienna happened in mid-July when brazen paramilitary groups accused of randomly shooting into a crowd of Social Democrats in Schattendorf, a small town near the Hungarian border, were swiftly acquitted by a conservative court. By nightfall, over 600 protesting workers had been killed and wounded by the Viennese police and the Palace of Justice set on fire. Despite the Social Democrats' resistance to the Austrofascist Ignaz Seipel, the Chancellor and his allies in the increasingly strident Christian Social Party of Austria were moving ahead with their extremist agenda.

For our book though, the Austrian "Days of Horror," as the repression of July 1927 has been called, have a different meaning. We have two historical markers for the year. One is the dismantling of the Minister of Education Otto Glöckel's progressive reforms in Vienna's public school system. The other is the opening of the Hietzing School where Anna Freud, the youngest daughter of Sigmund Freud, and Dorothy Tiffany Burlingham, the youngest daughter of the great American artist Louis Comfort Tiffany, created a small wonder in the world of 20th-century education. A seedbed for the new fields of child analysis and psychoanalytic pedagogy, Hietzing succeeded because a synergetic group of Austrian psychoanalysts and American teachers – progressives who respected children's independence of thought – disputed the prevalence of authoritarianism under the guise of traditional education. It was, as Erik Erikson (1980) said, "the best possible school." Five years later, the web of reactionary complicity that brought down Vienna's remarkable post-World War I recovery also closed down the school. Yet the moral, psychological, aesthetic and political associations that are inseparable from psychoanalysis, and all of which found a home in Hietzing, endured. Blending the historical with the personal, and social science with memoir, this book of new essays reflects the Hietzing legacy in all its richness.

Like psychoanalysis itself, we start with Sigmund Freud. Sifting through boxed decades of family memorabilia, Michael Burlingham (2017, p. 42) stumbled on

> a book of negatives I dimly remembered, photographs my father had taken as a teenager in Vienna… Viewing those photographs taken some 80 years ago was thrilling, especially when never-before-seen images of Sigmund and Anna Freud appeared on my computer screen.

The thrill is now ours. The photographs allow us to witness some private moments, to fall asleep in the sunshine with Freud, to smile back at Anna when she comes into view and to wonder if we have ever seen Freud smiling at us as he finally does (Figures I.1–I.4).

With nearly 100 varied and expressive photographs, including these four portraits of Sigmund Freud published here for the first time, the nine essays in "Freud/Tiffany" are, though eclectic, carefully assembled. Together, they paint a closely observed portrait of children and adolescents at school from the late days of Vienna's Social Democratic government, which ended roughly in 1934, to London during World War II. Anchored by the Hietzing School, and ranging from the intellectual fervor of Anna Freud's psychoanalytic circle to the brutality of Dachau where August Aichhorn's son was held, the authors chronicle a series of contrasts that played out in that intimate microcosm of society. The stories are less about open rebellion than about the alternations of pain and hope at the onset of social progress; their protagonists are, for the most part, determined children and adults striving to find the support of community in science, in exile and, ultimately, in the theories and practice of psychoanalysis. In "Bob's Diary, December 1931,"

Figure I.1 Freud napping in the sunshine.

Figure 1.2 Sigmund Freud, Mathilde Hollitscher, Anna Freud.

Figure 1.3 Freud smiling.

Figure 1.4 Freud on a stroll (Semmering).

Michael Burlingham describes and contextualises how Dorothy Burlingham's eldest son pared down a few months of his teenage years as a Hietzing pupil, patient of Anna Freud, and American boy of privilege caught between wit and naivete when faced by surrounding poverty. In "The Hietzing School as the Birthplace of a Psychoanalytic Theory of Adolescence," Florian Houssier revisits Anna Freud's own native talents. She neither hid nor simply endured the analysis by her father, but it set her on a journey to understand children, deeply, and their adolescence from the perspective of new psychoanalytic theory. In another story, "The Child in Mind and Body – the Writing of Anna Freud and Dorothy Burlingham in *The Psychoanalytic Study of the Child*," Dorothy Burlingham and Sigmund Freud share their fascination with blind children's own forms of visuality; the psychoanalysts repeated visits to Vienna's innovative *Israelitisches Blindeninstitut* (Hebrew Institute for Blind Children) confront them with the utter failure of educating blind children as a sort of null variants of sighted children – as though blindness contaminates everything from the body to the parental relationship, so too pathologising their inner lives closes off pathways to education.

With this volume, we focus as much on personal experience as on the work of the Hietzing teachers who led historic changes in the overlapping fields of psychoanalysis and education. Their personalities are striking: the "concise and unhesitating" style of Anna Freud; Dorothy Tiffany Burlingham and the legacy of New York's progressive cultural circles; the restless young German artist Erik Erikson (then Homburger) who taught science; Peter Blos' encounters with modern American education; and the deeply empathic August Aichhorn, who harnessed what Kurt Eissler (1951) called an "uncanny intuition" in the pursuit of therapeutic success with Vienna's *pülchern*. Ultimately, as much of Hietzing's significance can be attributed to the unique historical era of interwar Vienna as to the vision of its teachers. Surrounded by Adolf Loos' re-conceptualised uses of public–private space, plus the work of Maria Montessori, Siegfried Bernfeld, Alfred Adler, Otto Glöckel, Josef Friedjung, Lili Roubiczek-Peller, Eugenie Schwarzwald and Julius Tandler, the Hietzing School advanced the 20th-century's understanding of the whole child. The second generation of psychoanalysts located a new theory of adolescence in their patient-pupils; the nascent field of psychoanalytic pedagogy found its laboratory; and all shared a core belief in the child's capacity to become what Anna Freud (1930, p. 127) called "a free and self-reliant human being." In Vienna of the late 1920s, "you did something for people who didn't have money. Money didn't play such a great role. Nobody was really rich, but they cared more about others," Helen Schur (1995) told me. Schur (then Krauss) was a student at the University of Vienna's Medical School, where Freud taught. "What was it like?" she reminisced.

> It's very hard to describe. Vienna was a very progressive city and a very nice place to live, with a great lot of different cultural interests, painters,

> actors, writers, much interest in sport. We had a very good ice skating team, I think, world champions...And all those municipal buildings.

Seen from a distance on the train, say from Venice to Vienna, the *Gemeindebauten*, the community apartment buildings, still fill in the city's skyline – the spaces between the Prater's ferris wheel and the steeple of St Stephen's create a cityscape that evens out the contrast between the reconstructed Beaux Arts of the Hapsburg bourgeoisie and the flamboyance of the city's Art Deco. "Seventy-eight thousand apartments, at low rent and completely city-owned were built," said Hugo Breitner (1929) who had been Vienna's Housing Commissioner from 1919 to 1932. Over the course of Austria's First Republic, the community buildings were often named after socialist scholars or politicians or simply titled, like a poem. The Kongressbad in the 16th District, Vienna's enormous swimming pool for workers' families, was titled "Schwimm-, Sonnen- und Luftbad" in May 1928 and authored by, of course, *Gemeinde Wien* (the Vienna Community). With education at its core, the community movement swept up Viennese thinkers from Anna Freud to Ludwig Wittgenstein. "Am I doing child psychology?" asked the great philosopher. "I am making a connection between the concept of teaching and the concept of meaning" (Peters, 2012, p. 19).

In Vienna's 13th District, May 1928 saw the Hietzing School complete its full first year of education and validate, as Erik and Joan Erikson put it, "John Dewey's theory that children learn only where their interest is fully engaged and centered." The sixteen-year-old Bob Burlingham photographed this process. Photography invites viewers and readers to partake, intimately, in an artist's own experience of their subjects. In "A School for Trick Cyclists," one of Michael Molnar's most compelling photo essays to date, Bob looks after his peers who are chatting in the schoolyard, just outside Peter Blos' office window. The boy's father is off in America. His mother is as involved with the demands of the school – the Freuds, her relationships and psychoanalysis – as she is with him. "Bob was a very good-looking boy. He was very tall, as far as I could tell, and he also played cello," said his classmate Ruth Bernstein Hoch. Now, almost a 100 years later, both Burlingham and Molnar reveal how the gifted adolescent perceived himself and his friends, the Freud family included, at Hietzing (Figures I.5 and I.6).

Monarchist nostalgia aside (the Hapsburgs, Freud wrote in 1918 (p. 311), "left behind nothing but a pile of crap"), early 20th-century Vienna was the great home of European modernism in architecture, medicine, music and psychoanalysis. After the impressive election of the Social Democrats in 1919, idealistic economists, artists and intellectuals rebuilt the city, believing that socialism was the future. Otto Bauer, the sophisticated leader of the Austrian Social Democratic Party, spoke of the movement as a revolution in human fulfillment. Urban culture, the Social Democrats believed, should encompass the worker's total life, from individual and family life to public

Figure I.5 Bob Burlingham.

policy and the workplace. But post-war Vienna was more than an ideological playground. As the contemporary American economist Charles Gullick reported (p. 535),

> The socialists inherited a practically bankrupt city in May 1919. By July 1, 1921, the municipal finances were 'in the black,' prices charged to patrons of the municipal monopolies were greatly reduced as compared even with pre-war rates, and after the budget was brought into order in 1921 the credit of the city was always excellent.

The redistributive economic policies of Red Vienna's financial decision-makers, Robert Danneberg and Hugo Breitner, took hold, and surplus funds were invariably sent to institutions of social welfare. Vienna's position as a new independent state had served it well. As such, the city was called "Red

Figure I.6 Ruth Bernstein.

Vienna" in contrast to the emerging "Black Vienna" of the Austrofascists who would dominate, ruthlessly, in 1934. Meanwhile, "the absence of slums, the clean streets, the well-tended parks, … new workers' apartments and a number of very interesting schools for children and adults" impressed the young American psychoanalytic candidate named Muriel Gardiner (1983, p. 5). For Anna Freud's Viennese originality, the 1920s was fertile ground and the Hietzing School was on trend. Yet in "Step-by-Step," as Alexandra Steiner-Strauss titles her nimble essay, the author estimates that from the onset of World War I through the 1940s, and even to some extent today, Austrians hold conflicting attitudes toward the parties of the Left and of the Right. Largely illegal until 1938 but ominously present, right-wing political action took many forms from violent anti-Semitism to stringent authoritarianism. At the same time, modernism thrived in Vienna, leaping over cultural boundaries in psychoanalysis, public housing, music, art, everywhere.

With newly released photos from the US Associated Press of the late 1930s and early 1940s, Steiner-Strauss chronicles these stories of progress and regression. She corrects a blind spot in our understanding of Vienna's history and clarifies mechanisms by which both the best and the worst endure (Figures I.7 and I.8).

Figure I.7 The Matteotti-Hof, 1929.

Figure I.8 A Vienna *Gemeindebau*.

Very few works about the historic educational and psychoanalytic nucleus that the Hietzing School represents are available in English. The teachers went on to work out some of our most significant developmental models and theories of modern child and adolescent psychology. Fortunately, Thomas Aichhorn's essay, "August Aichhorn and his Hietzing Friends," draws on his personal expertise as his grandfather's primary archivist to establish how certain qualities of mutual support and self-reliance within this extraordinary group of people – Erik H. Erikson, Peter Blos, August Aichhorn and Kurt Eissler, plus Eva Rosenfeld, Anna Freud and Dorothy Burlingham – sustained them all both before and after World War II. Aichhorn has gathered the stories of their relationships from his grandfather's letters (sent and received), and most of their writing about themselves and each other, about Hietzing and psychoanalytic pedagogy, is built on their testimony. A more vivid portrayal of the psychoanalysts' daily life, pre- and post-exile, is hard to come by (Figure I.9).

In "Anna Freud and The Science of Unexpected Findings," Inge-Martine Pretorius distills a wide range of archives to show that the innovations in theory and practice seen at the Hampstead War Nurseries for London's children displaced during World War II, got their start in Vienna, at the Jackson Nursery in 1936 and the Hietzing school before that. Living precariously under

Figure I.9 August Aichhorn at the Jackson Krippe, 1937.

the Dolfuss and Schuschnigg regimes, and even after Germany's annexation of Austria in March 1938, Anna Freud maintained, perhaps paradoxically, that the Jackson Nursery had given her "the most beautiful year in Vienna, the best that I ever had" (Johler, Sommer & Steiner, 2016, p. 53). Pretorius took on the challenge of explaining this statement without concealing nor disguising Anna Freud's biography, and she locates the justification in Anna Freud's own research methodology: the pleasure came from her striking gift for identifying unobserved developmental patterns within the hundreds of categories used to measure the children's psychological and physical growth.

The story of "Young Dorothy Burlingham," as told by Paul Werner, took place in New York, in a family of the upper bourgeoisie not unlike the one into which she would marry, and out of which she would escape. Essentially driven by an influential culture that exalted young women for everything but their existence, Dorothy (who did not like her father very much) found resistance in psychoanalysis, in Vienna. But this resistance was not confined to the family dynamic of urban elites. The move to Red Vienna signified a shift away from the entrenched American value of individualism where the exercise of free will is, allegedly, merely a personal choice. "Before I was married," she wrote to Peter Heller, "I had this fantasy of adopting a whole lot of children and the kind of school I would have for them. I had a horrible schooling [and] I wanted to give them something that wasn't so horrible" (Burlingham, 1971). By the late 1920s, Dorothy Burlingham and Anna Freud had matched up their unique sensitivities to the needs of marginalised populations. With "The Child in Mind and Body – the Writing of Anna Freud and Dorothy Burlingham in *The Psychoanalytic Study of the Child,*" Nellie Thompson and Helene Keable's essay picks up the narrative at this point. Anna Freud and Dorothy Tiffany Burlingham shared an intellectual, and certainly deeply personal, fascination with the meaning and effects of childhood attachment. Each woman would write about it in her own way. Directed to Vienna's *Israelitisches Blindeninstitut* (Hebrew Institute for Blind Children) by Sigmund Freud who was particularly interested in the dream experience of blind children, Dorothy's research visits led her to two bracing conclusions: (1) the sighted world fails to appreciate or understand the accomplishments of blind children, and (2) blind children need alternative forms of education based on their own strengths and challenges. With this new cultural analysis of Burlingham's writings we see that, no matter her society legacy, her sense of social justice played a critical role in the pursuit of every child's right to dignity and respect.

Psychoanalysis and education are the twin poles of this collection of essays. Drawn in by the fascination of vintage photographs and personal stories, the authors persuade us to connect these themes and also the visual and the textual dimensions of historical analysis. From May through July 2017, the Freud Museum London hosted an exhibit called *Freud/Tiffany – Anna Freud, Dorothy Tiffany Burlingham and 'The Best Possible School'*. Viewers were as likely to encounter the original *Lehrplan* that Peter Blos handed to August Aichhorn, as a film of Julius Tandler opening the Vienna *Haus der Kinder*. Along with the actual gold signet ring Freud gave to Bob Burlingham, the first-ever public viewing of privately-held objects, original letters, paintings and photographs, autographs and unique toys that Anna Freud hand-carried from the Jackson Nursery to London, all recreated the Hietzing school's sense of space, surface, lighting and surroundings. As with this book, the interplay between psychoanalysis and education built a storyline that started with Sigmund Freud but did not end with him.

All of the essays were written specifically for this book. Each one explores how Anna Freud and Dorothy Tiffany Burlingham, separately or together, dispelled outmoded narratives of childhood and empowered educators to do the same. Bringing together the historic Freud and Tiffany legacies as never before, each of the well-established European and American scholars first offered their research at an international symposium held in May 2017 at the Anna Freud Centre in London. They had agreed to develop an original paper to meet a major unifying goal: to gather the names, the theories and the practices of early 20th century Austrian-American pioneers in psychoanalysis and education under one roof. The symposium was grounded in the work of Freud and Burlingham at the Hietzing School. From there, however, the discourse expanded to research innovations in childhood and adolescence, special populations, and the virtually incalculable impact of Vienna 1920s in culture and politics. This book is a product of that inspiring discourse (Figure I.10).

Figure I.10 Dorothy Tiffany Burlingham and Anna Freud, 1979.

Illustrations

Figure I.1 Sigmund Freud and Mathilde Hollitscher, photograph ca. 1931, Bob Burlingham, Collection of Michael J. Burlingham, New York.
Figure I.2 Sigmund Freud, Anna Freud, Mathilde Hollitscher, photograph ca. 1931, Bob Burlingham, Collection of Michael J. Burlingham, New York.
Figure I.3 Sigmund Freud smiling, photograph ca. 1931, Bob Burlingham, Collection of Michael J. Burlingham, New York.
Figure I.4 Sigmund Freud walking (Semmering?), b/w film strip of 5 images, 9.5 mm Pathé Baby, AgfaPhoto film, Collection of Michael J. Burlingham, New York.
Figure I.5 Bob Burlingham, b/w photograph, Peter Heller Album 3/25, Sigmund Freud Privatstiftung, Sigmund Freud Foundation Vienna.
Figure I.6 Ruth Bernstein, b/w photograph, Peter Heller Album 3/33, Sigmund Freud Privatstiftung, Sigmund Freud Foundation Vienna.
Figure I.7 The Matteotti-Hof, Vienna, b/w Associated Press photograph dated 2/14/1934, private collection.
Figure I.8 "Vienna Builds Ideal Community Houses in the Heart of the Slums." b/w Associated Press photograph dated 10/9/1929. "Vienna, headed by their popular mayor Karl Seidz (sic), has, in the heart of the slums, built homes for 6000 families. All constructed on the latest architectural and hygienic principles, and built from the proceeds of the city housing taxes for the years 1925/1928." Private collection.
Figure I.9 August Aichhorn at the Jackson Nursery, 1937, b/w photograph. Estate of August Aichhorn, Collection of Thomas Aichhorn, Vienna.
Figure I.10 Anna Freud and Dorothy Tiffany Burlingham in the Library at 20 Maresfield Gardens, October 1979. Photo by Michael J. Burlingham, collection of Michael J. Burlingham, New York.

References

Breitner, H. (1929) folder "Personnen," File C, document # 19/62. Archives of the Verein für Geschichte der Arbeiterbewegung, Vienna.

Burlingham, D. T. (1975) unpublished interview with Peter Heller dated June 13, 1975, folder "Burlingham, Dorothy T., 1974–1975" Box 2, Peter Heller Papers, Manuscript Division, U.S. Library of Congress, Washington DC.

Burlingham, M. J. (2017) An Incidental Collector. *Freud/Tiffany and 'The Best Possible School' – Exhibit Catalog.* London: Freud Museum London.

Eissler, K. R. (1951) *"New Preface" to August Aichhorn.* Wayward Youth. London: Imago Publishing Company.

Erikson, E. H. (1980) "Dorothy Burlingham's School in Vienna" in Schlein, S. ed. (1995) *Erik H. Erikson – A Way of Looking at Things.* New York: W.W. Norton.

Freud, A. (1930) "Four Lectures on Psychoanalysis for Teachers and Parents" in *The Writings of Anna Freud, Vol. 1.* (1974). New York: International Universities Press.

Freud, S. to Sandor Ferenczi. Letter # 772, November 17, 1918. In Falzeder, Ernst and Brabant, Eva, eds. *The Correspondence Volume of Sigmund Freud and Ernest Jones, Vol. 2,* p. 311.
Gardiner, M. (1983) *Code Name 'Mary' – Memoirs of an American Woman in the Austrian Underground.* New Haven, CT: Yale University Press, p. 35.
Gulick, C. A. (1938) Vienna Taxes since 1918. *Political Science Quarterly* 53/4: 533–556.
Johler, B., Sommer, M., & Steiner, A. (2016) *Anna Freud in Wien: Ein Rundgang zu Orten der Psychoanalyse.* Wien & Berlin: Turia & Kant.
Peters, M. A. (2012) *Education, Philosophy and Politics.* New York: Routledge.
Schur, H. (1995) unpublished interview by author.

Chapter 1

Bob's Diary, December 1931

Michael John Burlingham

The first school I remember was a private day school in Swiss Cottage, London, to which I walked every morning from my home in St John's Wood. This was followed by three years of public middle school in Princeton, New Jersey; two miserable years in boarding school in New York State; and two much happier years in Pennsylvania. Little did I know that my paternal grandmother and her father had also been sent to boarding schools, and hated them. When it came to my own children, I enrolled them in the Little Red School House, a private day school founded in 1921 by Elisabeth Irwin that has become a bastion of progressive education.

How, then, do I make sense of something as radical as what my father, his siblings and a handful of other kids experienced in Vienna from 1927 to 1932? Other than home-schooled children, who bypasses the school system entirely? Who gets a school founded and built around their needs? What kind of parent has the time, energy, finances and vision to do such things? Whatever the answers, whatever one may think of such a solution, surely one would agree that the Hietzing School was unusual for any time or place. In fact, in its particulars, it was unique, and the diary that my father kept while he was a student there provides a unique account of that experiment, and the larger, wider forces it embodied (Figure 1.1).

> In school these last days we have been reading Pepy's Diary and discussing its faults and contributions to the Engl. literature. And as it pleased me, the way he writes and tells I got the idea of writing a diary myself from now on. So to-day I went to a paper shop and bought this little booklet.

Thus, Robert Burlingham, Jr, known as Bob, starts his diary on December 1, 1931, a cold winter's Tuesday, writing by hand in black ink, since faded to dark gray. He wrote not from 17th-century London but from 20th-century Vienna, and his diary lasted not "from now on" but rather twenty-two days, ended by Christmas festivities, an early, characteristic false start, perhaps (Burlingham, 1989, p. 248). He would title it "December 1931 to January 1932." No great events are recorded, no plague, no war, no great fire, but

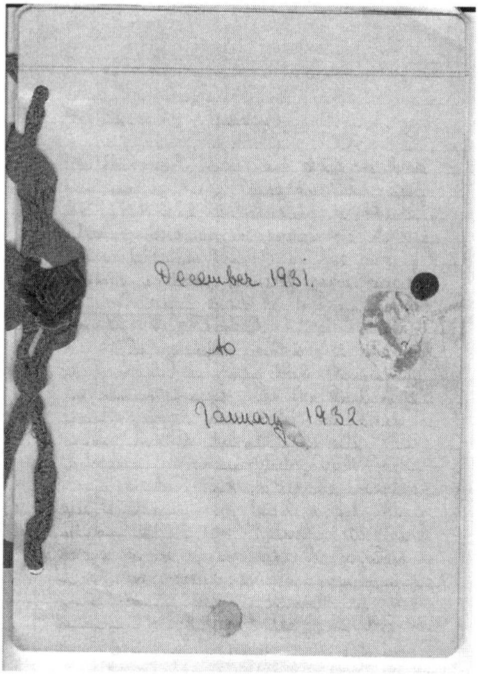

Figure 1.1 Bob's Diary. Original manuscript.

as my essay shows, there are good reasons to dive into this narrative of a sixteen-year-old American boy. I have transcribed Bob's diary exactly as it appears in the original, without corrections of any kind, whether for style, spelling or inconsistencies. Occasionally, I have put annotations within brackets for reasons of meaning or identification, but I have purposefully avoided the use of "sic." Like his siblings, by 1931, Bob was bilingual in English and German and sometimes used a German word in an otherwise English-language document.

On December 1, 1931, when he began to write, Bob was living at Berggasse 19 in an apartment two floors above the one occupied by Sigmund Freud and his family. Bob had a spacious bedroom to himself and once leaned out the window to record the view down the street with his new Leica rangefinder camera. I recently visited that same room and tried to recreate the view as it looks today with my digital Canon, so I know just how far out of the window he had to lean. Bob's photo reveals Berggasse with an orderly line of parked cars in a distant center aisle and an outdoor cafe with two tables of customers. Today, the view is much the same, though somewhat obscured by trees, and the dome of the telephone-exchange building in the far distance is gone (Figures 1.2 and 1.3).

Figure 1.2 View from Berggasse 19, 1931. Bob Burlingham.

Figure 1.3 View from Berggasse 19, 2016. Michael J. Burlingham.

It did not take Bob long to walk down two flights of stairs to his appointments with Anna Freud, his psychoanalyst for the past six years. Bob and his younger sister Mabbie were among Anna Freud's first ten child analysands, and their case studies figured prominently in her first book, *Introduction to the Technique of Child Analysis* (1927). Child analysis was then still in its infancy, and those early experiments in adapting classical analysis to the needs of children had virtually no precedent.

Bob and his siblings were also participants in another, related experiment in child development. It acquired various names, but in day-to-day life, it was simply "*die Schule*" (Bob used German terms to identify and label the negatives of photos he took from 1930 to 1932), where his teachers had thought fit to include *Samuel Pepys' Diary* in the English curriculum. Later, *die Schule* became known as the Burlingham-Rosenfeld School because Bob's mother, Dorothy Tiffany Burlingham, had put up the money to build a small schoolhouse in the backyard of Eva Rosenfeld's home at 11 Wattmanngasse. Eva was a close friend of Anna Freud's and in analysis with Professor, as Freud was known among his intimates. Eva had already been running her home along lines she described as a sort of Zellerhaus, an orphanage in Berlin for girls where she had been a teacher. A number of youngsters were boarding with Eva and her family, including Kyra, the daughter of dancer Vaslav Nijinsky, who had gone mad. Some of those children were in analysis; some joined the ranks of the schoolchildren. The Rosenfeld household was a lively place, bursting with youthful energy and, above all, music, which Eva (n.d., in Burlingham, 1989, p. 182) borrowed from Shakespeare in calling "our food of love" (Figure 1.4).

Figure 1.4 Portrait of Kyra Nijinsky by Serge Gres, 1935.

When Dorothy arrived to pick up Mabbie after her first sleepover at Eva's, the child ran onto the balcony shouting, "Hello, hello, I don't want to go home. I want to stay here!" (Burlingham, 1927). Today, the Rosenfelds' two-story row house remains, complete with decorative wrought-iron balcony. The schoolhouse is gone, however, demolished by a bomb in World War II.

It has also been called the Hietzing School after its location in that district of Vienna, where homes had been built for the workers who attended to the Kaiser in the nearby Schönbrunn Palace. And finally, due to its diminutive size, it was known as The Matchbox School. But it might as well have been called the Anna Freud School, as it was founded in part to nurture students who were in analysis, to be supportive of psychoanalytic values, and to foster learning through the kind of progressive education that John Dewey advocated. It had but twenty-six students and a short life span – just five years – but carried an outsize influence due to the backing of Anna Freud, a former schoolteacher herself, and the presence of Erik Erikson as one of the two principal teachers, along with Peter Blos. The close connection between education and child analysis, for Anna Freud, is seen in Bob's entry of December 1, when he calls his analytic hours "lessons" in his diary.

So what goes through the head of an adolescent in such circumstances, and what does he commit to paper? In his first entry, Bob mentions some of the current events shaping the wider landscape – the shocking bankruptcy earlier that year of the Austria's once-mighty *Credit-Anstalt* bank – and fears that the Austrian schilling would be devalued. He also indirectly referenced the abysmal economic condition of many Viennese in a theme repeated throughout the diary – the Austro-German effort that commenced that year to help unemployed and poor families in need of relief during the coldest months of the year, called the *Winterhilfe*.

But soon Bob turned to the kind of details presented by life as it's lived. His December 1 entry reads:

> Sigurd and Walter had a fight in school and Walters nose was all swollen when he came for his lesson with Mother. I am sure it was sigurd who aggravated him till he got mad, as Sigurd was allready so against our ideas about the "Winter Hilfe." After we left alone to consult, he ran down stairs and after fetching a Sandwich he sat down in his sloppy way and ate, & inbetween munching he made some remarks about our ideas. We thought we might feed poor children every noon in a room Felix [possibly Augenfeld, the architect] was to get for us. It certainly would be great if it were possible, but it doesn't look so.

"Mother" was Dorothy Tiffany Burlingham, an American woman in analysis with Professor. Intellectually intrigued, she had recently augmented her psychoanalytic portfolio with a training course in child analysis. Sigurd Baer and his brother Basti were Bob's fellow students, as was Walter Aichhorn, the son of analyst August Aichhorn, a Viennese expert on adolescence. From the diary, it would seem that Walter was either one of Dorothy's early analysands or someone she was privately tutoring. Again, it's hard to separate the educational from the psychoanalytic; Walter was, in fact, one of her first analysands.

In 1921, shortly before the birth of her fourth child, Dorothy had left her husband, Robert Burlingham Sr, a New York surgeon who was later diagnosed with bipolar disorder. As the granddaughter of Charles Lewis Tiffany, the founder of the eponymous jewelry and silver company, and as the youngest child of Louis Comfort Tiffany, the famous glass artist, she had the means to flee her husband, his destabilizing mood swings and her marriage (Figure 1.5).

Equal measures of desperation and open mindedness had led her to Vienna in 1925, ostensibly to seek psychoanalytic treatment for ten-year-old Bob. But it wasn't long before her other children followed Bob into analysis and she herself started analytic treatment, first with Theodor Reik, then with Sigmund Freud, an analysis that lasted twelve years.

When Dorothy arrived in Vienna on May 14, 1925, she put up at the five-star Bristol Hotel on the Ringstrasse, thinking she would return to the States in a few months' time. But Anna and Dorothy – the mother of children in

Figure 1.5 Dorothy Tiffany Burlingham 1925, by Franz Löwy.

analysis and their analyst – rapidly found common ground that evolved into a lifetime attachment. By 1929, Dorothy and her four children had moved into the fourth-floor apartment at Berggasse 19.

In late 1930, the two women bought a farmhouse on twenty acres which they called Hochrotherd, after that part of Breitenfurt, some forty-five minutes by car from Vienna. From their perch overlooking a valley, as I recently saw for myself, the city was visible on the horizon, nestled between blue-misted mountains.

The "simple," or "natural" life of the *Bauern*, or peasant, as Dorothy and Anna Freud (1930) imagined it, formed an important thread in their lives. At Hochrotherd, they wore peasant clothes and filled the farmhouse with striking examples of hand-painted folk furniture, now housed in the Freud Museum London. Peter Heller, an astute observer of the school he attended, later wrote that the Burlinghams cultivated "a stylization in the direction of the expensively unpretentious" (Heller, n.d., p. 6) (Figure 1.6).

Figure 1.6 Anna Freud and Dorothy Burlingham at Hochrotherd ca. 1931.

Anna Freud described the lure of country living in a letter she sent Dorothy in mid-August 1933, when Dorothy was taking Bob to Cherbourg for another trip back to the US. Since they first met, Dorothy and Anna had been separated only briefly.

> I like it about farm life that it brings everything down to a simple formula, even psychic things. For instance how could one express in town the difference between being one person alone or two together? One would have to talk about the libido etc. and narcissism. Here it is much simpler: to-day f.i. it took me twice as long to weed the young peas than it would have taken if you were here again. So you see!
>
> (Anna Freud, 1933)

Bob returned to his diary on December 2.

> Walter wasn't in school to-day. He seems to have hurt himself rather badly. In our 1st period in school Joan [Erikson] read our compositions aloud, and because mine was so bad (or I rather thought so), I had to look at the ceiling the whole time feeling as hot as a lobster. We certainly don't seem to know anything about the restoration period, and I was lucky, as she only asked me about the plot of St. Celaads Day [*Ode for Music on St. Cecilia's Day*]—by Pope.

Bob was keenly interested in music and had been taking cello lessons with Frieda Krause for about five years. At age fourteen, he had performed Léon Boëllmann's *Variations Symphoniques* at a recital held at the Klub Õsterreichischer Eisenbahn-Beamten. Bob was also studying piano under someone named Gretl, learning a Chopin prelude (Figure 1.7).

He continued on December 2, "Later I was even able to practice piano for 2 hours thoroughly." The following day, he went to hear French cabaret singer Yvette Guilbert. "It was the best evening yet, and she certainly has a lot of feeling in her although her voice is not beautiful."

On December 6, Vienna celebrated the anniversary of Mozart's death. Bob observed,

> Everywhere the musicians are playing his compositions. It seems so funny to me that a composer like him is not very popular in his lifetime. But as soon as he is dead everyone is so terribly sorry and he begins to get the publicity that he has reached 140 years after his death. Most every musician nowadays thinks that classical music is fading off and that dance music and the new style of composing (with out any background) will take its place.

Bob and his sister Mabbie were especially gifted in the visual arts. Erik Erikson's early life as a draftsman and painter was no doubt helpful to their

Figure 1.7 Portrait of Bob Burlingham and his cello, 1927 drawing by Erik Homburger Erikson.

artistic development, although Bob mentions him only one time in the Diary, on December 17: "After the recess, we had "Freie Arbeit"; History. Erik was tellephoning all the time and only looked in once."

The previous summer, at age fifteen, Bob had been presented with a Leica and began a series of extraordinary photographs that are preserved as negatives in two albums documenting this period in his life. He carefully

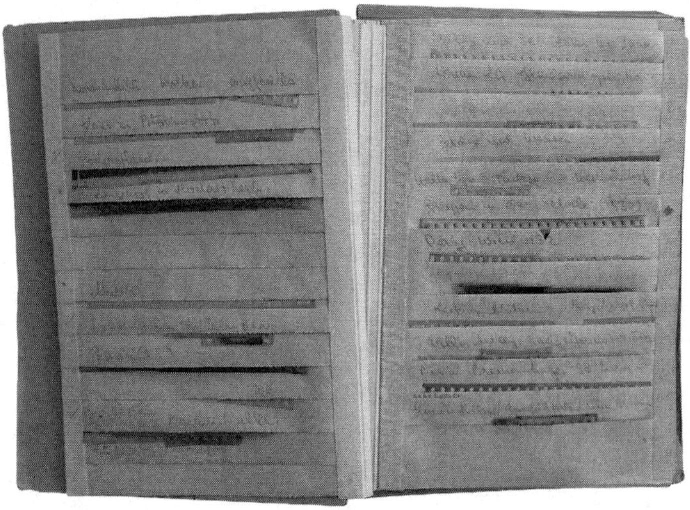

Figure 1.8 Bob Burlingham's book of negatives.

identified each strip of negatives as to subject; the very first image he took with the Leica, noted as such, was of the chalet his mother had rented for the summer of 1930 in Grundlsee, in western Austria (Figure 1.8).

Bob also had a Pathé Baby 9.5-mm movie camera and was protective of both instruments, once grudgingly allowing Peter Blos to borrow the Leica and another time refusing to lend the Pathé Babe to Margot Goldschmidt, the young woman whom his mother had hired to live with the family and care for her children while she immersed herself in psychoanalytic studies. In Bob's entry for December 4, he remarks, "Margot says I am not nice to her, and of course rather stingy. I didn't feel she would handle the Pathée, because she is so awfully cautious."

On December 16, he wrote, "I am planning to take photos of all the people I am writing about and whom I am in connection with." This he did, demonstrating a keen eye and consistency of vision surprising in someone so young (Figure 1.9).

He added,

> I want to paste the picture at the top of the page and write a short account of the person, his and mine connection, and about what I think his character is worth. Lets hope the pictures will turn out.

This he did not do, although he frequently passed judgment on his peers, as well as on himself.

Figure 1.9 Bob's photo of his brother Mikey, ca. 1931 at Hochrotherd.

One might expect to find Bob's account of his analytic hours to be given special weight in his diary. Instead, they are treated with no more or less emphasis than anything else. Analysis, he understood, was just another component of education, another subject in the curriculum – Explorations in Self-Knowledge, if you will.

Observations of Anna Freud, his analyst, are commingled with those of Anna Freud, his mother's closest friend, as well as with other details from everyday life. He began on December 1,

> My lesson with Anna Freud was the worst I have had since I returned from U.S.A. [earlier that year]. She didn't seem to understand that my [piano] lesson with Gretl yesterday could have been the cause for Gretl's getting mad.
>
> December 2: "My lesson with A.F. was very much better, and we talked a lot about Marianne's baby, and how miraculous it was that it didn't die." Marianne was Anna Freud's close friend, the daughter of the Freud family pediatrician, Oscar Rie, and the wife of Ernst Kris, a curator at the *Kunsthistorisches* Museum in Vienna; both Marianne and Ernst were members of the Vienna Psychoanalytic Society.

Bob continued,

> Just now I heard that Walters nose is much better but probably broken to my disgust. He was in the hospital all morning. Mother has just fixed Anna Freud a beautiful birthday-cake. She is giving her a pair of fire tongues for the hearth at Hochrotherd.
>
> December 3: "'Hoch Anna Freud!' It is really not imaginable for anyone, except for the person who has been through it all, to understand what analysis has done for me. If I think about the way I used to steal and lie, and that now just because I am able to <u>understand</u> why I did it, I am able to stop; well! it seems just as much a miracle, as that Mariannes baby (by the way also called Anna) got well."

Bob also understood – only too well – that he could give Anna Freud no greater gift than to affirm the "miraculous" powers of psychoanalysis. Bob's numerous photographs of a chubby, smiling, gurgling baby, identified as "Annerl," now suddenly make sense – as portraits of miraculous recovery from illness.

Within a few days, plans for the *Winterhilfe* had shifted from feeding children on a daily basis to raising money for a one-time delivery of food and clothing at Christmastime.

> December 4: I just had a sweet talk with Mother about everything under the sun. She talked a lot about the "Winter hilfe" and what we are going to do for the different families. She expects us to gather about 25S. not including the S50 I expect to give. With that we only expect to buy the food—at least as far as possible. Peter [Heller]s father [a confectioner] who generally gives us bonbons we are going to ask to just give us chocolate and little things to hang on trees for the *Winterhilfe*.
>
> December 5: To begin a nice Sunday well I have a very disagreeable cold and don't feel well at all.
>
> To day we had our test on the Restoration and Elizabethan period with Joan. The questions were; compare the Restoration period and its contributions [with the Elizabethan period and its contributions]. Then she gave us a list of writers whom we had to write about. I wonder how mine will be as it was very hard and we had too little time to write in.

Another theme running through Bob's diary was his lively interest in girls, of which there was no shortage at the school and in Eva Rosenfeld's home, with its steady supply of au pairs. Evidently, he no longer resembled the "passive-feminine character [whose] original object relationship with his mother [was] entirely overlaid with identification with her," as Anna had described him when he began analysis (Freud, 1928, p. 163). Much of her work since then, both within and outside of analysis, had been to clarify his sexuality.

December 3: Gretl Oskerhal was here to-day, and I like her pretty well. She certainly is lots of fun—but I guess nothing to fall in love with. Of course she is 20 again which makes it impossible this time. I don't want to fall in love with anyone like Trude, Hertha [Huber] or Ann [Niederhal], but want the next girl to be my age. I must be able to like somebody who also likes me a lot, without thinking she might get too dangerous.

Kept out of school by his cold, Bob turned to carving a female torso from a bar of soap. "In a way I seem to be able to carve quite well although I can not draw. I do it all by feeling and the touch—and after it was finished it really looked like a real body," he writes on December 8. During his week-long convalescence, Bob's thoughts turned introspective. He began to write about his dreams and go deeper into his analysis.

December 8: I had a dream last night for the 1st time since I have begun this diary. It was about Toria and lurili and me meeting them in Grundlsee again. They were very surprised at the way I looked at them—as I didn't ever want to see them but they were glad to see me.

December 9: I had two dreams last night again. It is really funny that I only dream on days I don't have hours with Anna Freud. My 1st dream was about lurili and that I went with her in my car to town. In the middle of the way she got out because of some reason I cannot remember, and took a taxi home. The 2nd was about me being at a dance. A lady (like one gets on the street to buy) sent her maid to my loge to ask me for a dance. In my lesson with Anna Freud I found out that all my dreams were about Mother, when she was out or went away from me (when I was 6 months old), and that she refused me, as I felt then. I wanted her milk that she had given me up to then and she refused. Mother tells me now that I refused any eatable when in that state & they had the time of their life trying to feed me.

December 10: Last night I have had a dream about Marlene Dietrich and meeting her on the street while going along with Ernsti [Halberstadt, Anna Freud's nephew]. She waved to me and I was so pleased that I waved back and went up to her forgetting Ernst. But he came up and dragged me on with him. Marlene Dietrich laughed and I was mad. Of course I was unable to remember this dream when with Anna Freud but just at 4 punctually I remembered it. Anna Freud said it meant the same as the previous dreams.

December 11: It is very funny, but these last days I have been able to dream a lot. Last night I dreamt that I was very strong and able to kill Sigurd, Walter, and Peter by throwing them off a roof so that they would just scalp them. I can't see what the dream means but I guess Anna Freud will be able to help me understand it. Well I have just been to A.F.'s, but there isn't so much to explain. All these dreams seem to

> mean the same. This last one meant that I wanted to kill the man that took me away from Mothers breast.

On December 14, he added:

> By the way in our lesson to-day we found out that I had very very strong feelings against this Christmas and that it was because I thought Mother was forgetting us and instead thinking about others—as I thought she did when I was young.

After six years of analysis, Anna Freud had evidently zeroed in on the period in Bob's life when his lifelong physical and psychological troubles began. At six months, he developed eczema so severe that he had to be covered from head to foot with thick tar salve to prevent himself from scratching. The eczema was followed by an allergic reaction to breast milk and cow's milk. For a while he could stomach only goat's milk, then he stopped eating entirely and had to be force-fed. He also experienced the first bout of asthma that troubled him for the rest of his life. These attacks were triggered by periods of separation from his parents, while in the care of nannies, but his reputable Park Avenue pediatrician advised Dorothy and Robert to go about their business and let the infant adjust to their schedule.

In February 1916, when Bob was six months old, his father was completing his surgical residency at Roosevelt Hospital in New York. Later, Dorothy would say the pressures of medical school were too much for her husband who, around then, began to manifest the bipolar disorder that ran in his mother's side of the family. Tension was in the air, therefore, and Bob was by all accounts extremely sensitive. Unfortunately, neither Dorothy nor Bob's doctors linked the child's asthma attacks to separation anxiety; or if they did, they decided to ignore it. This "wrong handling," as Dorothy wrote to Bob, would remain a source of regret for the rest of her life (Burlingham, 1941).

Under these trying circumstances, the search for solutions that brought Dorothy to Vienna commenced. Later, when she became a child analyst, her experiences as a mother informed the compassion she showed her analysands and their parents, particularly the mothers.

By December 15, Bob had recovered from his cold and returned to school.

> Every one was so pleased to see me and I felt very happy. We had a nice but discusted lesson with Joan. I certainly wrote the most awful "arbeit." She couldn't even read it I had written it in such ununderstandable Engl. Proffessor Freud gave us children for the "Winterhilfe S. 100." By the way, last week Grandfather and Grandmother [Mr. and Mrs. Charles C. Burlingham] together gave us to spend for the unemployed $100 or 700 Schillings which is quite a nice sum. We are of course very happy.

Bob noted on December 13 that the juggler Enrico Rastelli had died and also mentioned plans to put on a circus to raise money for the *Winterhilfe*.

> There was a question whether the circus we are playing for Christmas should be played here. But so that Mother does not over tyre again we think that it might be at the Jonases [home of fellow students Elisabeth and Mario Jonas].
>
> December 15: In our circus I am going to be a servant and show the people around. Dr. [Julius] Tandler spoke awfully well over the radio this evening about the "Winter hilfe" and that this Fryday every theater, kino and varietée is going to use <u>all</u> its income for the "Winterhilfe's" sake. All the workers on the stage and every employed man in these different subjects lets his earned money go for the "winterhilfe." He expects in this way to get a <u>lot</u> of money. I think the idea is marvellous and it really miraculous that all the workers will do it. Don't you! Good Night!
>
> December 16: This afternoon Eva [Rosenfeld] and Elisabeth [Jonas] came here for the circus Probe (rehearsal) and it seems to be getting on much better than I thought. I as a servant am to wear knickerbockers, a mustache, a pullover and a cap put on my head the wrong way around. Now I feel much more like doing it.
>
> December 17: All the boxes, I think there are 39, came to-day from Peter's father. Also a huge box of honey (about 30 kg heavy) came. It seems that there is going to be an awful lot to do. This dumb circus seems to be taking all the time up at present but I hope much more now for a good performance; at least I hope to do my part as well as I can.
>
> A.F.'s lessons are all filled with talking about the "Winterhilfe" plans. It sort of seems as if the "Winterhilfe" was covering up other much more important doings. No dreams of course.
>
> December 18: To-day I had my last lesson with Anna Freud before the Christmas holidays. I felt sorry in a way to brake off now that we are at the point of reaching something.

As the holiday approached, school discipline eroded, and the students amused themselves with passing *Liebesbriefe*, or love notes, to one another while their teacher was out of the room. Sigurd Baer and Bob sent messages to Elsa, "a sweet girl," Bob confided in his diary entry of December 17.

> December 20: Well! our circus did turn out very well. We got $136.95 from it for the "Winterhilfe" which is a lot. I feel awfully tired because we had a lot of work to do. I and Margot [Goldschmidt] stayed on till 9.30 to help fix up the house. It was really a lot of fun.
>
> December 22: Well! we have finished all the packages and filled up the boxes. To-morrow everything will be delivered.

> December 23: The boxes have all been delivered and [chauffeur] Herr Wimmer told me that the families are so poor and the houses so smelly that he won't want to eat anything for supper.

Bob's last entry noted that Anna Freud's nephew and his best friend, Ernsti Halberstadt, was due to arrive the following day from Hamburg.

When it became evident that he would not return to the diary, Bob tied a red ribbon through the holes in the left-hand margin of the pages, melted red wax over the ribbon and frontispiece, and stamped it with a diamond-shaped seal. He titled it, "December 1931 to January 1932," leaving a minor mystery, since the diary ended on December 23.

Once sealed, pages could be torn out but not added, so perhaps the diary did continue into 1932 and Bob decided to remove the additional pages. Or, possibly, he wanted the diary to seem more substantial than it was. In any event, this window on his world closed on the day before Christmas Eve 1931 – the record of an adolescent American under extraordinary circumstances (Figure 1.10).

One cannot conclude this chapter without noting some of the virtues reflected in this diary. I refer to the underlying interiority and earnest self-reflection, the casting inward for perspective, and the effort to know oneself better amid the tumult of day-to-day life. This, of course, was precisely the point of pairing psychoanalysis and education. Those responsible for the school's existence fervently hoped that its students would emerge as adults with the ability to look both within and without, and be that much better equipped to deal with life. Ninety-one years after the school bell first rang, that effort has not been forgotten.

Figure 1.10 Bob Burlingham's ring, gift of Sigmund Freud.

Illustrations

Figure 1.1 Bob Burlingham's Diary from a year at the Hietzing School, Collection of Michael J. Burlingham, New York.
Figure 1.2 View from the Berggasse toward Servitengasse, 9th District, Vienna, ca. 1930, Bob Burlingham, Collection of Michael J. Burlingham, New York.
Figure 1.3 View from the Berggasse toward Servitengasse, 9th District, Vienna, 2015, Michael J. Burlingham, Collection of Michael J. Burlingham, New York.
Figure 1.4 Portrait of Kyra Nijinsky, Serge Gres, 1935, oil on canvas, the Royal Ballet School Collections, UK.
Figure 1.5 Portrait of Dorothy Tiffany Burlingham wearing traditional Austrian clothing, sepia photo by Franz Löwy, 1925, Collection of Michael J. Burlingham, New York.
Figure 1.6 Anna Freud and Dorothy Tiffany Burlingham at Hochroterd, photograph, ca. 1932, Collection of Michael J. Burlingham, New York.
Figure 1.7 Portrait of Bob Burlingham with cello, pencil on paper drawing by Erik Homburger Erikson, October 10, 1927, Collection of Michael J. Burlingham, New York.
Figure 1.8 Book of Photo negatives, Bob Burlingham, 1930–1933, Collection of Michael J. Burlingham, New York.
Figure 1.9 Mikey Burlingham at Hochrotherd ca. 1931, b/w photograph by Bob Burlingham, Collection of Michael J. Burlingham, New York.
Figure 1.10 Bob Burlingham's ring, Sigmund Freud's gift of a Greek intaglio of Apollo, scarab in red jasper, Collection of Michael J. Burlingham, New York.

References

Burlingham, D. T. (1927) Untitled document of March 6, 1927. Privately held. Collection of Michael John Burlingham. Quoted in Burlingham, M.J. *The Last Tiffany,* p. 183.

Burlingham, D. T. (1941) Letter to Bob Burlingham dated October 28, 1941. Privately held. Collection of Michael J. Burlingham.

Burlingham, M. J. (1989) *The Last Tiffany: A Biography of Dorothy Tiffany Burlingham.* New York: Atheneum. Published in paperback as *Behind Glass: A Biography of Dorothy Tiffany Burlingham.* New York: Other Press, 2002. Published as an audiobook as *The Last Tiffany: A Biography of Dorothy Tiffany.* Wickford, RI: New Street Communications, 2015.

Freud, A. (1927) *Introduction to the Technique of Child Analysis.* Republished in the Classics in Child Development Series (1975). Manchester, NH: Ayer Co Publishers.

Freud, A. (1928) The Theory of Child Analysis. In *The Writings of Anna Freud,* Volume I (1973) New York: International Universities Press.

Freud, A. (n.d. 1933) Letter to Dorothy Burlingham. Privately held. Collection of Michael J. Burlingham.

Freud, A. and Burlingham, D. T. (1930) Quoted in Burlingham, M.J. *The Last Tiffany*, pp. 215–216.

Heller, P. (undated) Recollections of the Burlingham-Rosenfeld School, p. 6. Quoted in *The Last Tiffany*, p. 212.

Rosenfeld, E. (undated) untitled typescript, p. 15. Collection of Victor Ross. Quoted in *The Last Tiffany*, p. 182.

Chapter 2

A school for trick cyclists?

Michael Molnar

Figure 2.1 The small boy on the bike is Mikey Burlingham, Dorothy's youngest son. Bob identified the older boy only as "Willi" in his book of negatives from this period. It was taken in Poetzleinsdorf in 1932.

This photo is a rebus: it conjures up the term *trick cyclist*, which, in British slang, means "psychiatrist" (Figure 2.1).

What we see is curious. The tall boy is steering but can't see where the bike is heading. The little boy with his arms outstretched is facing the right way but has no control. He has to trust the other. It even seems as if he might have closed his eyes.

Partridge's *Dictionary of Slang* also cites a verbal use of *trick cyclist*: "He got himself trick-cycled out of the Army." This dates from World War II, when therapists such as Tom Main and Wilfred Bion were first trying out psychoanalytic methods on the armed forces. It brings to mind military comedies in which common soldiers find loopholes in the system that enable them to outwit the experts and authorities.

If the stunt in the photo is taken as a rebus, it enacts more than just a word. It demonstrates a predicament: the difficulty of two sides in an unequal relationship in maintaining their equilibrium.

The Hietzing School ethos was progressive and anti-authoritarian. The two main teachers, Peter Blos and Erik Homburger Erikson, were only a few years older than the oldest pupils. Erikson recorded "a strange confession" made by one pupil: "'In other schools it was fun to pin a paper on the teacher's coat. Here there's no fun in it any more'. We were too nice!" (Erikson & Erikson, 1980, p. 94).

Niceness may disarm, but does not eliminate the factor of authority. In even the most progressive of educations the child is subject to adult guidance, and guidance may blend into compulsion. This was an issue that Anna Freud and Eva Rosenfeld discussed:

> We really don't disagree; I also believe that the school must be compulsion. Our disagreement concerns only one point. I want the children to be made to want to do what they are supposed to do. You want them to be made to do what they don't want to do as well.
>
> (Anna Freud to Eva Rosenfeld 22.3.1929 *in* Heller, 1992, p. 112)

Like any child the young photographer Bob Burlingham was subject to his mother's will. Yet his own will, as inflected through his difficulties with her and the world, created the climate that culminated in her decision to take him and the other children to Europe, and eventually to Vienna. At the age of ten, he started his analysis with Anna Freud, and the analysis continued for the duration of his schooling at Hietzing. So he knew something about trick cycling and in both senses: it is recorded that he "raced down the Cobenzl – one of Vienna's steepest hills – standing on the seat of his bicycle" (Burlingham, 1989, p. 191).

Bob's photo of the cyclists brings to mind the young Jacques Henri Lartigue's photos of his family and friends fooling around in go-karts and other home-made contraptions, around the turn of the century. However, a telling difference is the stillness of Bob's cyclists. Lartigue presents motion as sheer delight: Bob's picture freezes it. That immobility is ominous. The lifeless street isolates the boys in a stasis out of time; the tall boy appears to be shouting at the small one as if they were locked in conflict; the bike seems stationary, each spoke of the wheels clearly visible. If it were moving, it is not clear which way it might be heading.

*

Other photographs show that Bob was in fact intrigued by peoples' movements and changes of expression. He took filmic series of action shots of fellow pupils, following their shifts from moment to moment. Eventually he would have a movie camera as well as his Leica to play with. This "play" is to be taken seriously and seen as experiments with mood, perception and distance. In this exploration of his surroundings, Bob's camera-eye framed family and friends; it recorded outings into the country; it surveyed from overhead a shop display and the cobbles of Berggasse below the windows of their fourth-floor apartment; and, most notably, it spied on groups of girls.

Polymorphous curiosity is a driving force in photography. At the school Bob's flirtations with various girls were notorious, while in his psychoanalysis Anna Freud was dealing with what she interpreted as his "tendency to homosexuality" (Burlingham, 1989, p. 172). How such theoretical constructs as tendencies or developmental phases might impinge on photography remains imponderable. In purely practical terms it is likely that the girls were a far better subject for photography than boys since they sat around together more in groups. Whatever the reasons – and they would tell us little about the images as such – Bob's filmic series concentrated on girls and their kabals. Each photo of the series is a sort of visual eavesdropping on mute conversations (Figure 2.2).

The cyclists were perhaps performing their trick for the photographer: the girls are not putting on a performance (or, if they are, it is for each other, not for the camera). In one frame the third girl looks straight at the camera, appearing neither pleased nor offended by its presence. The trio seems at first self-contained, then you notice a half hidden intruder, as if deputising for the unseen photographer – a boy slouched in the background. In one of the photos he intervenes and a girl turns to address him. In the other photos he is ignored or excluded.

When explaining his own photographic technique, Henri Cartier-Bresson would speak in terms of creative intuition and sensing the decisive moment. But in a filmic sequence there are several moments: the image is no longer

(a)

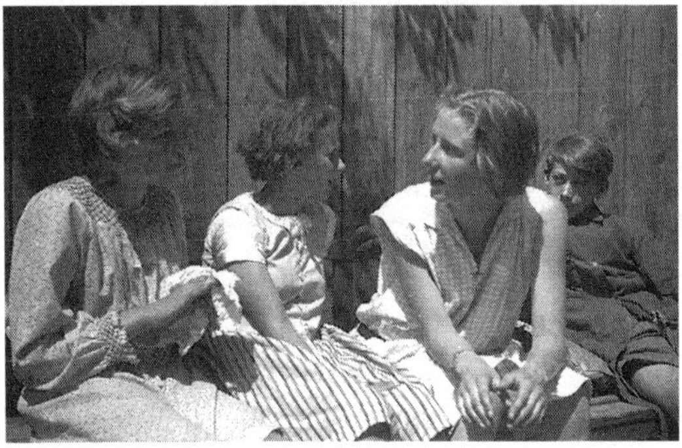

Figure 2.2 (a–c) (left to right) Mabbie Burlingham, Elisabeth Iona, Gerda Matthes.

(b)

(c)

Figure 2.2 (Continued).

self-sufficient. What lies in between the frames and connects them becomes part of our imaginary reconstruction of the picture. We are led to deduce a theme and story. Though each single shot is artfully angled and composed, the totality points in another direction. Bob allures the viewer of his sequences into a hunt for meaning.

*

A portrait emerges from a contest with self-consciousness, especially when done by a professional photographer such as Trude Fleischmann. We cannot know how she arrived at this particular pose, though we can be fairly confident she did not say to Dorothy Burlingham "Be yourself" or "Act naturally" or any such self-defeating instruction. If the portrait is commissioned and chosen, it is presumably a face the subject is satisfied to present to the world and to be represented by (Figure 2.3).

Figure 2.3 Dorothy Burlingham 1933 (Photographer: Trude Fleischmann).

This brooding image, chosen as a cover photo for Michael Burlingham's biography of his grandmother, becomes increasingly unsettling the longer one looks at it. Does her introspection express self-doubt or discontent with the world? And what is it about the effect of those two long hands – the right cupped round her jaw and showing the signet ring Freud gave her, the left hanging loosely, white against the black dress as if detached from her body, and displaying a wedding ring?

The Fleischmann portrait was taken in 1933. A year or two earlier Bob had photographed his mother, probably at the rented villa in Poetzleinsdorf next to the one the Freud family rented for the summers of 1931 and 1932. By putting her in the shade against the bright background of the sunlit garden, Bob emphasizes her dark skin and bright eyes, making her look like an American Indian, which was, incidentally, also how Peter Heller, another of Anna's child analysands, described her (Heller, 1990, p. xxiii; Figure 2.4).

The contrast of the two photos is striking, above all because here she is not "being herself" – in the sense of that introspective self-awareness visible in the posed portrait. She is relaxed and half smiling at the photographer, her son, and the restraint of her smile increases its effect and its implications.

Figure 2.4 Dorothy Burlingham.

The two portraits supplement each other, though the second becomes more interesting because of its back story, which is the interaction between the forty-year-old mother and the photographer, her sixteen-year-old son. In the historiography of psychoanalysis she has often been written off as a colorless adjunct to the Freuds. In the case of the Hietzing School, at least, this is impossible. She was its prime mover, founder and funder. Whatever the contingent causes of her happiness in this photo, she had at that time good reason for pride in an achievement which had demanded energy, determination and imagination.

There is no trace here of the doubt or self-criticism sensed in the Fleischmann portrait. The mood of this garden portrait can be attributed not just to accidental circumstances but to the bond between her and the photographer. Unlike women who only remain married "for the children's sake," it was precisely for their sake, and above all for Bob's sake, that she had separated from her husband and left America. And it was for their sake, and his sake, that the school had been set up. Her total devotion to them hardly required further proof nor did their total reliance on her.

What is remarkable about this portrait is the gleam of her eyes against her dark face. Their brightness affects the overall expression and confuses the viewer as to its intention. Could her smile be seen as some sort of plea or appeal to the photographer?

It was during these first years of the 1930s that Dorothy and Anna really became what would now be termed "an item." Together they acquired the country cottage at Hochrotherd and invested their spare time renovating it and cultivating its garden. Perhaps a devoted single mother might feel a certain guilt about this transfer of her attention away from her children or, on top of any residual guilt for having deprived them of a father and a full family life, some pangs of conscience at depriving them of the affection she had invested in Anna? From a certain angle, reading into the shadows of this portrait, I can imagine it as an appeal to her son for his understanding. Or even – a plea for his forgiveness?

Though subtleties of facial expression may be discernible even in a still photograph, their significance generally evades precise analysis or interpretation. Reading them is an act of imagination, in the sense that the historian Peter Burke uses that term:

> They [images] bring home to us what we may have known but did not take so seriously before. In short, images allow us to "imagine" the past more vividly.
>
> (Burke, 2001, p. 13)

In the case of Dorothy Burlingham, taking her seriously means taking her humor into consideration. The Freud literature presents her, if at all, primarily through her devotion to Anna and psychoanalysis, and her primary characteristic as unalloyed New England puritanism. Bob's photos bring other aspects of her character, gaiety, a sense of humor, into focus.

*

To some extent Anna Freud too has suffered from historiographical condescension. She too is often presented as a strict, over-serious and overshadowed character. Which is not how she and Dorothy appear here, on this short strip of 9.5-mm film taken with Bob's Pathé Baby movie camera. Like twins in their matching dirndls, the two women are walking down a hill in the country, both smiling radiantly. Dorothy is in slightly sharper focus than Anna, an accidental circumstance due, perhaps, to the unpredictable differential speed of the two, or to some difficulty in controlling distance and focus, though it is tempting to give the fact a metaphorical slant. As it is, the sight of these two happy women might well have placed Bob in a quandary as to his own distance and focus in relation to them. *Mutatis mutandis* he might be imagined like Freud's Leonardo, puzzling over the relationship of the Virgin to St Anna, those enigmatic sister-mothers, and over his own relationship to them both (Figure 2.5).

Figure 2.5 Film strip. Anna Freud and Dorothy Burlingham.

In Bob's photos of girls talking, his camera records a brief zoetropic series of images, bringing the girls' expressions and movements to flickering life. Here, where we have a real film, the strip of only five shots is too short to register any movement at all. The women are forever approaching the photographer; the scene is like a looped tape repeating the questions, what is going on here between the women and between the women and their photographer?

In dream interpretation, happiness in the manifest dream may translate into underlying anxiety. Interpreting this photo, I wonder how the photographer was reacting to the women's gaiety – or to their suppressed anxiety? Anxiety is contagious: what effect did their shared concern for his psychological wellbeing and sexual development have on him? And in addition to that, since the Hietzing School was a gynarchy underpinned by Anna Freud's passionate friendships with Eva Rosenfeld and Dorothy Burlingham, how did the adolescent photographer respond to these puzzling coordinates?

Another strip of film taken around the same time, consisting of Sigmund Freud walking down a similar section of road (*see* Figure 1.4, p. 4), reminds us of the men in the background of the School and the women's activities. Bob might have accepted his circumstances as normal if it had not been for his father's and his grandfather's absent presence, covertly or openly insisting on the boy's need of a father.[1] As it was, the women's concern over his development may in turn have been stoked by a parallel anxiety. Anna must have had some awareness of how her female friendships were viewed, not just by her parents but also by a wider circle, since she was already something of a public figure. Gossip or rumors can be dismissed as beneath contempt, but she could hardly have been untouched by her own parents' concern about her sexual life.

The two women have their eyes on Bob and his camera, and this sets up a curious equivalence. He, the problem child, knows himself to be an object of anxiety and inquiry to both his mother and her best friend, his psychoanalyst. Now this new movie camera, apart from all its other uses and pleasures, turns the tables on them both, turning him into the one who is questioning his questioners. The camera as a mechanism of defense...

Or of aggression? To capture a person's image gives power over them. Historically one of the most important functions of photography has been as an instrument of science, both in its narrow and its wider senses, that is, as a means of recording phenomena to be studied. The photos in Darwin's *The Expression of the Emotions in Man and Animals* (1872) are in the tradition that the psychoanalyst Willi Hoffer continued when he recorded the children of the Jackson Nursery in 1937 and, far more extensively, those of the Hampstead Nurseries in the 1940s. Whether in a scientific, artistic or journalistic context, the subject/object of photographs has often been seen and treated as raw material for some extrinsic moral or narrative purpose. In many of its uses, photography is inherently intrusive and controlling, even aggressive and authoritarian.

But to treat the interactions between Bob and the two women in terms of a binary power relation is inadequate. Whatever the photographer's intention, he cannot know exactly what his image might convey. There are too many contingent elements in the world for him to be able to control everything that enters the lens, nor can he decode the smiles he is recording without taking into account that they are aimed at him, and that he himself and his influence is reflected in them and the picture.

*

Don McCullin, photographing homeless people in London, refused to use long-focus lenses. He explained that he did not want to "steal" their image: "I wanted their trust and to become their voice" (McCullin, 1994, p. 96). Some moral aspects of photographic seeing and being seen resemble those of child analysis. Like the photographic subject unaware of the photographer's intentions, the child cannot give full and knowing consent. To gain their cooperation in the psychoanalysis requires respect, tact and finesse. Even then the analysis involves risks.

The long-term effects on the child's consciousness of having knowingly been under analytical observation are neither measurable nor predictable. How does the eye of the analyst affect the child's inner eye, its sense of itself in the world and as seen by the world? It is hard to imagine any outcome study that could deal with such a question. Because of all the complexities of time and change, and the absence of any definitive end product, those professions dealing with human development – psychoanalysis and education – may still be classified as impossible.

At first glance, photography, by contrast, deals with the certainties of a visual image. Yet when the certainties fall apart, we are left searching for what the photograph doesn't show – the hidden and the unseen correlates.

In a series of nine photos, Bob snapped this pair of teenagers, who are looking at something or someone out of the frame (Figure 2.6). He himself seems to have been concealed from them, perhaps indoors; the vertical bar at the left could be the frame of the door or window of his hiding place. In the act of seeing which is recorded here, and which is the essence of photography itself, the first photo sets up the seated boy and girl as proxies for both photographer and viewer of the photograph.

In the second shot the photographer has betrayed his own presence. Seeing is interrupted and replaced by confrontation – the girl who has detected him is giving him a hard stare that could be read as reproachful (Figure 2.7).

(a) (b)

Figure 2.6 (a, b) These two shots belong to a series of nine photos of a group of children gathered next to the wall. (Figures 2.7 and 2.8 are extracted from the same series.) Tinky Burlingham is seen standing on both, and on the lower photo the back of Priscilla de Forest's head. The seated boy and girl have not been identified.

Figure 2.7 Front, seated, Priscilla de Forest, Mabbie Burlingham. Back, standing, Tinky Burlingham. Others unidentified.

In the next shot, only part of her sleeve and left arm are visible. Bob shifts his focus from her and her disturbing look to the group of girls on the right, who are paying no attention to him. Presumably the photographer has no interest in a self-conscious subject; it is a natural unreflexive presence he is after.

Like Lartigue, Bob had a talent for timing and composition; the attentive girls against the white wall in an attractive play of light and shadow celebrate the unselfconscious delights of vision and the visible world. The girl on the left, by covering her eyes (which she uncovers later in the series), acts out this coded theme. As the series unfolds, the girls turn from the distant scene to their own shared concerns and conversation, and here Bob seems to be probing from a distance that we cannot cross some hidden secret they are sharing (Figure 2.8).

(a) (b)

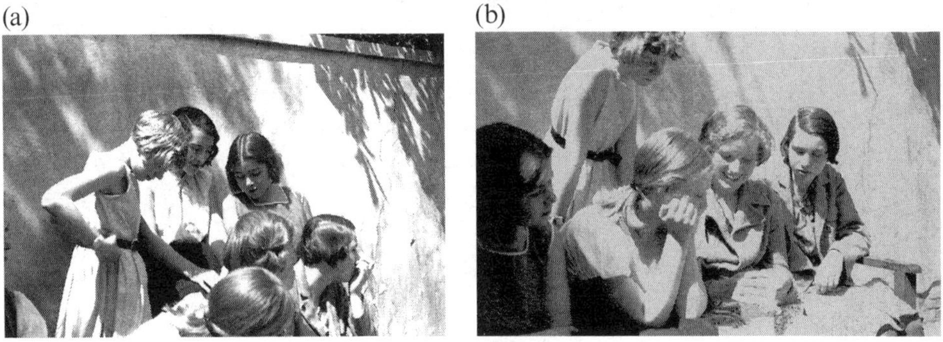

Figure 2.8 (a, b) From the same grouping as in Figure 2.7.

Probably he could hear what they were saying (he, too, was not using a telephoto lens). He might even have seen what they crowded together to look at, whatever it was hidden behind Mabbie's head or whatever she was then holding cupped in her hands. We the viewers only have access to what the image allows. Just as codes and whispers create mystery per se (however banal their actual meaning might turn out to be), the girls' interest in a hidden object incites in us a curiosity that takes us beyond the object as such, suffusing the entire scene with a sense of the mystery of the fleeting moment itself.

*

The difficulty in imagining the past at all, let alone vividly, is to see it as a present moment, and this is where Bob's photographs come in. They obviously do not *document* the Hietzing School in the sense that the children's projects or the adults' subsequent accounts do. What they give us instead is a means to imagine the school more vividly, in the sense suggested by Peter Burke. In doing so, in looking seriously at these traces and scattered moments of those involved, thoughts come to mind which the written records would not have aroused. Such as that question of the effects on the child's consciousness of being placed under observation, and, by analogy and more importantly, the after-effects of having once been under psychoanalytical observation.

The instigators of the Hietzing School were well aware of the social and political determinants of education; it was to avoid their effects and the state education system that the school was established. Their idealism was pragmatic and, at least as far as Anna Freud was concerned, was founded on a psychoanalytic understanding of child development and the limitations its stages imposed.

No doubt she had read the book Siegfried Bernfeld published in 1925 – *Sisyphos or the Limits of Education.* In his judgment schooling could only take you so far and terminates when the student becomes autonomous. In his foreword to the 1928 second edition, Bernfeld stated soberly: "The educability of the child is limited; so also is the ability to educate of the educator"[2] (Bernfeld [1925] 1928 [unpaginated p. ii]).

Anna's idealism was therapeutic rather than pedagogic: she wanted to spare children the negative experiences of her own childhood. On December 11, 1927, in the first letter to Lou Andreas-Salomé that mentions the new school, she wrote:

> It seems such a lovely aim; to free children from fear and make them at home in everything. For I remember so well how afraid I was of the unknown and how with understanding I overcame it.
>
> (Rothe & Weber, 2001, p. 551)

Earlier that year she had been corresponding with Lou about child analysis. In her letter of May 17, 1927, she admitted that she had always secretly had a bad conscience as far as Lou was concerned, because of their differing attitudes toward child analysis: "… I go so far into education and you always said, you had no desire to make children anything other than they were. I always want to make them different…" (ibid, p. 546)

It is possible that Lou's unwillingness to educate through analysis had its origins in her own happy childhood and her consequent lifelong self-confidence. It is as if she felt there was no need to teach children to be at peace with themselves and the world. Anna was unable to take that for granted: a child needed guidance. That Bob and Mabbie referred to their analytical hours with Anna as "lessons" fits in with her practice and intent.

Anna left no direct account of her work with the Hietzing pupils. She did leave accounts of her ideas on training young children, which make it clear that she was willing to take the side of their superego in their treatment, while remaining well aware of its dangers:

> The formation of the superego facilitates matters for those who are training and educating the child. Whereas up to this point they have carried on the struggle with a being absolutely opposed to them, they now have an ally in the enemy's camp. The educator of the older child can rely on this superego to support him, he knows that he and the superego will join forces against the child. Thus the child finds himself confronted by two authorities, the transformed part of his own inner personality, i.e., his new superego, and the ever-present love object of the outer world. He becomes unexpectedly docile and obedient. It is the docility thus achieved, the strict obedience which the parents or educator so often encourage for the sake of making their work easier, that can drive the child into extreme repression, into neurosis.
>
> (Freud, 1935, pp. 23–24)

Among the pupils who were her analysands, Peter Heller and Tinky Burlingham were no longer infants; Bob and Mabbie Burlingham already adolescents. At that age too, analytic intervention might still tend to foster obedience and docility, especially if analyst and mother were in close alliance. But the adolescent analysand does have their own resources, if not argument then concealment, to counter the attack (it is worth noting Anna's military metaphors – "an ally in the enemy's camp," "join forces against the child").

Whether Bob's perilous trick cycling on the Cobenzl ever featured in his analysis, we do not know. We do know, from his friend Ernst Halberstadt's memoirs, that when Bob scaled the outer wall of the school and clambered into an upper room through the window, his chief anxiety at that moment was – "Mother mustn't know" (Benveniste, 2015, p. 121).

In his reflections on his own analysis, Peter Heller's feelings were mixed and ambivalent. One persistent suspicion was that it had had an infantilising effect on him. The desire to help children conquer their fears and anxieties might result in overprotection. Years previously, in 1918, around the time she began her analysis with her father, Anna had confessed in a poem that analyzed her own self-protectiveness: "I was like the mother that weakens its own child / Through too much love..." The poem was entitled "Error" and the error was that of false mastery, of trying to play the part of fate, and of confusing one's fantasies with the real world: "Last night I first realized the error. / Instead of faithfully reproducing the world / I have made a likeness of my own self..."[3] (Spreitzer, 2014, p. 107).

*

The end of the Hietzing School came about naturally; the teachers had careers to pursue; the children were growing up; Bob needed to go on to a further education they could not provide. As for the end that Bernfeld foresaw, the pupil's autonomy – though it may, in its fullest sense, be classed among the impossibilities that confront psychoanalysis and education – this final photo might be taken as a representation of that ideal (Figure 2.9).

The girl sitting on the school step is perfectly self-contained, her right hand holding her left arm, bowed over the big book on her lap. This is the same girl (Priscilla de Forest) who in a previous series closed her eyes and shielded her face from the sun. Here she is partly in the shade but the book

Figure 2.9 Priscilla de Forest.

is a block of bright sunlight. Even so the shape of the print on the page can be made out, though not deciphered. It forms two vertical columns of text that seem to be center justified. Perhaps it is poetry.

***

Notes

1 Notes of a discussion in 1929 involving Sigmund and Anna Freud and Dorothy's husband Robert and his father illustrate the emotional background referred to here. *See* Burlingham (1989), pp. 200–204.

2 "Die Erziehbarkeit des Kindes ist beschränkt; die Erziehfähigkeit des Erziehers ist es gleichfalls..."

3 Quoted from "*Irrtum*" (my translation). Original: "Der Mutter glich ich, die das eigne Kind / Durch zu viel Liebe schwächt..." "Den Irrtum sah erst heute Nacht ich ein. Ich hab' / Anstatt die Welt getreulich nachzubilden, / Ein Abbild meines eignen Selbst gemacht..."

References

Benveniste, D. (2015) *The Interwoven Lives of Sigmund, Anna and W. Ernest Freud.* New York: IPBooks.

Bernfeld, S. (1928 [1925]) *Sisyphos oder die Grenzen der Erziehung.* Leipzig, Wien and Zürich: Internationaler Psychoanalytischer Verlag.

Burke, P. (2001) *Eyewitnessing: The Use of Images as Historical Evidence.* London: Reaktion.

Burlingham, M. J. (1989) *The Last Tiffany: A Biography of Dorothy Tiffany Burlingham.* New York: Atheneum.

Erik, E. H., & Erikson, J. (1980) Dorothy Burlingham's School in Vienna. *Bul. Anna Freud Centre,* 3(2):91–94.

Freud, A. (1935) Psychoanalysis and the Training of the Young Child. *Psychoanalytic Quarterly*, 4:15–24.

Heller, P. (1990) *A Child Analysis with Anna Freud.* Madison, CT: International Universities Press.

Heller, P. (1992) *Anna Freud's Letters to Eva Rosenfeld.* Madison, CT: International Universities Press.

McCullin, D. (1994) *Sleeping with Ghosts.* London: Jonathan Cape.

Partridge, E. (1984) *A Dictionary of Slang and Unconventional English* (8th edition, edited by Paul Beale). London: Routledge.

Rothe, D. & I. Weber [Hg.] (2001) "*... als käm ich heim zu Vater und Schwester*": *Lou Andreas-Salomé – Anna Freud Briefwechsel 1919–1937.* Göttingen: Wallenstein.

Spreitzer, B. (Hg.) (2014) *Anna Freud: Gedichte – Prosa – Übersetzungen.* Wien, Köln, and Weimar: Böhlau Verlag.

Note on photographs

The photographs are from the Collection of Michael J. Burlingham. I am grateful to him for his help with identifying the children and for having granted permission to reproduce the photos here. All photos except one (Figure 2.3) were taken by Bob Burlingham during his time at the Hietzing School. Though Bob was less than sixteen years old, as a photographer he had both artistry and technical skill and his photos are of remarkable quality. I have discussed them primarily in terms of the relationship between the photographer and his subjects, and not in aesthetic terms, but should add that I consider these images to have considerable merit in their own right, both singly and in conjunction with each other.

Chapter 3

The Hietzing years

Elizabeth Ann Danto

Wattmanngasse 11, Vienna

Seen from the outside, the Hietzing School, a small school that opened in Vienna's 13th District in 1927, looked more like a New England split-wood cabin than a traditional educational establishment. With just two floors of several rooms each, the school was endearingly nicknamed the "Matchbox" by students and faculty. Since both the school and its playground had been built in Eva Rosenfeld's former garden, behind her home on Wattmanngasse, their classes overlooked the one remaining walnut tree. Its "branches were a sort of balcony onto which the children climbed from the windows of the first floor," as Rosenfeld (1970) described it later. The children made up a small crowd at best, and in the school's early years, they all ate lunch together. Their school logo, which Bob Burlingham designed for the student journal, was an encircled sun with five rays shining on a mountain range. (Figure 3.1)

Inside, the upper floor was divided into two classrooms and a library, or rather a large classroom lined with library shelves, a *cartotheke* for collecting pictures, and posters about geography and grammar tacked on the wall. A fairly broad staircase, painted green, eased the upstairs–downstairs foot traffic. The lower floor was entered from the playground, had a small coat room to the left, the director's office to the right, and the community workshop with large tables and two workbenches at the end. Until the early 1930s, Peter Blos shared the director's office with Erik Erikson (then Homburger) and August Aichhorn for both curricular and administrative matters. Between 15 and 25 students attended at any one time; they were separated into a "younger group" and an "older group" which ended at the equivalent of sixth grade. Today it would be called a "micro-school." About a dozen more children were enrolled before the school closed in 1932. The founders' original goal was to implement Anna Freud's concept of a school "organized according to psychoanalytic principles" (A. Freud, 1927, p. 47). But how and why Hietzing came to figure as so much more than a mere addition to the history of psychoanalysis and education is a complex narrative. Archival documents and oral histories show, today, that Hietzing was a seedbed of modern

Figure 3.1 Lunchtime at the Hietzing School, 1927.

theory in child and adolescent mental health, from Erik Erikson's lifespan model of "identity" to the legal system's concept of "best interests of the child." In programmatic innovation, Hietzing led to the Jackson Nursery in Vienna, the Hampstead War Nurseries and the Hampstead Child Therapy Course and Clinic in London, and influenced a range of psychoanalytically informed schools and services across America. (Figure 3.2)

Figure 3.2 The School (Die Schule) 1928.

Founders and mentors

The Hietzing School opened in the Fall of 1927 in an outlying leafy district of Vienna. The idea grew, in part, out of the search that Dorothy Tiffany Burlingham conducted to find an adequate school for her twelve-year-old son Bob and her three younger children. "Before I was married," Burlingham (1975) told Peter Heller, "I had this fantasy of adopting a whole lot of children and the kind of school I would have for them. I had a horrible schooling [and] I wanted to give them something that wasn't so horrible." With her complicated marriage to Robert Burlingham ending, Dorothy had brought her children to Vienna in 1924 for respite, safety and psychoanalysis. Then, since "Dorothy's American children did not fit into the conventional schools of Vienna," as Anna Freud explained, "her obvious remedy was to found a modern school of her own" (A. Freud, 1980, p. 12). The modern school would be, arguably, a compromise between her father's own foundation at Laurelton Hall – an art school without curriculum, classes, rules or teachers – and the structured private schools she had attended in New York. Dorothy's vision fit a modernist educational ideology, in which teachers were urged to let pupils find what excites them and reward their pursuit of independent learning.

Founding the new school was not Dorothy's idea alone. While "Dorothy was implementing the best possible school," Erikson (1980, p. 3) said, "Anna Freud, of course, was discreetly omnipresent." The two women were joined by their friend Eva Rosenfeld. "[They] dreamed the whole idea up together . . . for children of different nationalities whose parents were in analysis or who were perhaps in analysis themselves." But Eva had an altogether different motive for starting the school. To the rhetorical question "Why a school?" she answered: "I never thought about my reasons for choosing that kind of monument for my daughter; I wanted to find comfort for my own sad heart in being with the young ones" (Rosenfeld, 1992, p. 16). Her fifteen-year-old daughter Mädi died that year in a sudden mountain accident.

A new progressive school was more in keeping with Eva Rosenfeld's career than she let on. "Her life's work – helping, teaching, healing ... with a fierce sense of justice," as her son Victor Ross (né Rosenfeld) described it, had been launched at Zellerhaus, a social work service for homeless girls in her native Berlin of the early 1900s. Eva moved to Vienna after marrying Valentin Rosenfeld, attended Freud's lectures and, after World War I, transformed part of her house into "a model of household and gardening management, a sort of 'research station' with deeper psychological functions for young women" (Ross, 1992, p. 26). One boarder was a patient of Eva's close friend, Anna Freud. Eva was actually close to both Anna and Dorothy, but at the time Anna felt so comfortable in Eva's home that, with her parents on a holiday in December 1926, she wrote to Lou Andreas-Salomé: "So that I won't be so alone in Berggasse, I'm moving with Wolf to Eva Rosenfeld's in Hietzing" (A. Freud, 1926 in Rothe and Weber, 2004, Letter # 290, p. 534). (Figure 3.3)

Figure 3.3 Eva Rosenfeld.

Before settling into the large fourth-floor apartment at Berggasse 19, the Burlingham family lived in a pretty cottage on the Semmering property of Dorothy's American friends, Ruth and Arthur Sweetser. Anna and Dorothy had grown closer; Anna was analyzing Bob and Dorothy was in analysis with Freud. On Eva Rosenfeld's advice, Dorothy had already hired Peter Blos, a pre-medical student at the University of Vienna who had grown up in a family of German intellectuals. He would tutor Bob and his younger sister Mabbie. The arrangement worked out so well that, at Dorothy and Anna's request, Blos left his biology studies to run the new Hietzing School in the spring of 1926. He had a teacher's diploma from the University of Heidelberg but no experience as an educational administrator. Still, the children trusted him, and this good relationship, combined with a lively interest in both art and science, offered the kind of pedagogical progressivism for which Dorothy hired him.

In 1927, Blos moved into the director's office. While "I personally had no interest in the psychoanalytic world," he said of those years, "I wished to get acquainted with August Aichhorn" (Blos, 1994, p. A-19) – insuring that, eventually, the school's program would be influenced to move in that direction. And in a sense, Sigmund Freud influenced that direction too.

Historically, Freud wrote about education from three positions: as the psychoanalytic theoretician himself; as father of Anna Freud, a teacher and emerging as a child analyst; and as a Viennese intellectual, a sometimes controversial but always collegial figure in the City's academic and political circles. "It is no wonder that psychoanalytic work was expected to be valuable in education. My personal role in this application has been slight … yet I appreciate the great social value which attracts my colleagues in the pedagogical field" (S. Freud, 1925, p. 274). These colleagues were reformist teachers like Siegfried Bernfeld and August Aichhorn, friends with both Sigmund and Anna, who wrote about the new psychoanalytically informed education for disenfranchised or disturbed youth.

August Aichhorn was a kind and serious mentor and, according to Anna Freud and many others, "an especially natural teacher." Aichhorn believed that adopting psychoanalysis in schools could resolve most pedagogical impasses. "When the psychic mechanisms revealed by psychoanalysis are familiar to the educator," he wrote in 1925 (p. 10), "what has been intuitive becomes a recognition of the forces involved. [Yet] for well-rounded work, he must take into consideration many other factors, psychiatric, sociological, economic and cultural." Aichhorn also noted that the most crucial factor in psychoanalysis, especially of adolescents, is the quality of the analyst's empathy and the clarity of reassuring questions experienced as authenticity. A child welfare specialist for the city of Vienna in the early 1920s, the more Aichhorn thought about the educational and psychological needs of stigmatised children, the more he sought to bring about environmental change. He converted the former refugee camp Oberhollabrunn, in Lower Austria, into an extensive residency and educational center for troubled youth, and then replicated this community strategy in St Andrä. Anna Freud was captivated. "He wasn't only able to reach children otherwise unreachable," she said. "He influenced a lot of us" (Coles, 1991, p. 46).

While still a young and newly certified teacher, Anna Freud would meet with Aichhorn every Friday to tour a range of social welfare agencies which grew rapidly under Vienna's Social Democratic government elected in 1919. They visited Siegfried Bernfeld, who also in 1919 founded *Kinderheim Baumgarten*, an educational refuge for Jewish war orphans. The ideas of Maria Montessori, socialism and psychoanalysis, were popular then, and Bernfeld knew how to merge them into the kind of empowering approach to education that would promote systemic change. He believed that social repression was an early impediment to children's development and that teachers generally reinforced the moral burden instead of lifting it. "[Because] childhood and youth are not purposeless, transitional stages on the way to maturity," he said, "… no theory of education can resolve the antipathy between the justified will of the child and the justified will of the teacher; on the contrary, education consists in this antipathy" (Bernfeld, 1973, pp. 9, 16). Like Aichhorn, Bernfeld was convinced that the flexibility

Figure 3.4 Siegfried Bernfeld, late 1930s.

and innovation of psychoanalysis could be used productively in education; in fact without it, education would simply perpetuate the status quo and stifle human growth. (Figure 3.4)

Though it was deeply influential, the *Kinderheim* was short lived. Willi Hoffer, who had volunteered there, took over from Bernfeld just as the school was closing down. Hoffer's later lectures on public education and his psychoanalytically based "Vienna Course for Educators," which reached teachers from the city's nursery, elementary and high schools, were informed by case illustrations from his *Kinderheim* work with the child refugees, many under five years' old, starving, handicapped or traumatised (A. Freud, 1966). Anna Freud was deeply moved by what she observed in these agencies. She said that Baumgarten was "the first experiment to apply psychoanalytic principles to education" (A. Freud, 1968, p. 7) and pursued this theme in her later *Lectures for Parents and Teachers.*

> Whoever wishes to discover the connection between unemployment, the housing shortage, and neglected children must [read] sociology. But the teacher who desires to learn more of the mental background of the individual child may obtain information through the new science of psychoanalysis.
>
> (A. Freud, 1930, p. 75)

The Hietzing School would offer her a place to put into practice what she had been believing, observing and conceptualising for almost a decade.

Teachers and learning

The summer of 1927 was not a good time to be in Vienna. Soldiers from Austria's protofascist *Heimwehr* ("Homeland Guards") were acquitted of their violent attacks on Social Democrats; a general strike was called and then crushed with heavy artillery; and the Palace of Justice was set on fire. But, as the founders of Hietzing discovered, it was ironically a good time to start a new school. Under the clerical conservative leadership of Ignaz Seipel, the increasingly strident Christian Social Party passed an education bill which, that summer, began dismantling Otto Glöckel's progressive reforms. As the Social Democrat's Minister for Education, Glöckel had sought to eliminate the *Drillschule* tradition of rote learning while modernising the schools – exactly what Dorothy had wanted for her children. The solution was to create a school of their own, and Dorothy had the money to build it, pay the teachers, buy the supplies and keep the project going for the next five years. "School starts tomorrow, full of children" she wrote gleefully to Max Eitingon on October 2nd (Burlingham, 1927 in T. Aichhorn, 2012, p. 80. Figure 3.5).

Dorothy's excitement about the new school had gathered strength over the summer. In discussions with the director, and of course Anna and Eva, she gave Peter Blos and Erik Erikson a free hand to develop their curriculum: it would be structured but, without grades, experimental and progressive yet thoroughly academic in its own way. Erikson had been hired as a second teacher after Blos successfully recruited more students.

Figure 3.5 Hietzing, the schoolyard in the afternoon.

In telling the story of Erikson's arrival at Hietzing, Blos made the point that his lifelong friend knew little about education but was "an artist of great talent… I believe more in giftedness than in training." Blos remembered, quite vividly, how Anna Freud first hesitated and then answered: "I want to meet your friend" (Blos, 1994, pp. A 34–35). By all reports, both Erikson and Blos were well liked as teachers. They were friendly and handsome, and gave the children confidence in their own research and artistic skills. Anna and Dorothy wanted students to develop skills that would promote their personal growth and be useful to society, rather than forcing them to learn what traditional standards regarded as significant. "So many teachers judge themselves by what they get children to learn," Anna later told Robert Coles (1991, p. 31). "But teaching is not only presentation of facts; it is persuading students to be interested in the world – a state of mind."

For Dorothy, the incentive may have been more personal. "My first school experience was rather tragic for me," she wrote to Peter Heller in 1974. "My memory was being put in a corner with a dunce cap on and told how stupid I was. This affected my whole life, and also my children's for I realized the importance of how one is taught." She wanted a school filled with literature and art – her father was Louis Comfort Tiffany, and she grew up immersed in the progressive worldview of an upper-class New York family. Robert Weeks de Forest, her cousin, had a leadership career that reached from the Charity Organization Society to the Metropolitan Museum of Art. The family placed within the city's avantgarde interested in psychoanalysis: at the time of Freud's sole visit to the United States in 1909, Dorothy's mother Louise and Robert's sister, the photographer Julia Brasher de Forest, were reading *Interpretation of Dreams* together – in German (M. J. Burlingham, 2017).

With this childhood exposure to reformist thinking, Dorothy was comfortable with the innovative educational design on which Peter Blos had decided. Students at the Hietzing School would have a project to work on regardless of their age. They would collectively choose a theme, for example, England, and then research every aspect of the theme from the history of a specific era to geography to, as Eva Rosenfeld (1970, p. 38) describes it, "a thorough study of the language, drawing, map-reading, poets and painters, natural and cultural history and so forth. For certain subjects, the children would study together and for others, they remained apart." Group projects, most of which combined art and language skills, were part of a broader effort to learn how a culture works and to cultivate forms of critical thinking. This model of social interaction and group learning was key to a pedagogy developed by John Dewey, and adapted by Peter Blos as he shaped the school-wide curriculum. Though class schedules varied over the years, basics like math, drawing, Latin and languages were usually taught first

Figure 3.6 On the school steps with Peter Blos.

thing every morning for two hours, with the rest of the day spent on work in small groups and English. Blos deliberately set aside the afternoon hours for "free work." For one project, Mario Iona (1983) remembered, girls and boys crowded around a work table in the library, excitedly building a model of the "apparent orbits of the sun throughout the seasons" they had learned in Erikson's science class. (Figure 3.6)

Hietzing's perspective did not direct the teachers to give up texts that had long been a mainstay of humanist education, but it did mean approaching study topics differently. Books, models, and pictures from the library *carthoteke*'s stack of National Geographic magazines were used for images of animals and their habitats, landscapes and people around the globe. At bi-weekly community meetings, students reported on their wide-ranging free work studies from geography and history, to nature study or physics. The reports would then be collected and reviewed (but not graded) and, some years, added to the school newsletter. Student tasks were evaluated not just for academic skills, like math and literacy, or sports, but also for social and emotional skills. "They are then amazingly capable of drawing all the facets of learning the mandatory 'three Rs' into the focus of a given project and of mastering otherwise dreary-to-learn skills," observed Erikson (1980, p. 5). (Figure 3.7)

Figure 3.7 Sports in Türkenschanzpark.

Joan and Erik Erikson (Erikson, 1980, p. 5) remembered the system vividly:

> We taught by [John Dewey's] Project Method. This called for an ingenious combination of playful new experience, careful experiment, and free discussions while it conveyed a sense of contextuality for all the details learned. The whole school would become, for example, the world of the Eskimos. All subjects were then related to Eskimo life – geography, history, science, math and, of course, reading and writing. The Project method was [based on] Dewey's theory that children learn only when their interest is fully engaged and centered.

Like the other teachers, Marie Briehl was drawn to the new school by Deweyism, which she had studied in New York, and by child analysis for which she was training with Anna Freud in 1927. She came from an activist family and related well to Hietzing, in part because she felt that Dewey's method of "learning by doing" was central to a new concept of teaching, and in part because, she said, "it was my understanding that [the Freuds] were Social Democrats and [Anna] knew about my Socialist background" (Briehl, 1984, Track 11). Of the school's three English teachers, Dorothy Burlingham and Esther Menaker taught literature while Briehl focused on language. Briehl liked what she saw as the lack of competitiveness in the classroom, the friendly relationship between teachers and pupils, and the positive effects of decreased anxiety on student learning. Esther Menaker did too. "I was impressed by the lack of authoritarian atmosphere and by the camaraderie between teachers and students," Menaker (1990) wrote to Peter Heller. Interestingly, Menaker's recollections of the Hietzing atmosphere lack the edge with which she described her ongoing misgivings about Anna Freud and the field of child analysis in Vienna. "One day when the students were playing in the yard, someone threw a snowball that hit Peter Blos in the eye. His self-control and absence of anger – although he was firm in his disapproval – was admirable" (Menaker, 1990). And Blos was also well organised. As Dorothy certified, Blos' "ability to find new methods of making children work independently and carry out the teaching schedule was excellent" (Burlingham, 1934). About to turn over the school's leadership to August Aichhorn in 1931, he wrote: "The timetable [and] the number of hours for specific topics remain the same. We will begin the regular schedule on the first day. Geometry repetitions would be the final hour on Saturday. But you can easily change Eissler's hours" (Blos, 1931). Kurt Eissler was one of the two math instructors; the other math teacher was from the local *Realschule* (Hoch, 2016). (Figure 3.8)

Clearly, none of these teachers wanted to be mere stakeholders in a new school. They found that Hietzing offered, for the most part, a modernist, child-centered education that used a collective approach to learning and a meaningful academic curriculum. By giving its students the time and space to attend their analytic sessions, it afforded them an empathic, non-threatening environment. In a sense, the Hietzing ethos was abiding by one of Freud's precepts on human society. We need both freedom and discipline but it is authoritarianism that inhibits our empathy for others. "Strict ethical demands would not do so much harm," Freud wrote in 1930 (p. 134), "if education were to say: This is how we must behave in order to be happy and to make others happy." Education restores the coveted balance between freedom and social structure. And teachers, who show children that empathy comes with understanding of ourselves and others, enhance our human capacity for happiness.

Vienna's interwar environment matched well with the Hietzing objectives. Red Vienna, as the era from 1919 to roughly 1934 is known, advanced new-sprung professions of utilitarian architecture, public health policy and

Figure 3.8 Hietzing School logo.

professional social work, and emphasised the significance of culture for a city of workers. The governing Social Democrats invested in medical and dental clinics, family assistance and alcoholism programs, aid to children and maternal consultation centers. With its handsome public housing, social welfare programs for families, its art and music, the city projected public commitment and civic pride. Above all, however, school reform stood out as the centerpiece of socialist cultural politics. The movement swept up Viennese thinkers from Sigmund Freud to Ludwig Wittgenstein. "Am I doing child psychology?" asked the great philosopher. "I am making a connection between the concept of teaching and the concept of meaning" (Peters, 2012, p. 19).

Bernfeld and Aichhorn's educational projects intersected with these reforms both in ideology and in implementation. Similarly, when Anna Freud sought to further the child's capacity to become "a free and self-reliant human being" (A. Freud, 1930, p. 127), she virtually echoed the social democratic goals advanced by Otto Glöckel. Glöckel's plans for a network of *Arbeitsschule* (activity schools) and for boosting *Selbsttätigkeit* (self-motivation) were based on a simple idea: education for independence. Or, as she told Robert Coles (1991, p. 5): "Those five years [teaching in an elementary school] ... gave me a chance to learn from the children – and learn that children not only need to be taught but need to have a chance themselves to teach." The Project method, exactly.

Psychoanalytically aware education

From the student perspective, the Hietzing environment was mindful of psychoanalysis, meaning mostly that classmates knew who was, and who was not, in analysis. The teachers' actual involvement with analysis varied widely: some like Marie Briehl, Kurt Eissler and Erik Erikson were in training analysis; some like August Aichhorn and Dorothy Burlingham were already accomplished practitioners; and others like Peter Blos hadn't even started. Analysis and education co-existed; the boundaries between the two seem to have been drawn but with some ambiguity. As Marie Briehl explained,

> The staff met to discuss curriculum, and also individual students and their progress or difficulties in conferences with Anna Freud and Dorothy Burlingham. Marie Bonaparte stopped in occasionally. Some children were in analysis for emotional or behavioral difficulties. Nevertheless, the aim of the school was education and social relations among students, and between pupils and teachers.
>
> (Briehl, 1983)

Tinky (Katrina) Burlingham attended Hietzing from the very beginning and captured the atmosphere well: "Yes, there was a connection between analysis and the school's educational ideas but personal analysis and analysis in general was not brought into the classroom," she told Peter Heller, adding "School was academic and fortunately removed from analytical interpretations" (Burlingham-Valenstein, 1982). Her mother agreed. Dorothy corroborated Briehl's recall of staff meetings, later telling Peter Heller that

> it [was] conceivable that the analysts discussed how some child or another need[ed] something – but that certainly wasn't the purpose... We did not make any systematic or explicit connection between the pedagogical side and the analytic side. On the contrary, I think one tried to do the opposite. It was to be as normal a school as possible with an emphasis on enjoying literature, art and so forth.
>
> (Burlingham, 1975, p. 6)

Despite the stated boundary between analysis and the educational agenda, the school's atmosphere was, as Erikson (1980, p. 3) said wryly, "hospitable to a psychoanalytic orientation." Both students and teachers were aware that some, if not most, of the children had near daily appointments. Bob Burlingham had his "lessons" with Anna Freud; Ruth Bernstein visited Jenny Waelder-Hall every afternoon except Friday; Walter Aichhorn was in analysis with Dorothy. Anna Freud also counted Peter Heller, Ernst Freud, Reinhard Simmel, Priscilla de Forest and the Sweetzer children among her patients. During the staff meetings (on which Erikson, Briehl, Heller and Dorothy reported), the names and circumstances of children who were experiencing emotional or behavioral difficulties were brought up. But even then, clinical exchanges and individual interpretations were considered out of line. The boundary applied to the instructional staff as well. In this, they amplified on a salient principle of psychoanalytic pedagogy that teachers must be aware of their inner worlds in order to help children and adolescents cope with theirs. (Figure 3.9)

Figure 3.9 Schoolyard, behind the Rosenfeld home.

Some students were personally opposed to the presence of psychoanalysis even though they liked the school. Others like Anne Nederhood and Kyra Nijinsky were uninterested. At age 12, Elisabeth Iona and her twin brother Mario did enjoy Hietzing's co-ed alternative to what she called "the very conventional and old-fashioned" secondary education in the city. Their parents ran the international Laxenburg-Hellerau dance school near Vienna and had sent the children to a progressive primary school. Elisabeth was not in analysis and was very emphatic about it. She was also religious. "There seemed to be an emptiness created by the analysis," she commented. "I would not have liked that done to me. I valued my interior life" (Iona-Lewis, 1982). The witty Victor Ross was even more adamant.

> I was not in analysis, not conscious of analysis, and had none of the hang-ups that the unanalyzed had vis-à-vis the analyzed. I thought that analysis was a minor misfortune that befell some, like the dentist, and that if one did not have to go, so much the better.
>
> (Ross, 1989)

Aside from the psychoanalytic perspective, in retrospect most students felt that the education at Hietzing had helped them form a progressive worldview. Elisabeth Iona, with all her objections to psychoanalysis, said that Hietzing's values "opened my eyes to a wider world... It showed us different ways of thinking; it taught us tolerance and understanding. We met so many different kinds of people. It taught us to 'see large'" (Iona-Lewis, 1982). For Basti (Sebastian) Baer, whose mother taught music at Hietzing, the school's "liberal and creative atmosphere" stayed with him all his life. He told Peter Heller: "I believe that my own values of antiracism, individualism and the absolute need for freedom while rejecting the cult of personality, stemmed from the school" (Baer, 1989). Elisabeth and Basti may well be alluding to the *Weltanschauung*, the kind of ethic that undergirded the development of Red Vienna and allowed the city to emerge from the devastation of World War I with what the social psychologist Marie Jahoda called "not so much a theory as a way of life ... pervaded by a sense of hope that has no parallel in the 20th century" (Jahoda, 1983, p. 343). The Social Democratic Party believed in the future but focused on the present. "It was not just a promise to be redeemed later but an activity that encompassed life as a whole in the here and now," Jahoda wrote. She spoke of modern housing, symphony concerts for workers and summer camps for urban children – how the social democrats enriched the lives of hundreds of thousands. This was, arguably, the same momentum that seized child analysis and psychoanalytic pedagogy. From Anna Freud to Maria Montessori, to Lili Roubiczek-Peller and Eugenie Schwarzwald, Josef Friedjung, Wilhelm Reich, Karl and Charlotte Bühler and the contributors to the new *Zeitschrift für Psychoanalytische Pädagogik* (*Journal*

Figure 3.10 Games in the Schoolyard.

of Psychoanalytic Pedagogy), all explored the interplay between school reform, child analysis and human freedom.

"Back in Vienna then, we were all so excited – full of energy, Anna Freud told Robert Coles" (1991, p. 9). "It was as if a whole new continent was being explored. We were the explorers, and we now had the chance to change things." (Figure 3.10)

Marie Jahoda remembered the parallel, darker side of this era as well: "So much were we involved in this all-embracing movement that we did not pay enough attention to the wide gulf that separated us from the other side in Austria's deeply split culture – until it was too late" (Jahoda, 1983, p. 343). No question that Red Vienna ebbed as Black Vienna, the moniker for Austria's conservative and ever more reactionary sector, grew in strength and violence. The Christian Social Party dominated the University of Vienna, transforming the Medical School (where Freud taught) into an anti-Semitic, anti-scientific and anti-democratic stronghold for Austria. Among students and faculty alike, the anti-liberal political climate at the University was controlled by a coalition of German-nationalist parties of the Right namely the *Christlichesoziale Partei*, the *Grossdeutsche Volkspartei* and the *Landbund* (Heiss, 1993; Taschwer, 2015). By 1932, the Medical School was firmly in the hands of the Austro-Fascists and over eighty percent of the faculty was gone. So too was Hietzing.

A legacy of theory

In April 1933, two months after Hitler's takeover in Berlin, Freud summed up the political mood. "We are in transition toward a rightist dictatorship, which means the suppression of social democracy," he wrote to Ernest Jones

(Freud, 1933, p. 716). No wonder that the Hietzing School, born of social democracy, had closed down the year before. When the time came to move into the Austrian school system, all the children passed the state exams (D. T. Burlingham, 1934). The exile had begun. Most of the American teachers like Briehl and Menaker went home. Eva Rosenfeld had already moved to Berlin and then left for England. Erik and Joan Erikson fled to Boston, and Peter Blos to New York. Kurt Eissler, the last candidate to be admitted to the Vienna Psychoanalytic Society under Freud, left for New York in 1937. Anna Freud stayed with her family in Vienna until 1938, and August Aichhorn never left the city.

The particular kind of pedagogy they had embraced at Hietzing was complex and, in its founders' estimation, motivated by psychoanalysis but not psychoanalytic in itself. For Anna Freud and Dorothy Burlingham, there was no contradiction between the collectivity of the Project Method and the individualism of child analysis. Most significantly however, for all the path-breaking work the two women did later, they were among a sizeable number of early 20th- century analysts who drew on their years at Hietzing to develop later theories of depth and on-going influence.

Today psychoanalytic writers of note, like Florian Houssier (2009) in France, regard Hietzing as the birthplace of a unified psychoanalytic theory of adolescence. Anna Freud's role is decisive, says Houssier (Houssier & Marty, 2010), for whom she represents a nodal point in the metapsychology of adolescence; her work lies at the critical intersection between August Aichhorn and Siegfried Bernfeld on the one hand, and the next generation, namely Peter Blos and Erik Erikson, on the other. Her articulation of children's rights in both "Beyond..." (1973) and "Before" (1979), the best interests of the child, originated in the emancipatory ethos of Red Vienna. Today, the Hietzing staff roster reads like the register of classical theorists on adolescent development. They remained colleagues, friends and mentors in exile after the mid-1930s, and each one gained from the other to investigate the adolescent mind. Notes from their shared experience in staff meetings stretched Marie Briehl's advances in child analysis. Anna Freud wrote about adolescent reactions as prototypes, in themselves, of developmental disturbance. Peter Blos drew on August Aichhorn, Anna Freud and Erik Erikson for *On Adolescence* (1962). Kurt Eissler published on technique in the treatment of adolescents. And Erik H. Erikson, the Pulitzer Prize winner who pushed the central concept of the social environment's influence on human development, taught and trained at Hietzing. That experience made plain that the teacher "should ask himself not where his work touches the work of the analyst or the worker in child guidance, but where and how it in itself gives him the opportunity to make use of his new knowledge" (Erikson, 1930, p. 15). Applying this to himself by posing the perennial question "Who am I?" Erikson began to merge his own two self-concepts – the artist and the teacher – into one vocation, the psychoanalyst. Later, this question provided Erikson with the prompt he needed for Stage 5 in human psychosocial development: adolescence, or the dueling memes of identity and role confusion. "In our memory of the Hietzing school," Erik and Joan Erikson (Erikson, 1980) recapped together, "we experienced that rare joy which is evoked where a setting permits us to respond to the growth potentials of young people as they reveal and develop our own potentials."

The Hietzing School was, as in a seeming epitaph by Marie Briehl (1983), the "not-to-be forgotten accomplishment of Anna Freud and Dorothy Burlingham."

Acknowledgments

The author wishes to thank Dr Claudia Lament, the Association for Child Psychoanalysis, and Taylor and Francis Co. for their kind permission to reprint this article originally published in *Psychoanalytic Study of the Child,* Issue 71(1), pages 137–148.

Illustrations

Figure 3.1 Lunchtime at school, b/w photograph, Peter Heller Album 3/16, Sigmund Freud Museum, Collection of the Sigmund Freud Privatstiftung, Vienna.

Figure 3.2 "Die Schule" (The school), sepia photograph, Eva Rosenfeld Album, Sigmund Freud Museum, Collection of the Sigmund Freud Privatstiftung, Vienna.

Figure 3.3 Eva Rosenfeld, b/w portrait from the 1920s, Peter Heller Album, Sigmund Freud Museum, Sigmund Freud Foundation, Collection of the Sigmund Freud Privatstiftung, Vienna.

Figure 3.4 Siegfried Bernfeld, b/w photograph by Ernst Wolff, ca.1939, Collection of Dr. Daniel Benveniste, Bellevue, Washington State.

Figure 3.5 The Hietzing School Yard, b/w photograph, Peter Heller Album 3/23, Sigmund Freud Museum, Sigmund Freud Foundation, Collection of the Sigmund Freud Privatstiftung, Vienna.

Figure 3.6 Pupils and Teachers on the School Steps, Eva Rosenfeld Album, Sigmund Freud Museum, Collection of the Sigmund Freud Privatstiftung, Vienna.

Figure 3.7 Sports in Türkenschanzpark, b/w photograph, Collection of Michael J. Burlingham, New York.

Figure 3.8 Hietzing School logo, wood or linoleum cut by Bob Burlingham 1929, Collection of Michael J. Burlingham, New York.

Figure 3.9 Game time, the Hietzing School, b/w photograph, Peter Heller Album 3/24, Sigmund Freud Museum, Sigmund Freud Foundation, Collection of the Sigmund Freud Privatstiftung, Vienna.

Figure 3.10 Students in Hietzing, photograph, Peter Heller Album 3/22, Sigmund Freud Museum, Collection of the Sigmund Freud Privatstiftung, Vienna.

References

Adam, E. et al. (1983) *Die Schul- und Bildungspolitik der österreichischen Sozialdemokratie in der Ersten Republik*. Vienna: Österreichischer Bundesverlag.

Aichhorn, A. (1925) *Wayward Youth*. New York: The Viking Press (1965). Originally published as *Verwahrloste Jugend*. Vienna: Internationaler Psychoanalytiches Verlag.

Aichhorn, T. (2007) La pédagogie psychanalytique viennoise. In Marty, F. and Houssier, F. eds, *Éduquer l'adolescent* [Educating the Adolescent]. Nîmes: éditions Champs Social, pp. 187–200.

Aichhorn, T. (2012) *Anna Freud/August Aichhorn. 'Die Psychoanalyse kann nur dort gedeihen, wo Freiheit des Gedankens herrscht' Briefwechsel 1921–1949* [Anna Freud/August Aichhorn. 'Psychoanalysis can thrive only where there is freedom of thought' Correspondence 1921–1949]. Frankfurt: Brandes & Apsel.

Baer, S. (Basti) Letter to Peter Heller dated July 9, 1989, folder "Questionnaire undated," Box 2, Peter Heller Papers, Manuscript Division, U.S. Library of Congress, Washington DC.

Bernfeld, S. *Sisyphus, or the Limits of Education* (1973) University of California Press, pp. 9, 16. Originally published as *Sisyphos oder die Grenzen der Erziehung* (1925).

Blos, P. (1931) Letter and memorandum to August Aichhorn, dated September 7, 1931 and titled "Lessons plan through December 1931." Estate of August Aichhorn. Collection of Thomas Aichhorn, Vienna.

Blos, P. (1962) *On Adolescence: A Psychoanalytic Interpretation*. New York: The Free Press.

Blos. P. (1994) *An Autobiographical Essay*. Unpublished memoir. Peter Blos Papers, unprocessed. Oskar Diethelm Library, DeWitt Wallace Institute for the History of Psychiatry, Weill Cornell Medical College.

Briehl, M. (1983) Letter of March 31, 1983 to Peter Heller, folder "Questionnaire, undated" Box 2, Peter Heller Papers, Manuscript Division, U.S. Library of Congress, Washington DC.

Briehl, M. (1984) Interview by Lucille Ritvo (1984–85) electronic transcript and sound tape. Oral History Collection of the Boston Psychoanalytic Society and Institute Archives.

Burlingham, D. T. (1927) Letter to Max Eitingon dated October 2, 1927. In Aichhorn, T. (2012) *Anna Freud/August Aichhorn. 'Die Psychoanalyse kann nur dort gedeihen, wo Freiheit des Gedankens herrscht' Briefwechsel 1921–1949* [Anna Freud/August Aichhorn. 'Psychoanalysis can thrive only where there is freedom of thought' Correspondence 1921–1949]. Frankfurt: Brandes & Apsel.

Burlingham, D. T. (1934) "Certificate." Peter Blos Papers, unprocessed. Oskar Diethelm Library, DeWitt Wallace Institute for the History of Psychiatry, Weill Cornell Medical College.

Burlingham, D. T. (1974) Letter to Peter Heller dated May 9, 1974, folder "Burlingham, Dorothy T., 1974–1975" Box 2, Peter Heller Papers, Manuscript Division, U.S. Library of Congress, Washington DC.

Burlingham, D. T. (1975) Interview with Peter Heller dated June 13, 1975, folder "Burlingham, Dorothy T., 1974–1975" Box 2, Peter Heller Papers, Manuscript Division, U.S. Library of Congress, Washington DC.

Burlingham, M. J. (1989) *The Last Tiffany: A Biography of Dorothy Tiffany Burlingham*. Atheneum.

Burlingham, M. J. (2017) personal communication with the author.

Burlingham-Valenstein, K. E. (1982) Response to Peter Heller. Folder "Questionnaires," Box 2, Peter Heller Papers, Manuscript Division, U.S. Library of Congress, Washington DC.

Coles, R. (1970) The Measure of Man – Profile of Erik H. Erikson. *The New Yorker*. November 7, 1970.

Coles, R. (1991) *Anna Freud – The Dream of Psychoanalysis*. Reading, MA: Addison Wesley/The Radcliffe Biography Series.

Erikson, E. H. (1930) "Psychoanalysis and the future of education". In Schlein, S. ed., (1995) *Erik H. Erikson – A Way of Looking at Things*. New York: W.W. Norton.

Erikson, E. H. and Erikson, J. (1980) "Dorothy Burlingham's school in Vienna". In Schlein, S. ed., (1995) *Erik H. Erikson – A Way of Looking at Things*. New York: W.W. Norton.

Freud, A. (1926) "Letter to Lou Andreas-Salomé dated December 21, 1926". In Rothe, D. A. and Weber, I. (2004) *"... als käm ich heim zu Vater und Schwester"- Lou Andreas-Salomé - Anna Freud: Briefwechsel 1919–1937* [As if I came home to father and sister: letters of Lou Andreas-Salomé and Anna Freud]. Göttingen: Wallstein Verlag.

Freud, A. (1927) "Introduction to psychoanalysis: lectures for child analysts and teachers, 1922–1935". In *The Writings of Anna Freud, Volume 1* (1974). New York: International Universities Press.

Freud, A. (1930) "Four lectures on psychoanalysis for teachers and parents". In *The Writings of Anna Freud, Volume 1* (1974). New York: International Universities Press.

Freud, A. (1966) A short history of child analysis. *The Psychoanalytic Study of the Child* 21: 7–14. New Haven, CT: Yale University Press.

Freud, A. (1968) Willi Hoffer In Memoriam. *Psychoanalytic Study of the Child* 23: 7–11. New Haven, CT: Yale University Press.

Freud, A. (1980) Dorothy Burlingham 1891–1979. In Memoriam. *Psychoanalytic Study of the Child* 35: 2–6. New Haven, CT: Yale University Press.

Freud, A., Goldstein, J. and Solnit, A. (1973) *Beyond the Best Interests of the Child*. New York: The Free Press.

Freud, A., Goldstein, J., Solnit, A. and Burlingham, D. T. T. (1979) *Before the Best Interests of the Child*. New York: The Free Press.

Freud, S. (1925) *"Foreword" to August Aichhorn's* Wayward Youth. *SE* 19: 274.

Freud, S. (1930) Civilization and its discontents. *SE* 21: 134.

Freud, S. (1933) Letter to Ernest Jones dated 7 April, 1933. *The Complete Correspondence of Sigmund Freud and Ernest Jones, 1908–1939*, ed. R. Andrew Paskauskas (1993). Cambridge, MA: The Belknap Press of Harvard University Press, #222, p. 716.

Friedman, L. J. (1999) *Identity's Architect: A Biography of Erik H. Erikson*. New York: Scribner.

Galatzer-Levy, R. and Galatzer-Levy, I. (2007) August Aichhorn – a different vision of psychoanalysis, children and society. *Psychoanalytic Study of the Child* 62: 153–179. New Haven, CT: Yale University Press.

Heiss, G. (1993) Pan-Germans, better Germans, Austrians: Austrian historians on national identity from the First to the Second Republic. *German Studies Review* 16/3: 411–433.

Hoch, R. B. (2016) unpublished interview with E. Danto and A. Steiner-Strauss, March 31, 2016, London.

Houssier, F. (2010) *Anna Freud et son école - Créativité et controverses* [Anna Freud and Her School – Creativity and Controversies]. Paris: Editions campagne première.

Houssier, F. and Marty, F. (2009) Drawing on psychoanalytic pedagogy: The Influence of August Aichhorn on the psychotherapy of adolescents. *The Psychoanalytic Quarterly* LXXVIII/4: 1091–1108.

Iona, M. (1983) Response to Peter Heller. Folder "I-M miscellaneous, 1982–1990", Box 2, Peter Heller Papers, Manuscript Division, U.S. Library of Congress, Washington DC.

Iona-Lewis, E. (1982) Letter to Peter Heller dated September 9th. Folder "Questionnaires", Box 2, Peter Heller Papers, Manuscript Division, U.S. Library of Congress, Washington DC.

Jahoda, M. (1983) The emergence of social psychology in Vienna: an exercise in long-term memory. *British Journal of Social Psychology*, 22/4: 343–349.

Marty, F. and Houssier, F. eds. (2007) *Éduquer l'adolescent* [Educating the Adolescent]. Nîmes: éditions Champs Social.

Menaker, E. (1990) Response to Peter Heller dated May 27, 1990. Folder "I-M miscellaneous, 1982–1990", Box 2, Peter Heller Papers, Manuscript Division, U.S. Library of Congress, Washington DC.

Midgley, N. (2008) The 'Matchbox School' (1927–1932): Anna Freud and the idea of a 'psychoanalytically-informed education'. *Journal of Child Psychotherapy* 34/1: 23–42.

Peters, M. A. (2012) *Education, Philosophy and Politics*. New York: Routledge.

Rosenfeld, E. (1970) Unpublished Memoir, folder "Rosenfeld, Eva Marie, 1972–1977, undated" Box 2, Peter Heller Papers, Manuscript Division, U.S. Library of Congress, Washington DC.

Rosenfeld, E. (1992) Recollected in Tranquility. In Heller, P. *Anna Freud's Letters to Eva Rosenfeld*. Madison, CT: International Universities Press.

Ross, V. (1989) Response to Peter Heller. Folder "Questionnaires," Box 2, Peter Heller Papers, Manuscript Division, U.S. Library of Congress, Washington DC.

Ross, V. (1992) 'Eva Marie Rosenfeld (1892–1977): a woman of valor. A personal memoir'. In Heller, P. *Anna Freud's Letters to Eva Rosenfeld*. Madison, CT: International Universities Press.

Rothe, D. A. and Weber, I. (2004) *"... als käm ich heim zu Vater und Schwester"- Lou Andreas-Salomé - Anna Freud: Briefwechsel 1919–1937* [As if I came home to father and sister: letters of Lou Andreas-Salomé and Anna Freud]. Göttingen: Wallstein Verlag.

Taschwer, K. (2015) *Hochburg des Anti-Semitismus – Der Niedergang der Universität Wien im 20. Jahrhundert* [Stronghold of Anti-Semitism – The Demise of the University of Vienna in the 20th Century]. Vienna: Czernin Verlag.

Young-Bruehl, E. (1989) *Anna Freud: A Biography*. London: Macmillan.

Chapter 4

August Aichhorn and his Hietzing friends

Thomas Aichhorn

Dorothy Burlingham's letter to Max Eitingon takes a particularly enthusiastic turn on October 2, 1927:

> The school starts tomorrow with plenty of children – Eva [Rosenfeld] has made a charming home for it, and her own personality I feel is the centre point of the whole school – surely my children have opportunities and I am so happy for them.

The new educational endeavor would open soon at Wattmanngasse 11, Eva Rosenfeld's villa in Vienna 13th District called Hietzing. While the founder's names – Anna Freud, Dorothy Burlingham and Eva Rosenfeld – are those most often associated with the school, August Aichhorn played a central role of much greater scale than has been recognised.

In Vienna of the 1920s, August Aichhorn was bound to become a major figure at Hietzing. First and foremost, he was a teacher. As director of two consecutive public residences for adolescents, he had set up large schools where new educational principles could be tested out and implemented. Beyond these early experiments in education, Aichhorn's network of personal and professional relationships already included the school's three founders and two main teachers. By 1927, Aichhorn was ready to transfer his original ideas to a new setting. (Figure 4.1)

The scope of August Aichhorn's leadership and activities has never been adequately acknowledged until now. Peter Blos, more than anyone else, pointed this out in his previously unpublished 1975 report *An Intimate History of The School in the Wattmanngasse, Vienna 1927 to 1932.*

> It had often been suggested that I write down my reminiscences about the School because its history had been intimately related to the early years of child analysis. Quite apart from this fact, I was a participant observer as well as a moving spirit in this enterprise which brought me into personal contact with two of the outstanding personalities in the Vienna psychoanalytic community: Anna Freud and August Aichhorn.
>
> (Blos, 1975, p. 1)

Figure 4.1 Portrait of August Aichhorn ca. 1930 by Günther Baszel.

Blos' memoir confirms Aichhorn's crucial influence on Hietzing from the very beginning.

At this point, with new archival documents coming to light, it is fortunately possible to reconstruct the substance and impact of Aichhorn's position at the Hietzing School. His relationships with Anna Freud, Dorothy Burlingham and Eva Rosenfeld, and with Peter Blos and Erik H. Erikson, fill out the story in moving detail.

August Aichhorn at the Hietzing School

I will let Bob Burlingham (1928), Dorothy Burlingham's eldest son and a Hietzing pupil, introduce August Aichhorn's presence at the school, in his essay called "OUR SCHOOL – by Bob."

> My dear readers, I hope you will get an impression of our school from this letter... Herr Blos and his friend Herr Erik Homburger [Erik H. Erikson] were our teachers... We liked last year very much. Our Nature study was specially interesting and we heard a lot about the life and growth of animals. To illustrate the lessons Herr Erik

> drew so many posters, that by the end of the year they covered all our walls...To write about this year is much more difficult, because it is not yet ended... The little ones have their lessons all together and their teacher Herr Erik plays piano sometimes, while they are quietly working. Our class is quite different. We have a teacher for each subject: Mother and Mrs. Briehl for English, Herr Blos for Nature Study and Geography, Herr Erik for German, History and Drawing, Herr Goldscheider for Latin, Arithmetic and Geometry, Frl. Traute for Sports. Sometimes Herr Aichhorn pays us a visit to talk with us about many interesting things. Every Wednesday afternoon all the children gather at school for a pleasant social time of singing, playing and discussing our school affairs and problems. I hope we will learn much by the end of the year.

Though he had set aside his formal pedagogical career, at Hietzing Aichhorn brought together some of his favorite occupations: he returned to teaching with his chosen classes on "Performing Geometry," he held group discussions with the pre-adolescents and he was a trusted member of the administrative and curricular team. As he was about to leave in September 1931, Peter Blos, then the school's director, sent Aichhorn a list of instructions. (Figures 4.2 and 4.3)

> The timetable remains the same, except that the individual hours are lost, which will be repeated several times in the first weeks of school. The number of hours for the individual subjects also remains the same. We will start on the first day with the regular schedule. Your performing geometry would be on Saturday in the last hour. You still need to work out an exchange with [K. R.] Eissler's hours.

Aichhorn was always an original thinker. Unconstrained by the standard government statutes and teaching regulations when he was first appointed to organise and direct a large children's residence in the former refugee camp at Oberhollabrunn, in 1918, Aichhorn transformed the facility into a model of pedagogical reform. Initially, it was to be a holiday recovery center for 3,000 schoolchildren, to run from July 15 through September 30, 1918. Then, in October, Aichhorn was selected to set up a welfare education center in the same camp. He completely re-designed the form and content of the lessons to suit the abilities and interests of the students. Even social learning and the "Project Method" of teaching, characteristic of the Hietzing School, were already structured into the schooling at Oberhollabrunn. And years before joining the formal psychoanalytic profession, Aichhorn was using psychoanalytic categories to understand the relationship between teachers and students, and among students themselves (Mende & Aichhorn, 1983, pp. 109ff.).

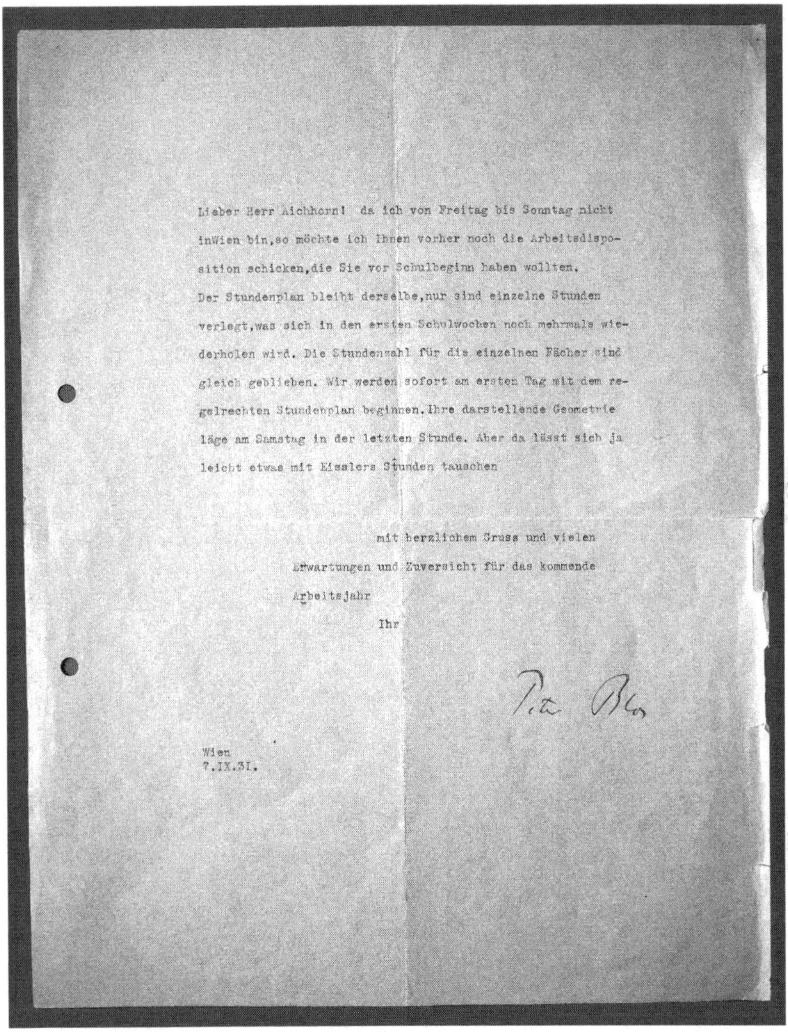

Lieber Herr Aichhorn! da ich von Freitag bis Sonntag nicht inWien bin,so möchte ich Ihnen vorher noch die Arbeitsdisposition schicken,die Sie vor Schulbeginn haben wollten.
Der Stundenplan bleibt derselbe,nur sind einzelne Stunden verlegt,was sich in den ersten Schulwochen noch mehrmals wiederholen wird. Die Stundenzahl für die einzelnen Fächer sind gleich geblieben. Wir werden sofort am ersten Tag mit dem regelrechten Stundenplan beginnen.Ihre darstellende Geometrie läge am Samstag in der letzten Stunde. Aber da lässt sich ja leicht etwas mit Eisslers Stunden tauschen

mit herzlichem Gruss und vielen Erwartungen und Zuversicht für das kommende Arbeitsjahr

Ihr

Wien
7.IX.31.

Figure 4.2 Lesson plan guidelines, from Peter Blos to August Aichhorn, 1931.

In 1929 though, with Hietzing entering its second year, Aichhorn's friend Anna Freud said that the field of psychoanalytic pedagogy was only in its infancy. Her lecture of the same year articulated his own position well. Originally, some analysts thought that children subjected to a highly structured education would simply internalise meaningless prohibitions. Yet the consequences of rejecting – or at least not participating in – education proved to be equally untenable. As Anna Freud and certainly Aichhorn saw it, the study of the neglected youth showed that a completely unrestrained instinctual

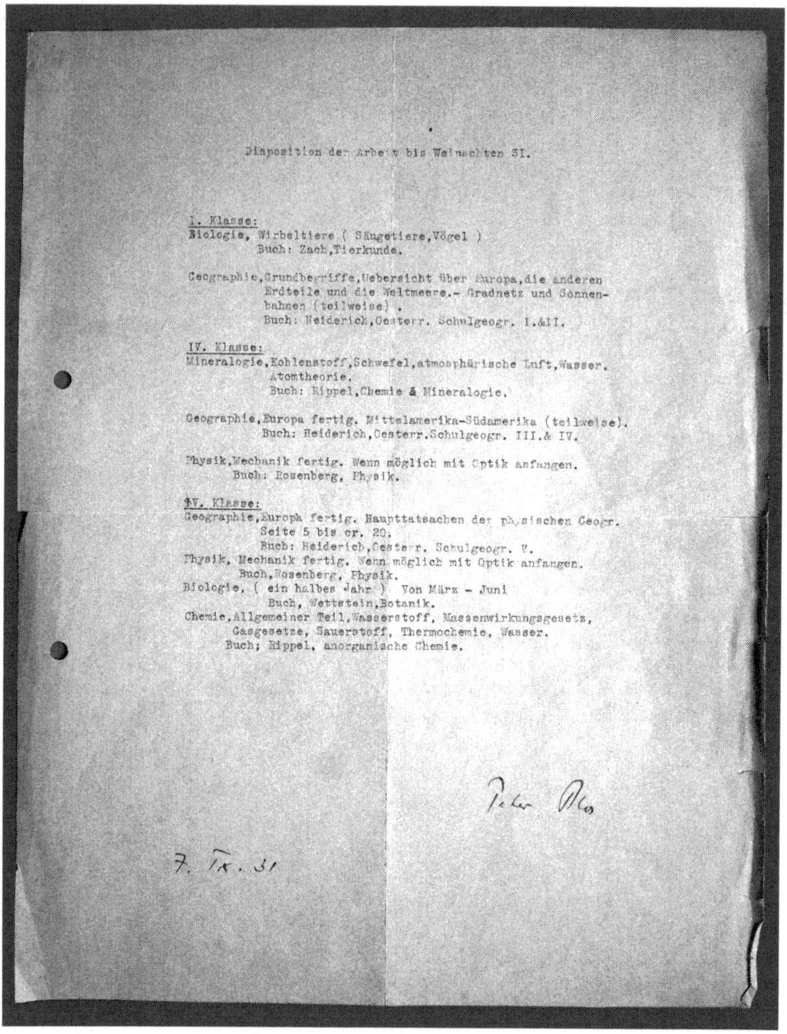

Disposition der Arbeit bis Weinachten 31.

I. Klasse:
Biologie, Wirbeltiere (Säugetiere,Vögel)
Buch: Zach,Tierkunde.

Geographie,Grundbegriffe,Uebersicht über Europa,die anderen Erdteile und die Weltmeere.- Gradnetz und Sonnenbahnen (teilweise) .
Buch: Heiderich,Oesterr. Schulgeogr. I.&II.

IV. Klasse:
Mineralogie,Kohlenstoff,Schwefel,atmosphärische Luft,Wasser. Atomtheorie.
Buch: Rippel,Chemie & Mineralogie.

Geographie,Europa fertig. Mittelamerika-Südamerika (teilweise).
Buch: Heiderich,Oesterr.Schulgeogr. III.& IV.

Physik,Mechanik fertig. Wenn möglich mit Optik anfangen.
Buch: Rosenberg, Physik.

V. Klasse:
Geographie,Europa fertig. Haupttatsachen der physischen Geogr. Seite 5 bis cr. 20.
Buch: Heiderich,Oesterr. Schulgeogr. V.
Physik, Mechanik fertig. Wenn möglich mit Optik anfangen.
Buch,Rosenberg, Physik.
Biologie, (ein halbes Jahr) Von März - Juni
Buch, Wettstein,Botanik.
Chemie,Allgemeiner Teil,Wasserstoff, Massenwirkungsgesetz, Gasgesetze, Sauerstoff, Thermochemie, Wasser.
Buch; Rippel, anorganische Chemie.

Peter Blos

7. IX. 31

Figure 4.3 Lesson plan for December 1931, Peter Blos.

development, uninhibited by the educator's will or by emotional ties to the teacher, would not be healthy; indeed, asocial and criminal tendencies could emerge. Roughly speaking, therefore, the neurotic person had too much education, and the neglected had too little. Aichhorn was not a champion of anti-authoritarian education but he did believe in a balanced approach to the needs of children, as he had already tried in Oberhollabrunn. (Figures 4.4 and 4.5)

Figure 4.4 View of Oberhollabrunn, 1919.

Figure 4.5 Oberhollabrunn staff with August Aichhorn and his family.

Aichhorn took over from Peter Blos as the school's principal in 1931, a position he maintained until Hietzing closed in 1933 (Aichhorn, 1938). This may have been connected to an official authorisation to continue running the school, which was probably started without official permission by the Vienna City School Board. Anna Freud too was concerned and in, March 1929, wrote to Eva Rosenfeld: "As for the question of certification for the school, we should also talk to Aichhorn once more. He too thinks one shouldn't start the next year without it" (Heller, 1992, p. 109). Aichhorn persevered but in August 1932, Anna Freud had to tell Rosenfeld: "Yesterday Aichhorn was here and was especially nice. He follows your plans with great interest. He is really making tremendous efforts on behalf of the school" (Heller, 1992, p. 162).

Anna Freud

Anna Freud and August Aichhorn met in 1921. It was the psychoanalyst Lou Andreas Salomé (she stayed in Vienna during the Fall and Winter months) who introduced them, inviting Anna Freud to accompany her and visit Aichhorn in his new position at the St Andrä an der Traisen children's residence. Instead, Anna Freud went by herself and reported back to Andreas-Salomé: "My dear Lou, I really did spend three days with Aichhorn's thieves, vagabonds and brigands and have returned quite fulfilled by all that I have seen" (Rothe & Weber, 2001, p. 14). She continued:

> Aichhorn is a truly unusual and remarkable person, one who is very approachable, personally. You were absolutely right and I am very glad of it. Mistrust and petty-mindedness, which I had almost wanted to ascribe to him initially, are infinitely far from his true self. He possesses a far deeper understanding of Psychoanalysis than he himself appears to admit and he is far more analytic in his work than his accounts would lead one to believe.... I am hugely impressed and taken with him and I hope I shall be able to speak with him often and thoroughly. (Rothe & Weber, 2001, p. 15)

Anna Freud got her wish. Their personal and professional relationship grew, and three years later, once Aichhorn returned to Vienna (the St Andrä institution was shuttered in January 1923), the two met weekly to discuss analysis and doubtless pedagogy (Figure 4.6). She offered Lou a lively description. "Last Saturday evening with Bernfeld and Aichhorn was especially nice," she wrote.

> The conversation turned toward the connection between politics and pedagogy, and strangely, even though they had very different starting points, they share the same goal: the communist school settlement. Too bad I did not yet know Aichhorn in his Oberhollabrunner time. He came closest to realizing this ideal as leader of 1000 children and 300 adults. His current sphere of influence is unfortunately nothing compared to that.
>
> (Rothe & Weber, 2001, p. 375)

Nevertheless, "he is positively inundated with a multitude of interesting cases – both on a personal and analytical level" (Rothe & Weber, 2001, p. 152).

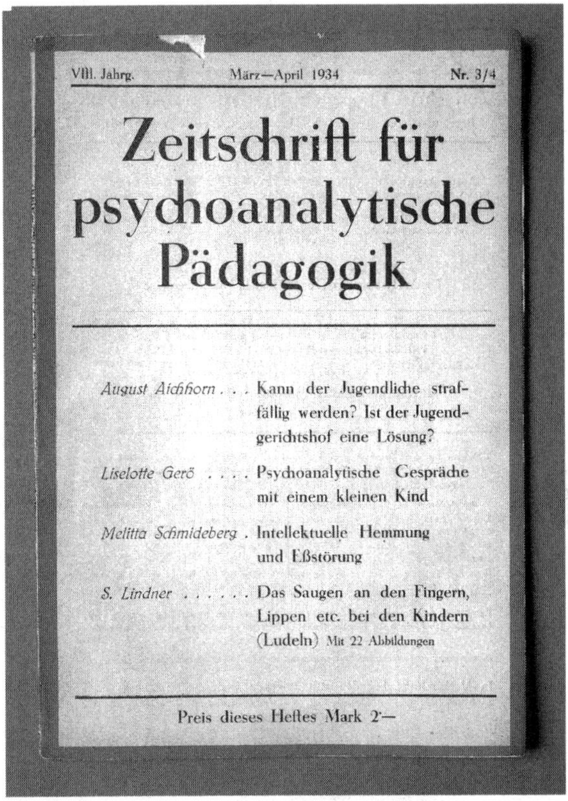

VIII. Jahrg. März—April 1934 Nr. 3/4

Zeitschrift für psychoanalytische Pädagogik

August Aichhorn . . . Kann der Jugendliche straffällig werden? Ist der Jugendgerichtshof eine Lösung?

Liselotte Gerö . . . . Psychoanalytische Gespräche mit einem kleinen Kind

Melitta Schmideberg . Intellektuelle Hemmung und Eßstörung

S. Lindner . . . . . . Das Saugen an den Fingern, Lippen etc. bei den Kindern (Ludeln) Mit 22 Abbildungen

Preis dieses Heftes Mark 2·—

Figure 4.6 Zeitschrift für psychoanalytische Pädagogik, 1934.

In moving ahead with these "human and analytically interesting cases," Aichhorn confirmed his belief that setting up local educational counseling offices in Vienna's fourteen district youth offices would give him more latitude than a standard government post. In this sense, as the American social worker Ernst Federn said of Aichhorn many years later, "Psychoanalytic social work [...] began with the care of delinquent and neglected youths in the 20 years ago by August Aichhorn in Vienna" (Federn, 2000, p. 1). Aichhorn was the sole provider of educational counseling until 1926 when he was joined by two doctors. His intention was to identify and treat developmental disorders as early as possible, thereby preventing later institutional referrals (Göllner, 2003). Then, with Anna Freud's participation ensured, the Vienna Psychoanalytical Association also opened its own "child and youth advice center" and Aichhorn ran it from his retirement in 1932 (pressured by Julius Tandler, Vienna's Minister for Social Welfare) until 1938. All the while, Aichhorn and Anna Freud continued to meet weekly. "The

Fridays with Aichhorn are not discussions, but above all hiking trips," she recounted these events, as always in those days, to Andreas-Salomé.

> He takes me to the most remote districts and shows me institutions and welfare facilities and the people who manage them. All this is extremely interesting and a look into a totally unique, oftentimes very strange world ...I have visited a youth welfare office and the juvenile court. Strangely enough psychoanalysis is well recognized and respected at public facilities though they are public institutions.
>
> (Rothe & Weber, 2001, pp. 274ff.)

Psychoanalysis had indeed become so "well recognised and respected" in Viennese education circles that Anna Freud was invited to deliver the series of lectures for the municipal after school care teachers. The lectures became her 1930 book *An Introduction to Psychoanalysis for Pedagogues.* To Max Eitingon, Anna Freud (1928) wrote: "Aichhorn, who is holding a large public course for pedagogues has remarkable numbers of participants." These lectures wouldn't remain isolated events, but were the beginning of a periodic seminar for municipal and Montessori kindergarten teachers held by Anna Freud and Dorothy Burlingham. (Figure 4.7)

Like so much of the era of catastrophes caused by the Nazi occupation of Austria in 1938, the Vienna Association and all its institutions closed, and Anna Freud fled with her family to London. Though Aichhorn remained in Vienna, his contact with Anna Freud was interrupted for years. Finally, on September 17, 1945, she was able to write to her friend.

Figure 4.7 August Aichhorn and Dorothy Tiffany Burlingham at the Jackson Krippe, Vienna 1937.

> I was very happy to get your letter.[1] It is very good to know that you are all right ... and that your work continues. Somehow, I always felt sure that you would manage to work whatever the outer circumstances were, and that under all conditions people would need you and your help... You would be pleased how highly people here think of your book[2] and that it is one of the standard works for students. If you think that it is possible to have an Institute again, then I am sure you are right. Anyway, I would always trust your judgment of any situation.[3] I have worked a good deal with children during the war (we organised two big residential war nurseries). With love and greetings, yours sincerely Anna Freud.
>
> (Aichhorn, 2012, p. 168)

Two years later, when both Aichhorn and Anna Freud planned to attend a 1947 meeting of European Psychoanalysts in Amsterdam, she wrote:

> If you were to come, we would elope and take a long walk on the beach or sit together somewhere that's as close to a Viennese coffeehouse as we could find. I remember so well how you first told me of Hollabrunn at a coffeehouse... After seeing photos of the opening celebration [of the Vienna Psychoanalytic Society], that you don't look much different than in the past. But me? I feel, I have changed quite a lot in these numerous and troublesome years.
>
> (Aichhorn, 2012, p. 241f.)

Instead of Amsterdam, the friends met in Lausanne. Their moving correspondence continued until they met again in 1948.

Eva Rosenfeld

Anna Freud had been searching for a foster home for a child patient and, in November of 1924, Siegfried Bernfeld suggested that Eva Rosenfeld's might be suitable. The two women met and soon became friends. Anna Freud's letter from the following Spring points to the quality of their friendship:

> And besides all that, me, I was so sure you were going to come that I counted on my own company only until 9:30. And now I have to get accustomed to myself again. I don't even know who has kept you away from me: Aichhorn after all?
>
> (Heller, 1992, p. 100)

Indeed, a relationship between Eva Rosenfeld and Aichhorn probably preceded the introduction of Anna Freud. Rosenfeld worked with the Vienna Settlement group to which Aichhorn was attached as an educational consultant. And they shared the same interests, as Rosenfeld's social work experience had started in Berlin at the *Zellerhaus*, a home for neglected alcoholic youth.

With Eva Rosenfeld resettled in England following the war, she was among those who actively supported Aichhorn with a range of donations – money, books, chocolates and cigarettes, and even clothes for his wife. "I take it from your letter that you have not completely forgotten Vienna," he wrote, "and thank you for your participation and your appreciative words" (Aichhorn, 1946a). Although available documents show that Aichhorn and Eva Rosenfeld, whom he called "Mrs Rosenfeld," were friends, little is known beyond a shared interest in education and in Anna Freud. But even before their mutual friend Siegfried Bernfeld referred a patient of Anna Freud's to Eva Rosenfeld's quasi-foster-home, Aichhorn had already met her. In an intriguing note from 1925, Anna Freud asked her friend: "I don't even know who has kept you away from me: Aichhorn after all?" (Heller, 1992, p. 100).

Aichhorn, whose postwar educational activities aimed to embed psychoanalysis within social welfare organisations, resumed the correspondence with Rosenfeld. "The scope of the [Vienna Psychoanalytic] association has expanded significantly since before 1938," he wrote (Aichhorn, 1947a).

> In addition to training the next generation of candidates, plus out-patient and educational counseling, our courses in psychoanalysis are generally accessible to carers, guidance counselors and teachers. We have a seminar for educational advisors of the municipal youth welfare office and the vocational counselors of Vienna's employment office, for the police nursery women and for the kindergarten teachers. Twenty-eight educators from "Jugend am Werk" receive targeted instruction. 'Jugend am Werk' organizes and trains unemployed male and female youth ages 14 to 16 years in different districts. Individual lectures are held at the local adult education centers and institute for science and art...Tell me what interests you most.
> (Aichhorn, 1947b)

Aichhorn retired from all his official positions in 1932, but like those few colleagues who could return from exile to Vienna, he sought to shape the training of psychoanalysts and social workers. As he told Rosenfeld, "My old colleagues from the youth offices have now risen to prominent positions and so – though maybe not officially – I am able to realize much of what I thought of as mere day-dreams. This fills me with great joy" (Aichhorn, 1947a).

Dorothy Tiffany Burlingham

Soon after Dorothy Burlingham arrived Vienna in the Spring of 1925, Theodor Reik, her first analyst, wrote to Aichhorn:

> ...there is an American here, greatly interested in educational theory and who would like to get acquainted with the prized Austrian schools, or respectively, the educational facilities. Could you help

> her with this? When could she see you? And where? She would prefer something between 9 to 4 p.m. but will naturally accommodate to fit your schedule.
>
> (Reik, 1925)

Dorothy was facing a challenging resettlement until she embraced the idea of starting a new and specifically modern school, in part for her own children and in part to expand on the latest ideas about pedagogy.

Like Anna Freud, or perhaps with her, Dorothy Burlingham accompanied Aichhorn on information-gathering trips to the Vienna youth office in the late 1920s. The Hietzing School opened and Aichhorn's son Walter enrolled as a pupil. He entered analysis with her and may have been Dorothy's first exercise in child analysis. (Figure 4.8)

Dorothy gave Aichhorn English lessons and many years later, in 1949, both recalled these exchanges fondly. "It is a great disappointment to me that I haven't seen you all these years. I often think of the English lessons I gave you" (Burlingham in 1949). Aichhorn (1949) answers: "I too think of our English lessons frequently, and would be pleased to welcome you to Vienna again someday." Burlingham and Aichhorn had resumed their amicable correspondence after the war. "I admire you for the way you have worked for analysis and its future in Austria," she wrote (Burlingham, 1946). She noted the sense of relief among those, Aichhorn and a few former students of the school included, who had safely survived the war, and added information on her children. And she was comfortable enough with him to bring up her relationship with Anna Freud:

Figure 4.8 Walter Aichhorn.

> I have been very ill with tuberculosis for the last two years but thanks to Anna Freud's care I am getting well and I am beginning to work and to be out again. I have not seen any of the children since 1940.

Interestingly, Aichhorn acknowledged the women's relationship, and his straightforward way of sharing his own pain echoes their mutual trust.

> I can imagine what comfort and help Fräulein Freud's loving care brings to you … I am glad about your sympathy and the appreciation of my work. The hardest part is surely behind me. What follows may be laborious and sometimes troublesome, but it cannot be compared to what came before.
>
> (Aichhorn, 1946b)

Peter Blos

Peter Blos was a handsome young biologist who, in 1927, jumped at the chance to run a school with Anna Freud and Dorothy Burlingham and settled, about six years later, on his way to New York and psychoanalysis. "The psychoanalytic milieu in which I lived had begun to fascinate me, even though a personal analysis was not contemplated nor suggested until much later… It was understood that I would be advised in my decisions by Anna Freud, Dorothy Burlingham and August Aichhorn," he remembered (Blos, 1975, pp. 8, 12).

At his suggestion, Anna Freud hired his best friend Erik Erikson (then Erik Homburger) as a second teacher, and the school opened in the Fall of 1927. (Figure 4.9)

Then, about six months into the school year, Blos met August Aichhorn. The "momentous experience" changed his life. Like Anna Freud and Dorothy Burlingham before him, Blos toured Vienna's child guidance clinics (*Jugend-Beratungsstellen*) with Aichhorn. "I was privileged to observe him in action, interviewing children, adolescents and parents, as well as advising the professional staff" (Blos, 1975, p. 9). Blos admired Aichhorn's personal style, his therapeutic efficacy and his empathic understanding of young clients. Sometimes the two men would take a long trolley-car ride through Vienna or share a beer at Aichhorn's apartment. At times, they read Freud together. Whatever Blos did not understand – which was almost everything, since he admittedly knew nothing of psychoanalytic theory at this time – Aichhorn explained patiently and with "irrefutable and magical simplicity." In contrast, Blos remembers holding Anna Freud in awe. "I hardly ever turned to her for advice," Blos recalled, "even though she was always most responsive and made herself easily available." Instead, he consulted with Aichhorn about school problems or personal matters. "My relationship to him was more natural and congenial" (Blos, 1975, p. 19). Aichhorn's influence on the Hietzing School was instantly recognisable.

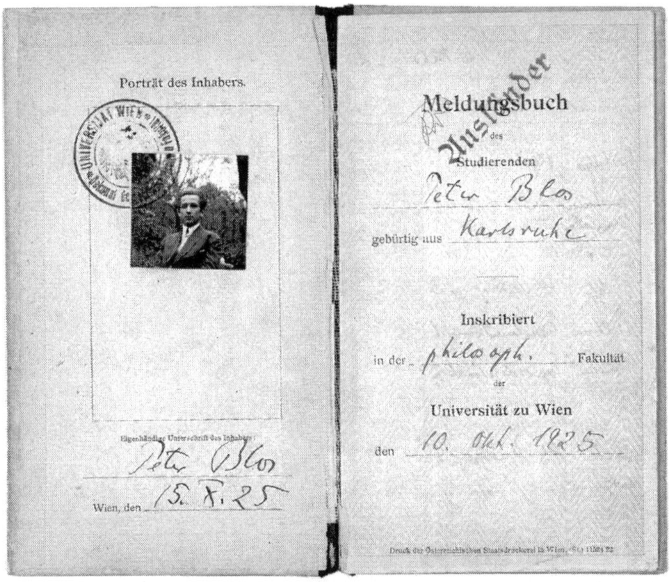

Figure 4.9 Peter Blos at the University of Vienna, 1925.

August Aichhorn was not a man of routine. It is no surprise then, with analytic regularity and attentive passivity at odds with his basic temperament, he was far more helpful with delinquent teenagers than with neurotic adults. As a mentor, however, he was very effective, and, in 1930, he finally persuaded Blos to start a personal analysis. "Now, there is no other way open to you but to go into analysis; go," Aichhorn said. "I went. I knew he was right" (Blos, 1975, p. 20). Blos never forgot. Two decades later and rapidly becoming an expert on adolescence in his own right, along the same lines as his mentor, Blos wrote to a Viennese friend:

> Dear Toby – by now you have my last letter[4] and I send this one only to tell you that I could not resist sending another package to you for August Aichhorn. […] I am very curious how you could deliver the package […] and how you found my old friend.
>
> (Blos, 1946a)

That Aichhorn would receive the gift was not inevitable in 1946. Aichhorn had intended to leave Vienna through Hitler's Germany and to go to Switzerland or Sweden, in case of an occupation of Austria. But on March 11, 1938, August Aichhorn Jr was arrested because of his political activities protesting National Socialism. He was transferred to the Dachau concentration camp on May 24, 1938. Though why Aichhorn did not leave Vienna cannot be verified with absolute certainty, we now believe that the decision revolved around this arrest of his older son. Although August Aichhorn Jr was released from the concentration camp on September 20, 1938, he remained under the control of the Gestapo and had to report regularly to the state police. He could no longer find work, and consequently he and his family needed their father's financial support. They lived in constant danger during the Nazi era, and in the summer of 1944, when the situation threatened to become critical, the family left Vienna for the countryside (see Ash, 2012).

It was under these conditions that Aichhorn thanked his "old friend" Peter Blos profusely.

> Through these long years of separation, you have not only maintained a feeling of friendship towards me, but are so concerned about our (physical) well-being even though it isn't quite as bad as you may imagine. We gladly accept our restricted level of sustenance for having been freed from the almost unbearable pressure and constant danger of being sent to a concentration camp. I will not write about everything we endured; we survived the war and that is what's important, although my older son sustained permanent injury. He has not lost his optimism, which never left him in Dachau. I certainly do not need to explain what Dachau is.
> (Aichhorn, 1946c)

Writing from New York of the mid-1940s, Blos' response (Blos, 1946b) to Aichhorn's powerful letter laid out stark contrasts to their former Viennese environment. As a lay analyst, Blos and his colleagues in education, welfare and kindergarten work, were either ignored or unsupported by the mainstream psychoanalytic society. And almost a half century later, Peter Blos still depicted Vienna vividly. "Your grandfather was like a father to me when I was in Vienna (from 1925 to 1934)," he wrote to me, in anticipation of our personal appointment in New York. "Since I have no time for interviews (I am too old, 92 years) … all requests are met with a negative response. I consider meeting with you 'a special case'." (Blos, 1996). He emphasised Aichhorn's mentorship when discussing school problems, and his support in quarrels with Anna Freud, Dorothy Burlingham and Eva Rosenfeld. It was Aichhorn, Blos said, who warned him about Erik Erikson's problematic character.

Erik H. Erikson

Aichhorn closed his March 1946 letter to Peter Blos with an ambiguous remark: "Please give my regards to Homburger [Erikson], even though he may not have me in fond remembrance" (Aichhorn, 1946c). They had not seen each other for years. Erikson was living in San Francisco, and though very successful, Aichhorn told Blos, still clinging to his old idiosyncrasies. Apparently, this tension dated back to their Hietzing days, when

Aichhorn already found Erikson more problematic than Blos. Even the Hietzing students had noted contrasts between the two men, but differently. In one instance, Ernest Freud, Freud's grandson, preferred Erikson. "Peter Blos was a bit too outspoken for my liking. Whereas Erik Erikson was gentle and likable... [Blos] was respected for his knowledge and his flair for running the Burlingham School. But he was not likeable enough for me" (Benveniste, 2015, p. 177). But Mabbie Burlingham claimed the opposite that Erikson "couldn't pass a mirror without looking into it." Freud said: "And it was absolutely true. He was a vain person. Good old Erik." (Figure 4.10)

A year after the school closed, with Erikson preparing his 1933 emigration to Boston, an important task remained: the letter to August Aichhorn. The letter opens with an avowal of the "moral defeat" he sees in his detachment from Aichhorn during their Vienna years. He had learned a lot of course, and their first discussions were promising. Then he asked Anna Freud to take him into analysis and everything else was abruptly interrupted. "With this act," Erikson wrote,

> I followed the leaden weight of my childhood which I spent with my mother alone with my aunts, without [a] father. You will easily recognize this same fateful constellation in the Vienna aunt-ensemble in whose transmission network I was caught.
>
> (Erikson, 1933a)

Figure 4.10 Hietzing faculty portrait with Erikson and Blos.

For a long time, Erikson felt unable to explain this sense of having betrayed Aichhorn. Eventually though, he focused on his own father's disappearance that left the three-year-old boy alone with his mother. For the sake of her freedom, his mother had the father declared dead. Erikson claimed to have forgotten all this until the age of seventeen and, consciously at least, he thought of his step-father as his actual father. "It was my unconscious knowledge of the betrayed father which made me withdraw from you, whose guidance I would have liked to have followed," Erikson continued. "Now I am travelling to America …And so I think, I should be allowed to make clear to myself the fatality of not robbing myself of an important teacher a second time; should be allowed to explain it to the person I have experienced it with, him being an analyst after all – and beyond that, hopefully something akin to a fatherly friend" (Erikson, 1933a).

While he had read Erikson's analytical deliberations with great interest, Aichhorn thought it best to answer less analytically. Analysis may offer great liberation and while one could, with its help, explain everything and exonerate oneself, at times prudence suggests we relinquish that aid and look at life the way others see it. "It does not seem all that important to me that you, dear Erik, discover all the underlying motives for what you are calling your 'betrayal.' For they will be just as readily and comfortably be at your disposal when your next 'betrayal' comes – and you are thereby granting yourself absolution," Aichhorn (1933) wrote.

> …If possible, I would suggest you develop a certain self-mistrust. That is, as soon as you are impulsively driven to seek someone's affection, to establish relationships, – you should be cautious and examine your motivations first, namely as an analytic. With a letter, with a conversation you establish ties, maybe raise expectations in your counterpart, make connections – and then ultimately fail… Every person with pronounced narcissism requires this form of self-mistrust, has to ask the question: What do I actually want from someone? Just narcissistic satisfaction? Is it truly the establishing of a real relationship? Only this mistrust can bring you to a point where you consider the other's position beforehand, become more careful and will not require you to "betray" the other. Please consider this my best wish for you in the time of your farewell.
>
> (Aichhorn, 1933)

Erikson's next letter carried all the strength missing from the first.

> Before I depart I would like to thank you for your advice, which I wholeheartedly and fully accept. You will know that it will be hard to put into practice. I would not accept the way in which you're trying to get at me

> 'unanalytically' as easily. [...] In spite of what you say, you really continued my analysis, at the same time disparaging my analytic zeal. Only one thing was even more unnecessary, namely my letter. If that is what you were trying to say, I'm afraid you are right. Incidentally, always, your Erik Homburger".
>
> (Erikson, 1933b)

Forty years later Erikson would remember:

> It was by teaching school that we[5] found our vocation in the area of child psychoanalysis and education, while regular and intimate contact with the great August Aichhorn first opened our eyes to the problems of youth".
>
> (Erikson, 1974, p. 711)

In conclusion

That August Aichhorn played a far more important role for the Hietzing School than was previously known can now be seen in the archival letters and documents. They record, virtually in situ, Aichhorn's experience as a teacher and psychoanalyst as well as on his personal relationships with Anna Freud, Dorothy Burlingham, Eva Rosenfeld, Peter Blos and Erik H. Erikson.

These surviving letters and documents offer only fragmentary insights into the personal and professional connections between the Hietzing School teachers, both during and after the life of the school. Nevertheless, they document the genuinely friendly and collegial relations, unaffected even by the political interruption of their exchanges in 1938. As soon as possible, the group re-established personal contact with the same, or even greater, spirit of familiarity and friendship.

Illustrations

Figure 4.1 Portrait of August Aichhorn, Günther Baszel, ca. 1930, oil on canvas, Collection of Thomas Aichhorn, Vienna

Figure 4.2 Peter Blos to August Aichhorn, lesson plan guidelines, Estate of August Aichhorn, Collection of Thomas Aichhorn, Vienna

Figure 4.3 Lesson plan for December 1931, Peter Blos, Estate of August Aichhorn, Collection of Thomas Aichhorn, Vienna

Figure 4.4 View of Oberhollabrunn, b/w photograph, Estate of August Aichhorn, Collection of Thomas Aichhorn, Vienna

Figure 4.5 August Aichhorn with family and Oberhollabrunn personnel, b/w photograph, around 1919, Estate of August Aichhorn, Collection of Thomas Aichhorn, Vienna

Figure 4.6 *Zeitschrift für psychoanalytische Pädagogik*, Volume 8, Nr.3/4 March-April 1934, Estate of August Aichhorn, Collection of Thomas Aichhorn, Vienna

Figure 4.7 August Aichhorn with Dorothy Tiffany Burlingham at the Jackson Nursery, Vienna 1937, Estate of August Aichhorn, Collection of Thomas Aichhorn, Vienna

Figure 4.8 Walter Aichhorn, ca. 1931, Bob Burlingham, b/w photograph, collection of Michael J. Burlingham, New York

Figure 4.9 Peter Blos, University of Vienna student identification card, Peter Blos papers, Oskar Diethelm Library, DeWitt Wallace Institute for the History of Psychiatry, Weill Cornell Medical College, New York

Figure 4.10 Hietzing School photo with Erik Erikson and Peter Blos, Peter Heller Album, Sigmund Freud Museum, Collection of the Sigmund Freud Privatstiftung, Vienna

Notes

1 To the best of our knowledge, Aichhorn's preceding letter to Anna Freud has not survived.
2 Aichhorn's "Verwahrloste Jugend" was translated into English in 1935. It was so popular that, as Michael Burlingham writes in The Last Tiffany, "...for a time this book was better known in America than The Interpretation of Dreams" (Burlingham, 1989, p. 187).
3 This may refer to Aichhorn's re-opening of the Vienna Psychoanalytic Association (letter lost) in April 1946.
4 Letter lost.
5 Erikson is referring to his work with Peter Blos at the Hietzing School.

References

Aichhorn, A. (1933) Letter to E. H. Erikson dated September 17, 1933. Estate of August Aichhorn, Vienna.

Aichhorn, A. (1935) *Wayward Youth*. New York: The Viking Press.

Aichhorn, A. (1938) Curriculum Vitae dated March 28, 1938. "School of the American Mrs. Burlingham, XIII., Wattmanngasse 11; Director: Schoolyears 1931/33." Typescript in the Estate of August Aichhorn, Vienna.

Aichhorn, A. (1946a) Letter to Dorothy Tiffany Burlingham, dated June 24, 1946. Estate of August Aichhorn, Vienna.

Aichhorn, A. (1946b) Letter to Eva Rosenfeld dated July 24, 1946. Archive of the British Psycho-Analytical Society. P33/A/02.

Aichhorn, A. (1946c) Letter to Peter Blos dated March 16, 1946. Estate of August Aichhorn, Vienna.

Aichhorn, A. (1947a) Letter to Eva Rosenfeld dated February 1, 1947. Archive of the British Psycho-Analytical Society. P33/A/02.

Aichhorn, A. (1947b) Letter to Eva Rosenfeld dated March 31, 1947. Archive of the British Psycho-Analytical Society. P33/A/02.

Aichhorn, A. (1949) Letter to Dorothy Tiffany Burlingham dated May 27, 1949. Estate of August Aichhorn, Vienna.

Aichhorn, T. (ed.). (2012) *Anna Freud / August Aichhorn "Die Psychoanalyse kann nur dort gedeihen, wo Freiheit des Gedankens herrscht" Briefwechsel 1921–1949.* Frankfurt: Brandes & Apsel.

Ash, M. (ed.). (2012) *Materialien zur Geschichte der Psychoanalyse in Wien 1938–1945.* Frankfurt: Brandes & Apsel.

Benveniste, D. (2015) *The Interwoven Lives of Sigmund, Anna and W. Ernest Freud.* New York: International Psychoanalytic Books.

Blos, P. (1946a) Letter to Toby List dated February 16, 1946. Estate of August Aichhorn, Vienna.

Blos, P. (1946b) Letter to August Aichhorn of December 8, 1946. Estate of August Aichhorn, Vienna.

Blos, P. (1975) "An intimate History of The School in the Wattmanngasse, Vienna, 1927 to 1932" Typescript. Peter Blos Papers, Manuscript Division, U.S. Library of Congress, Washington D.C.

Blos, P. (1996) Letter to Thomas Aichhorn, of February 26, 1996; archive of Thomas Aichhorn, Vienna.

Burlingham, B. (1928) *Unsere Weinachtszeitung 1928*, pp. 1–2. folder "Weihnachtszeitung, school Christmas journal, 1928–1929" Box 2, Peter Heller Papers, Manuscript Division, U.S. Library of Congress, Washington D.C.

Burlingham, D. T. (1927) Letter to Max Eitingon, letter dated October 2nd, 1927. In Aichhorn, T. (2012) *Anna Freud / August Aichhorn*, p. 80

Burlingham, D. T. (1946) Letter to August Aichhorn dated January 6, 1946. Estate of August Aichhorn, Vienna

Burlingham, D. T. (1949) Letter to August Aichhorn dated May 19, 1949. Estate of August Aichhorn, Vienna.

Burlingham, M. (1989) *The Last Tiffany.* New York: Atheneum Macmillan Publishing Company.

Erikson, E. H. (1933a) Letter to August Aichhorn dated September 7, 1933. Estate of August Aichhorn, Vienna.

Erikson, E. H. (1933b) Letter to August Aichhorn dated September 29, 1933. Estate of August Aichhorn, Vienna.

Erikson E. H. (1974) Peter Blos: Reminiscences. In Schlein, S. (ed.), (1987) *Erik H. Erikson. A Way of Looking at Things. Selected Papers.* New York, London: W.W. Norton & Company, pp. 709–712.

Federn, E. (2000) *"Was ist psychoanalytische Sozialarbeit und wozu wird sie gebraucht?"* [What is psychoanalytic social work and what is it used for?] Presentation of January 18, 2000 to the Wiener Psychoanalytische Vereinigung. Unpublished.

Freud, A. (1928) Letter to Max Eitingon dated November 28, 1928. Anna Freud Papers in the Archive of the Library of Congress, Washington.

Freud, A. (1930) *Einführung in die Psychoanalyse für Pädagogen.* In: Schriften, Band 1: 79–138.

Göllner, R. (2003) Psychoanalytisch-pädagogische Praxis ohne Ideologie vom "Schädling". August Aichhorns Erziehungsberatung zwischen Jugendamt und Psychoanalytischer Vereinigung. *Luzifer-Amor*, 16 (31): 8–36.

Heller P. (1992) *Anna Freud's letters to Eva Rosenfeld*. Madison, CT: International Universities Press.

Mende, J., & Aichhorn, Th. (1983) "Pädagogische 'Alternativbewegung in der Ersten Republik." In: Mende, J. (ed.), *Alternativschulen in Wien*. Vienna: Verlag für Gesellschaftskritik.

Reik, T. (1925) Letter to August Aichhorn, dated April 25, 1925. Estate of A. Aichhorn, Vienna.

Rothe, D., & Weber, I. (eds.). (2001): ... *Als käm ich heim zu Vater und Schwester. Lou Andreas-Salomé – Anna Freud, Briefwechsel 1919–1937*. Göttingen: Wallstein Verlag.

Chapter 5

Anna Freud and the science of unexpected findings

Inge-Martine Pretorius

Of Anna Freud's three major ventures in early childhood care and research, the Jackson Nursery formed a natural bridge between the Hietzing School in Vienna and the Hampstead War Nurseries in London. With her characteristic enthusiasm, optimism and curiosity, she lent her psychoanalytic knowledge to programs where the children thrived and the teachers were inspired. The Hampstead War Nurseries, created for London's children displaced during World War II, followed the Jackson Nursery in Vienna. Working there with toddlers living below poverty, Anna Freud and her team acquired a rich array of insights, some unexpected, which they continued to research and refine in Hampstead.

The Jackson Nursery

In her 1926 *Introduction to the Technique of the Psycho-analysis of Children*, Anna Freud documented her innovative method of direct observation. The book was based on four lectures she had first presented to the Vienna Institute of Psychoanalysis and covered in-depth notations on the behavior of children from infancy to toddlerhood. "What was not available to us," she remarked, "... was detailed knowledge of the important development between age one and two" (A. Freud, 1980, p. xiii). The Jackson Nursery would begin to fill this gap. Anna Freud called it an "experimental nursery" group because "at that time, group care for children of that age was unheard of" (A. Freud, 1971, p. 226). She explained:

> Our wish was to gather direct (as opposed to reconstructed) information about the second year of life, which we deemed all important for the child's essential advance from primary to secondary process functioning; for the establishment of feeding and sleeping habits; for acquiring the rudiments of superego development and impulse control; for the establishment of object ties to peers.
>
> (A. Freud, 1978, p. 731)

With funding from Edith Banfield Jackson, an American physician and analysand of Sigmund Freud, and Dorothy Tiffany Burlingham as well as political support from the American Ambassador to Austria, George Strausser Messersmith, Anna Freud's project took shape (Lynn, 2003). It was named the *Jackson Krippe* (Jackson Nursery) to avoid the rising anti-Semitism in Vienna (Krivanek, 2014). The nursery opened on February 1, 1937 within the *Montessori-Kinderhaus* (Montessori children's house) at number 5a Rudolfsplatz in Vienna's First District.

The *Krippe* was a day nursery for children aged twelve to seventeen months, who could move independently or at least crawl (Freud, 1980). They were from Vienna's poorest families; most of their fathers were "beyond the dole" (Freud, 1980, p. xiii). The nursery aimed to nurture the children's well-being and physical condition, to promote their sociability, and for the staff, to research child development (Krivanek, 2014). Anna Freud and Dorothy Burlingham co-directed the *Krippe* while Edith Jackson and Josefine Stross, both physicians, attended to the children's medical care. Julia Deming was responsible for feeding schedules, along with a number of Austrian and foreign professionals and volunteers (Freud, 1978). (Figure 5.1)

Figure 5.1 Anna Freud holding a child in the Jackson Nursery, 1937.

Anna Freud believed that treating psychological disturbances early in childhood would prevent the development of later pathology. She was particularly interested in learning about children's independent eating, toilet mastery, sleep patterns and aggression. In view of this research agenda, the *Krippe* staff used Index Cards to record their observations of, for example, the children's eating habits, which were then discussed, along with the progress and problems of individual children, at weekly meetings. Monthly seminars covered more theoretical concerns such as data collection methodology, the benefits of objective behavioral observations vs "analytic method," the use of "first impressions" to confirm or contradict psychoanalytic assumptions (Kennedy, 1988, p. 272). According to Hansi Kennedy,

> With hindsight, there is no doubt that these observations were from the beginning, not mere records of observed behaviour but a method of collecting data on the basis of pre-existing knowledge: an attempt to observe children's behaviour with aimed at confirming or contradicting psychoanalytic assumptions.
>
> (1988, pp. 272–273)

While daily life at the *Krippe* included parents, some of whom received food and help in finding accommodation, difficult social conditions and work commitments often precluded them from spending much time in the nursery (Krivanek, 2014). Anna Freud supported parental involvement because she believed that family contact would help staff understand the children better and, for the children, reduce the artificial separation between home and nursery. Anticipating what she would later confirm as the child's adverse reaction to a sudden and unprepared separation from the mother (Kennedy, 1988), mothers were especially encouraged to stay with their children for a settling-in period. Here, mothers could learn new ways of caring for the physical and emotional health of their children. Some of the children were sickly: a few had rickets while others were underweight and bad eaters. An American researcher had shown that young children ate a balanced diet when allowed to choose their food independently, and Anna Freud agreed that encouraging children toward self-regulation would lead to greater pleasure in eating. Breakfast became a buffet of drinks, bread, fruit and chocolate. Free to play with food and spill their drinks at first, within three months the children had acquired self-control, ate more and with greater pleasure (Kennedy, 1988).

Some children learned about personal hygiene only at the nursery and others regressed to wetting themselves after joining the nursery. Helping the children achieve or regain toilet mastery was discussed at a staff meeting on

December 2, 1937. Which adult best helped a child learn to use the potty: an adult to whom the child had formed an attachment or another familiar staff member? A lively discussion ensued, with staff disagreements over the impact of attachment in the course of this developmental achievement (Krivanek, 2014).

With its research program, inspired leadership and community of learning, the Jackson Nursery soon became an international training institution. Miss Pira, the Director of a Montessori School in the Netherlands, was just one of the many professionals who wished to observe and acquire Anna Freud's new model (Krivanek, 2014). Yet the nursery was forced to close almost as quickly as it opened, soon after Germany's annexation of Austria on March 12, 1938 (Kennedy, 2009; Krivanek, 2014). In May 1938, Anna Freud told Edith Jackson that the Jackson Nursery had given her "the most beautiful year in Vienna, the best that I ever had" (Anna Freud, in Johler, Sommer, & Steiner, 2016, p. 53). The following month, the Freud family was forced into exile.

But Anna Freud did not leave the Jackson Nursery behind: ten little children's cots and some wooden toys were stowed away in her luggage bound for London. Most of the other nursery toys went to England with Dorothy Burlingham (Kennedy, 2009; Young-Bruehl, 2008). The breakfast counter found its way to the War Nurseries and later the Hampstead Clinic Nursery School (Kennedy, 1988). Even today, some wooden toys from the Jackson Nursery remain in use for the Parent-Toddler Groups at the Anna Freud Centre. (Figure 5.2)

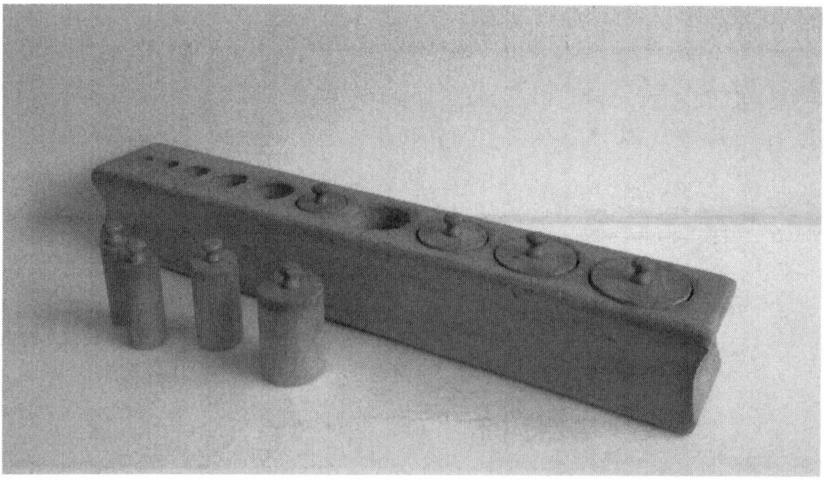

Figure 5.2 Cylinder block toy from the Jackson Nursery, still in use in the Anna Freud Centre Parent-Toddler Groups.

The Hampstead War Nurseries

In 1939, as World War II was breaking over London, Anna Freud and Dorothy Burlingham opened the three residential homes that became known as the Hampstead War Nurseries (Hellman, 1983). Expanding on their experience at the Hietzing School and the Jackson Nursery, they used psychoanalytic knowledge to enhance the education and welfare of children. Anna Freud and Dorothy Burlingham supervised the London centers while Alice Goldberger was in charge of New Barn.

Adults can generally cope with rationing but children experience emergency conditions differently. The Hampstead War Nurseries (HWN) first "Annual Report of a residential war nursery" (Burlingham & Freud, 1942b) describes this. The lack of essential foods in early childhood is widely known to cause lasting physical damage, Burlingham and Freud wrote, but "it is not yet generally recognised that the same is true for the mental development of the child." The authors continued: "Whenever certain needs are not fulfilled, lasting psychological malformations will be the consequences; these essential elements are; the need for personal attachment, for emotional stability and for permanency of educational influence" (Burlingham & Freud, 1942a, p. 2). To meet these overall goals, the HWN had four main aims: (1) a therapeutic aim of repairing the damage already caused by the children's wartime experiences; (2) a preventative aim of avoiding further harm by providing the security of a stable environment with opportunities to maintain relationships with parents; (3) a research aim of studying the children's reaction to the war, separation from families, responses to communal living and to investigate patterns of nursery life that could be a model for peace-time education; and (4) a training aim of teaching people forms of education based on psychoanalytic child development (Burlingham & Freud, 1942a). The residential homes marked Anna Freud and Dorothy Tiffany Burlingham as pioneers in the care of young children. Beyond meeting the children's physical and educational needs, they recognised – and met – their need for psychological and emotional care.

In January 1941, the Children's Rest Centre opened at 13 Wedderburn Road, Hampstead (Kennedy, 2009). Friends donated money and a charitable Swedish organisation provided equipment to shelter about thirty children from London's East End which the Blitz had reduced to rubble. The Centre's basement was converted into a reinforced shelter with a communal bedroom for twenty-seven beds and cribs. Anna Freud stressed that these were not shelter-beds, but peace-time, spring-mattress beds, built in tiers of two or three, and so large that a child could sleep at each end "without their feet touching in the middle" (Freud, 1973a, p. 4). In contrast to the prevailing practice of settling children to sleep upstairs and waking them to move into the shelter when the sirens started, this ingenious arrangement allowed them to maintain their sleeping routines undisturbed by the bombing raids. (Figure 5.3)

Figure 5.3 The Childrens' Rest Centre.

Two months later, the American Foster Parents' Plan for War Children, Inc. (FPP), a New York war charity, began financing the HWN. Like the Jackson Nursery funders, the FPP requested Monthly Reports. The first report was sent off in February 1941, followed by fifty-five more. Further financial and in-kind support from the British War Relief Society and the Red Cross made possible the opening of two more shelters later that year (Freud, 1973a).

The second nursery, the Babies' Rest Centre at 5 Netherhall Gardens in Hampstead, opened on July 3, 1941. Twenty-nine infants and toddlers, from ten days to two-and-a-half years, arrived in the first year. The children were admitted carefully and gradually, so that each new arrival could be received by a group of children who had already settled. The decision to keep sibling pairs together meant, at times, that a few children older than two-and-a-half years could not be accepted (Freud & Burlingham, 1973a). As the war continued, the Babies' Rest Centre ultimately accommodated up to fifty babies and toddlers. (Figure 5.4)

A country house called New Barn became the third nursery. It opened in August 1941 near the town of Chelmsford in Essex. New Barn was "a charming, friendly, modern building with all necessary conveniences" including "terraced lawns for perfect playgrounds, outhouses, vegetable and berry garden, a huge orchard with three little chicken houses" (Freud, 1973a, p. 80). At first, the home was designated as an evacuation residence for thirty older children, who – it was thought – could manage without daily parental contact. However, when the German bombing range expanded in July 1944, almost all the children were moved from London to New Barn. (Figure 5.5)

Figure 5.4 The Babies' Rest Centre.

Figure 5.5 Children napping outdoors at New Barn.

Of the 103 children housed in the nurseries in 1941, most were between one and five years old but some were as young as one week and others up to age ten (Freud, 1973a). One was a little girl from West Africa who, "because of her colour, had difficulties in being accepted, either in a private billet, or in a boarding school" (Freud, 1973a, p. 87). Some of the children were homeless and others considered "billeting problems." Their mothers may have developed physical or mental illnesses. Like the children at the Jackson Nursery, they came from highly vulnerable families.

Therapeutic and preventative aims

When the Viennese child psychologist (and fellow exile) Ilse Hellman first visited the Children's Rest Centre on Wedderburn Road, she was especially impressed by the HWN's unique methodology. In particular, Anna Freud emphasised that "although residential, [the HWN] was not run on institution lines." Her goal was to "re-establish for the children what they have lost: the security of a stable home with its opportunities for individual development" (Freud, 1973a, p. xxv). Hellman had worked with delinquent children at the Children's Tribunal in Paris before joining Karl Bühler in 1936, but knew little about psychoanalysis (Hellman, 1990). She was unprepared for what she encountered:

> It seemed very strange to me. Naturally, the whole approach to children was based on psychoanalysis principles, and it was quite unlike anything I have seen before. The children's behaviour and what was expected of them, was very different from other nurseries in terms of discipline and "do's and don'ts." I'll never forget when I first arrived. It was during the children's lunch-time, and all the one-and-a-half to two-year-olds were eating with their hands. They sat around a big table, and they could choose what they wanted to eat. Usually in a children's home you put some food on a plate and tell them to eat it up! But here there was a little buffet, and they could say what they wanted to eat, and if they did not want it anymore, no one minded.
>
> (Hellman, 1990, pp. 7–8)

Hellman, who oversaw the Toddler Department of the HWN from 1941 through 1945, later trained at the Institute of Psychoanalysis in London (Hellman, 1990).

Research

Beyond the HWN's innovations in wartime childcare, the settings also provided excellent platforms for observation, research and teaching. The longitudinal studies have endured as some of the most significant studies of child development (Burlingham & Freud, 1942a). Children could be observed, almost from birth, with or without their mothers, being breast- or bottle-fed, separated or reunited with parents, and relating to mother substitutes and peers (Freud, 1951). So too could the stages of libidinal and aggressive development, the process of weaning and acquiring toilet mastery, the acquisition of language and the development of various ego functions (Freud, 1966). The influence of communal life on child development and, on a larger scale, the impact of war events like sirens, air raids and bomb damage on their libidinal and aggressive development could be studied (Seifert, 2009). Some research questions, like significance of attachment, had started at the Jackson Nursery in Vienna and were later resolved at the HWN.

Hannah Engl (later known as Hansi Kennedy and co-director of the Hampstead Clinic) had fled Vienna for London at age sixteen and soon began working in the HWN. Though she had not worked at the Jackson Nursery, the data collection was similarly based on detailed, direct observation. "We were encouraged to write down our observations on index cards," she reminisced in 1993. These observations were grouped into categories and then integrated into the overall theoretical framework, itself continually modified by new observations and resulting information. This is how "a set of observations was compiled on each child, recorded by different observers and in different settings" (Kennedy in Miller & Neely, 2008, p. xxiii). Today, hundreds of these cards written in English, German and Yiddish and, sometimes a mixture of languages, are archived at the Anna Freud Centre. (Figure 5.6)

Anna Freud and Dorothy Burlingham based at least three major books on these recorded observations: "Young children in war-time. A year's work in a residential war nursery" (Burlingham & Freud, 1942b), "War and Children" (Freud & Burlingham, 1943) and "Infants without families: the case

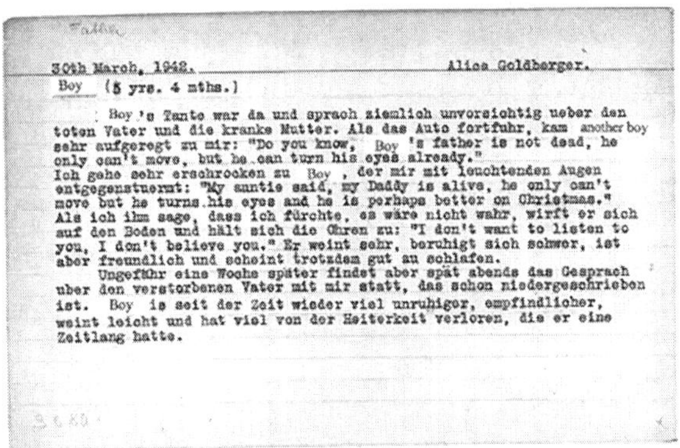

30th March, 1942. Alice Goldberger.

Boy (5 yrs. 4 mths.)

Boy's Tante war da und sprach ziemlich unvorsichtig ueber den toten Vater und die kranke Mutter. Als das Auto fortfuhr, kam another boy sehr aufgeregt zu mir: "Do you know, Boy's father is not dead, he only can't move, but he can turn his eyes already."
Ich gehe sehr erschrocken zu Boy, der mir mit leuchtenden Augen entgegenstuermt: "My auntie said, my Daddy is alive, he only can't move but he turns his eyes and he is perhaps better on Christmas." Als ich ihm sage, dass ich fürchte, es wäre nicht wahr, wirft er sich auf den Boden und hält sich die Ohren zu: "I don't want to listen to you, I don't believe you." Er weint sehr, beruhigt sich schwer, ist aber freundlich und scheint trotzdem gut zu schlafen.

Ungefähr eine Woche später findet aber spät abends das Gesprach uber den verstorbenen Vater mit mir statt, das schon niedergeschrieben ist. Boy is seit der Zeit wieder viel unruhiger, empfindlicher, weint leicht und hat viel von der Heiterkeit verloren, die er eine Zeitlang hatte.

Figure 5.6 Child observation card from the HWN.

for and against residential nurseries" (Burlingham & Freud, 1944). Taken together, the books blend empirical data with psychoanalytic interpretation and draw significant conclusions about the effects of war on individual children. *Young Children in War-time* (Burlingham & Freud, 1942b), the first book, starts with a wide-ranging description of children who were evacuated and forced to live in nurseries, and ends with recommendations for helping children prepare for similar evacuations. Even today, the book's wealth of psychological data helps us understand a child's experience in crises like divorce or parental illness.

Infants Without Families (Burlingham & Freud, 1944; Freud, 1973b), the third and final volume, entreats us to value the attachment needs of growing children. The book compares of the psychological and emotional development of children living within families, with those living in residential nurseries. It takes the reader deep into the children's feelings of longing and distress, and looks at how their behavior and functioning changes in reaction to the forced separation from their parents. Over the years, Anna Freud built up a detailed theory of the child's relationship to key figures and the importance of attachment in personality, cognitive and emotional development (Edgcumbe, 2000). (Figure 5.7)

Figure 5.7 Anna Freud and Sister Sophie Dann feeding infants at the HWN, 1942.

Major findings

How do children react to war? Anna Freud and Dorothy Burlingham concluded that the child's response was profoundly determined by the mother figure's absence, presence and state of mind. More powerful than the war itself, the broken attachment is what produces anxiety and trauma.

This and other major scientific findings emerged from unexpected observations and insights as Anna Freud and the HWN staff pursued their research agenda.

Children's reactions to the war

In 1941, a photo of a distressed child with the caption "Bomb shocked child – England" was widely publicised by the *New York World Telegram*. When Edna Blue, Executive Chairman of the Foster Parents Program, enclosed it in a letter (Blue, 1941) to Anna Freud and Dorothy Burlingham, they wrote back: "We have little knowledge of such states in children" (Freud, 1973a, p. 73). In contrast to conventional wisdom suggesting that scenes of aggression and violence would sadden or upset a young child, Anna Freud held children might actually turn toward and become excited by destruction. In other words, children react to violence differently from adults.

The HWN Reports relay many stories of children reacting to dangerous events with far more pleasure than fear. For instance, in May 1941, an unexploded bomb landed in a garden neighboring on the Children's Rest Centre (Freud, 1973a, pp. 43, 165). In January 1945, a US fighter plane narrowly cleared the roof of New Barn. The pilot escaped and survived, but the plane crashed in a nearby field and burned out (Freud, 1973a, p. 466). The children were excited; they were simply not frightened by these events. (Figure 5.8)

Figure 5.8 Children conveyed to a safe playground on Hampstead Heath after a May 1941 bombing.

The FPP wrote to Anna Freud and Dorothy Burlingham suggesting that photos of distressed or "bomb shocked children" might generate more financial support. Dorothy Burlingham's response is imbued with the same advocacy and idealism that motivated the creation of the Hietzing School and Jackson Nursery.

> Can we not find ways and means of interesting people to the fascination and even thrill of real facts? It is a thrilling fact that a human being, a little child, can be bombed out and smile ten minutes afterwards, or sleep peacefully while a bomb makes a big crater in a garden less than fifty yards away: or that love for a parent is so great that it is a far greater shock for a child to be suddenly separated from its mother than to have a house collapse on top of it. Can we not make a new kind of propaganda not only for the present time but for after the war as well? A propaganda for the real needs of a child based on what we are able to find out of the child during these years of war and strain.
>
> (Burlingham, 1941, Letter from the Anna Freud National Centre for Children and Families)

Elaborating on what Burlingham called "the real needs of the child," the Monthly Reports identified five types of anxiety with which children might react to the air raids (real anxiety, instinctual anxiety, moral anxiety, displaced maternal anxiety and anxiety following loss of the father). Each type was linked to the child's developmental stage and to the reaction of surrounding adults (Freud, 1973a). Of course, children did suffer from certain wartime factors like removal to a shelter, anxious mothers, the disruption of family life and separation from fathers. Again, however, these affective factors hurt them more than the bombing events. She hypothesised that the parents who managed to remain relatively calm protected the children from emotional damage. During the Blitz, children

> showed no signs of fear themselves. The situation is very different with two of our children who were brought in by excessively nervous mothers, women who had developed states of severe anxiety after having been bombed, one at home and one in a shelter.... These women naturally imparted their own fears to their children. But even these children, after separation from their mothers, quickly lose their state of tension and settle down into ordinary life.
>
> (Freud, 1973a, pp. 8–9)

Children should be shielded from war, of course, but Anna Freud changed the reasoning. Since children already know about chaos, destruction and aggression, the problems occur when the forces of "civilised" society encourage them to repress this knowledge. War events, in themselves, do not cause the distress. She wrote:

> Children have to be safeguarded against the primitive horrors of the war, not because horrors and atrocities are so strange to them, but because we want them at this decisive stage in their development to overcome and estrange themselves from the primitive and atrocious wishes of their own nature.
>
> (Freud, 1973a, p. 163)

Children's reactions to separation from their parents

For children, broken family attachments cause greater stress than war. Repeating this theme throughout the Monthly Reports, Anna Freud wrote:

> The war acquires comparatively little significance for children as long as it only threatens their lives, disturbs their material comfort, or cuts their food rations. It becomes enormously significant the moment it breaks up family life and uproots the first emotional attachment of the child within the family group. London children, therefore, were on the whole much less upset by the bombing than by evacuation to the country as a protection against it.
>
> (Freud, 1973a, p. 172)

As her theory played out, the form of family separation took on greater significance than the fact. First, with no separation, children regarded incidents of war as ordinary accidents of life. Second, family separation had a greater impact on the child than earlier research anticipated. But third – and particularly urgent – abrupt separations from parents were traumatising. An abrupt separation left the child feeling precariously empty and vulnerable. Indeed, local education authorities found that many of the evacuated urban children reacted to the abrupt separation by starting to bed-wet, sleepwalk or acting out (Armytage, 1976). "To lessen the shock of the breaking up of family life," nurseries should facilitate new attachments or "a really good substitute for the mother relationship" (Freud, 1973a, p. 127).

This "substitute mother," a staff member to whom the child would be introduced at the nursery, eased separation. Anna Freud identified "abruptness" of the separation as the core trigger, and this aimed to prevent trauma by slowing down the process where possible. Biological mothers were encouraged to visit while the child's attachment shifted from one mother figure to another. "Long-drawn-out separation may bring more visible pain," she observed, "but it is less harmful because it gives the child time to accompany the event with reactions, to work through his own feelings over and over again and find outward expression for his state of mind" (Freud, 1973a, p. 209).

Mothers could feed their children at the nursery, put them to bed on the first day and, if possible, for the next week or two. As Hansi Kennedy recalled, this method contrasted starkly with the prevailing opinion that children should be left and not visited for one or two weeks (Kennedy, 1988).

Maintaining relationships with parents and siblings

Besides facilitating the parent visits, the nurseries kept sibling groups together, organised the children into "artificial families" and gave young children the freedom to choose their own food. The Babies Rest Centre in London had been started, in part, to help working mothers maintain regular contract with their babies and toddlers (Kennedy, 2009). Nursing mothers could stay for at least two weeks and breastfeed their new-borns (Seifert, 2009). Twenty-one mothers, with twenty-eight children of the older children between them, lived in and worked as house-keepers.

Unlike most British residential nurseries at the time, the Centre's buildings stayed open at all hours and parents could sleep there overnight. "Parents … are used to obeying hospital rules regarding visiting," Anna Freud wrote in February 1941.

> They were surprised and delighted when they heard that we are glad to have them come at any time. If their occupation allows, they can come freely to take their children out for walks, bathe them and put them to bed in the evening, share meals without any undue insistence on our household routine. In practice this only happens during weekends when our home sometimes takes on the character of a coffee house, club or restaurant.
>
> (Freud, 1973a, p. 10)

In July 1944, most of the children were evacuated from London to New Barn. Because fuel rationing made visits more difficult, Anna Freud organised a monthly bus service for "Parent Sundays." Families were welcomed to spend the day together, share lunch and tea and actually stay overnight at the country house. Even if the mother's or father's visit ended in upset, these repeated shorter separations allowed children to overcome the grief of departure. Anna Freud observed:

> This slower method of overcoming the shock of separation [is] much less harmful to the child than the traumatic one usual in evacuation, when many little children who have never been away from their mothers for a single night are suddenly taken from them, not to see then again for weeks or even months.
>
> (Freud, 1973a, p. 10)

Figure 5.9 Parents visiting their children at New Barn. Anna Freud and Dorothy Burlingham are seated at the back.

"Artificial families"

The small "artificial families of children" or "family groups" came about all at once. In planning the Babies Rest Centre, Anna Freud and Dorothy Burlingham had decided on 1:4 ratio of carers to infants and toddlers. Each group had its own "substitute mother" responsible for all basic needs of child (Freud, 1973a, p. 220). Interestingly, Anna Freud did not expect the children to seek out mother substitutes since they had regular family visits. After about nine months, however, carers noticed that individual children would show a strong preference for a particular worker, regardless of who actually dressed, toileted, washed and played with them. Their disappointment at a "lack of stable mother relationship" was expressed by soiling or wetting themselves (Freud, 1973a, pp. 217, 220).

The children clung possessively to their substitute mothers and were fiercely jealous of "siblings" in their family group. No sooner had they accepted their own group, then they raged at the other family groups and tried blocking their own substitute mother from interacting with the others. The profound disruption concerned Anna Freud. "For a while we really thought our grand innovation had been a great mistake" (Freud, 1973a, p. 221). Nevertheless, after about three weeks, the children grew to trust their substitute mothers, and the frenzy gave way to more stable and comforting attachments. Anna Freud commented,

> The result of this arrangement was astonishing in its force and immediacy. The need for individual attachment with the feelings which had been lying dormant came out in a rush and in the course of one week all six families were completely and firmly established.
>
> (A. Freud, 1973a, p. 220)

Organising the children into family groups had a dramatically positive effect on their development. Those who had regressed or were slow to progress developed rapidly, especially in toilet mastery (Freud, 1973a, p. 221). Attachment to a specific mother substitute encouraged the child to relinquish infantile wishes. Intriguingly, these attachments had no consequences for the child's relationship with their visiting parents. Although the nursery lacked "father substitutes," Anna Freud employed men who had not gone to war because they were conscientious objectors (Hellman, 1990). James Robertson, a social worker, worked there and took most of the photos archived at the Anna Freud Centre. "It is quite difficult to conceive from today's perspective, when most residential care of young children is organised around family groups," Hansi Kennedy commented, "how innovative this idea was more than half a century ago" (Kennedy, 2009, p. 314).

The baby's buffet

Meals should be delicious and adults should avoid regulating when, what and how a child eats. If children could really enjoy their food, Anna Freud thought, they risked fewer eating disturbances later on. So at the HWN, toddlers were allowed as much choice as food rationing permitted and, indeed, they chose a balanced diet. Some compensated on Tuesday for what they had left out Monday, others finished the first course – if they were allowed to put it aside – after eating their pudding. "Chocolate, sweets, dried fruit, marmalade, and jam" came in parcels from the FPP (Figure 5.10), the Red Cross of private donors (Freud, 1973a, p. 151). These precious food items, no longer available in England, were mostly allocated to sick or undernourished children. With a newly acquired sense of their own needs, the children put on weight satisfactorily (Edgcumbe, 2000). Dr Hannah Fischer, who worked in the HWN, depicted the scene vividly:

> There was a choice. There was coffee – not real coffee but a hot drink made from corn – cocoa, water, warm or cold milk, fruit juices, all kind of drinks. The children could choose for themselves. Also they had different cheeses, sausage, eggs. In wartime it wasn't so easy to get these things. And they had fruit, cereals and porridge, everything you eat at breakfast. And they were also offered chocolate. It was very interesting

> what we found out about that consuming of chocolate. When they were new in the nursery, they would start eating heaps of chocolate. After a few days, no more chocolate. On the whole, the children would choose a fairly good kind of breakfast. Which means that the body says what is needed. You could really let the children decide on their food because on the whole they chose a very balanced meal.
>
> (Fischer, 2010)

Dr Fischer was impressed by Anna Freud's sensitivity to the affective needs of small children. Because they drew a symbolic equivalence between food and mother, infants should be granted the same self-determination as the toddlers at their buffet. In this moving story, Dr Fischer depicts feeding an infant who was separated from his mother:

> One day, Miss Freud came when I was feeding G, a little boy of 1 year 3 months. It was very hard to feed him; it took a long time (I had spoken about him at the meeting) because he would put his thumb in his mouth after every spoonful. It was an annoying habit, of sucking on his thumb after every spoonful. So Anna Freud sat down and watched me feed him and explained: G had been separated from his mother by

(a)

(b)

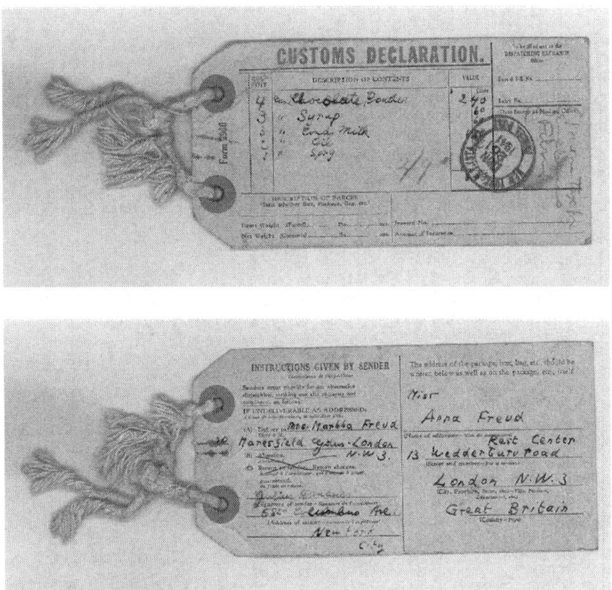

Figure 5.10 Shipping labels from food parcels for the HWN.

> war conditions. He had been breast fed until this sudden interruption and now he was being given food from a bottle or a spoon. Since he had always experienced food by sucking at the breast, now he was trying to recreate the breast experience by putting his thumb in his mouth. "If you stop him now," Anna Freud said, "he will develop terrible eating problems later on – and that would be worse." I asked how the feeding should progress. She assured me that, when "he starts to feed himself he will stop using the thumb." And he did. He gave up the thumb. He did it by himself.
>
> (Fischer, 2010)

The system worked well. Pleased with the experiments, Anna Freud wrote about the newly gained benefits of autonomy and food choice.

> All children who have been treated in this manner from their first year onwards, become, without exception, good eaters of a well-balanced diet. They eat and drink with pleasure; they do not keep food in their mouths unchewed; they do not dislike vegetables either raw or cooked; and they show such healthy appetites that visitors might suspect that we have been starving them.
>
> (Freud, 1973a, p. 526)

Informal training

Like Hannah Fischer, most of the staff were young refugees from Germany, Austria and other European countries. To give them skills that they could use after the war, Anna Freud initiated training activities within a few months of opening the nurseries (Dyer, 1983). Short lunchbreak discussions covered topics like children's war games and war conversations, thumb sucking and toilet mastery, aggression, and parental attitudes toward the war. Sometimes individual children and their problems were discussed (Freud, 1973a, pp. 22–23). In 1941, these discussions evolved into a "purely private and unofficial training scheme," a pragmatic and comprehensive course that included the psychoanalytic model of the mind (Freud, 1973a, p. 122). In-service rotations gave them experience in all the nursery departments (babies, toddlers, nursery children and ill children) as well as the kitchen, housekeeping and administrative offices. Kennedy reminisced,

> The highlight of these courses was a weekly Wednesday afternoon meeting with Anna Freud where problems with individual children were discussed, and possible ways of dealing with the child suggested by her. Anna Freud visited the Nursery every day and often following such a discussion, would spend time specifically observing this

> child and bring her observations and further thoughts to the next meeting.
>
> (Kennedy, 1993, quoted by Miller & Neely, 2008)

The nursery work was very demanding and, like most war-time nurseries, HWN experienced a rapid staff turnover. Staff regularly worked ten-hour shifts and four had to share a single bedroom when the children moved to the country house. Two chicken houses were converted into staff sleeping quarters, "the sitting nests … serving as built-in bookcase" (Freud, 1973a, p. 421). Despite these drawbacks, the training course ensured that the HWN "never lacked working students; vacancies were in constant demand, and applicants frequently had to be refused or placed on a waiting list" (Freud, 1973a, p. 537).

Beyond the nurseries

Of the 100 children who were living in the HWN, sixteen did not return to parent(s) when the war nurseries closed in 1945. Almost 200 children were admitted between 1941 and 1945. Of these, approximately one-fifth came with their mothers and remained in the nurseries for periods ranging from one week to five years (Freud, 1973a). While Anna Freud's own work in the HWN was unpaid, she recorded her gratitude to the FPP in the final report.

> We are aware of the fact that no other nursery establishment in wartime England had been provided for on an equally generous scale, or has been granted such freedom in determining which of the pressing needs in their sphere of work should have priority.
>
> (Freud, 1973a, p. 531)

From the beginning of her productive career, Anna Freud set her sights on "an enlightened analytic upbringing of children." She refined the psychoanalytic treatment of the emotionally disturbed child and sought, persistently, to safeguard the welfare of children, reduce the risks to which they were exposed and prevent interferences with their development.

In the Jackson Nursery in Vienna, she began her studies on child development and the systematic use of observation. She studied separation and substitute caregivers, libidinal development, and the impact of the internal and external work on the child. In the HWN in London, she continued her work on the child's reaction to war and separation from the parents. At both the Jackson Nursery and the HWN, she disputed prevailing views: she encouraged parents to spend time with their children in the nurseries and allowed very young children agency over their eating. She provided each child with a mother substitute to meet their need for a stable relationship and consequently. Reviewing her work three decades later, Anna Freud was "glad to note that … many of the findings presented here as new, have become familiar tenets on which a much more critical view of residential upbringing and its consequences for personality development [is] based" (Freud, 1973b, p. xx). Our ongoing review of her pioneering work in this essay and beyond confirms Robert Wallerstein's (1984, p. 65) testimonial that Anna Freud was indeed a "radical innovator."

Acknowledgments

The author would like to thank the Freud Museum London and the Anna Freud National Centre of Children and Families for permission to reproduce archival photographs and to quote selected passages from archival materials.

Illustrations

Figure 5.1 Anna Freud holding a child at the Jackson Nursery in 1937, b/w photograph by Willi Hoffer, Freud Museum, London
Figure 5.2 Cylinder block wood toy from the Jackson Nursery (still in use in the Anna Freud Centre Parent-Toddler Groups), The Anna Freud National Centre for Children and Families
Figure 5.3 The Children's Rest Centre of the Hampstead War Nurseries, b/w photo, HWN Archives, The Anna Freud National Centre for Children and Families
Figure 5.4 The Babies' Rest Centre of the Hampstead War Nurseries, b/w photo, HWN Archives, The Anna Freud National Centre for Children and Families
Figure 5.5 Children napping outdoors at New Barn, b/w photo, HWN Archives, The Anna Freud National Centre for Children and Families
Figure 5.6 Child Observation card written by Alice Goldberger and dated March 30, 1942 from the Hampstead War Nurseries, The Anna Freud National Centre for Children and Families
Figure 5.7 Anna Freud and Sister Sophie Dann feeding babies in the Hampstead War Nurseries in 1942, b/w photograph by James Robertson (?), The Anna Freud National Centre for Children and Families
Figure 5.8 Children conveyed to a safe playground on Hampstead Heath after a May 1941 bombing. The garden of the Children's Rest Centre was unsafe due to an unexploded time-bomb in the neighboring garden (Freud, 1973a, pp. 43, 165), b/w photograph by James Robertson, The Anna Freud National Centre for Families and Children
Figure 5.9 Parents visiting Sunday at New Barn. Anna Freud and Dorothy Burlingham are seated at the rear, b/w photograph by James Robertson, The Anna Freud National Centre for Families and Children
Figure 5.10 Front and back labels from food parcels sent to Anna Freud for the Hampstead War Nurseries, color photograph, The Anna Freud National Centre for Families and Children

References

Armytage, W. H. G. (1976). Psychoanalysis and teacher education: Part III. *British Journal of Teacher Education*, 2:95–111.

Blue, E. (1941). Letter dated 11 April 1941 to the Hampstead War Nurseries. The Anna Freud Centre Hampstead War Nurseries Archives.

Burlingham, D. (1941). Letter dated 14 May 1941 to the Foster Parents Plan for War Children. The Anna Freud Centre Hampstead War Nurseries Archives.

Burlingham, D., & Freud, A. (1942a). Annual Report of a Residential War Nursery. The Anna Freud Centre Archives.

Burlingham, D., & Freud, A. (1942b). *Young children in war-time, a year's work in a residential war nursery*. London: Allen & Unwin.

Burlingham, D., & Freud, A. (1944). *Infants without families: The case for and against residential nurseries*. London: Allen & Unwin.

Dyer, R. (1983). *Her father's daughter, the work of Anna Freud*. New York & London: Jason Aronson.

Edgcumbe, R. (2000). *Anna Freud: A view of development, disturbance and therapeutic techniques*. London: Routledge.

Fischer, H. (2010). Interview with Dr. Hannah Fischer by Elizabeth Ann Danto and Birgit Johler.

Freud, A. (1926). Introduction to the technique of the psycho-analysis of children'. In *The psycho-analytical treatment of children* (1946). London: Imago.

Freud, A. (1951). Observations on child development. *Psychoanalytic Study of the Child*, 6:18–30.

Freud, A. (1966). A Short History of Child Analysis. *Psychoanalytic Study of the Child*, 21:7–14.

Freud, A. (1971). Residential vs. foster care. In *The writings of Anna Freud, Vol. 7. Problems of psychoanalytic training, diagnosis and the techniques of therapy* (pp. 223–239). New York, London: International Universities Press. (original work published in 1967).

Freud, A. and Burlingham, D. T. (1973a). Infants without families and reports on the Hampstead nurseries 1939–1945. In *The writings of Anna Freud, Vol. 3*. New York, London: International Universities Press. (Original work published 1944 in collaboration with Dorothy Burlingham).

Freud, A. (1973b). Infants without families: The case for and against residential nurseries. In *The writings of Anna Freud: Vol. 3. Infants without families: Reports on the Hampstead nurseries: 1939–1945* (pp. 541–559). New York: International Universities Press. (Original work published 1944 in collaboration with Dorothy Burlingham).

Freud, A. (1978). Edith B. Jackson: In memoriam. *Journal of the American Academy of Child and Adolescent Psychiatry*, 17:730–731.

Freud, A. (1980). Dorothy Burlingham. *Psychoanalytic Study of the Child*, 35: x–xix.

Freud, A., & Burlingham, D. (1943). *War and children*. Medical War Book: New York.

Hellman, I. (1983). Work in the Hampstead War Nurseries. *International Journal of Psycho-Analysis*, 64:435–439.

Hellman, I. (1990). *From war babies to grandmothers. Forty-eight years in psychoanalysis*. London: Karnac.

Johler, B., Sommer, M., & Steiner, A. (2016). *Anna Freud in Wien: Ein Rundgang zu Orten der Psychoanalyse.* Wien & Berlin: Turia & Kant.

Kennedy, H. (1988). Thirtieth Birthday celebrations of the Anna Freud Nursery School. *Bulletin of the Anna Freud Centre*, 11(4):271–275.

Kennedy, H. (2009). Children in conflict: Anna Freud and the War Nurseries. *The Psychoanalytic Study of the Child*, 64:306–319.

Krivanek, R. (2014). "Vertrautheit mit dem Kleinkind ist das Ziel". Die Arbeit und Forschung in der Jackson-Krippe (Wien 1937/38). *Lucifer-Amor Zeitschrift zur Geschichte der Psychoanalyse*, 27:71–107.

Lynn, D. J. (2003) Freud's psychoanalysis of Edith Banfield Jackson. *Journal of the American Academy of Psychoanalysis*, 31:609–625.

Miller, J. M., & Neely, C. (Eds.). (2008). *The psychoanalytic work of Hansi Kennedy: From war nurseries to the Anna Freud centre* (1940–1993). London: Karnac.

Seifert, K. (2009). Die Projekte und Institutionen Anna Freuds. In: Diercks, Chr. u. S. Schlüter (Hg.) *Die grossen Kontroversen in der Psychoanalyse. Sigmund Freud Vorlesungen 2007* (S. 245–254). Wien: Mandelbaumverlag.

Wallerstein, R. S. (1984). Anna Freud: Radical innovator and staunch conservative. *The Psychoanalytic Study of the Child*, 39:65–80.

Young-Bruehl, E. (2008). *Anna Freud: A biography* (2nd ed.). New Haven, CT: Yale University Press.

Chapter 6

The Hietzing School as the birthplace of a psychoanalytic theory of adolescence

Florian Houssier

In the history of psychoanalysis to date, Anna Freud is often presented with ambivalence, and criticism is leveled as much at her person as at her theory. In France in particular, her ideas are associated with a psychoanalytic ego psychology and often despised as a kind of (de-) formed defense of the Freudian revolution.

This broad dismissal comes at a risk to psychoanalysis, namely the loss of a critical aspect of Anna Freud's work, her unique theorisation on the psychoanalytic understanding of the adolescent. This area of clinical investigation owes her a great deal (Houssier (2007, 2010). In this chapter, I amplify on my earlier (2010) argument that the repression of Anna Freud's contributions stems from conflicts, within the field of psychoanalysis, about her analysis by her father. The analysis of a young woman handling the infant–adolescent struggle may well carry echoes of Freud's self-analysis and his own adolescent journey (Houssier 2007, 2010). (Figure 6.1)

The path that brings the daughter of the creator of psychoanalysis to take an interest in adolescence rests on a set of circumstances, mixing personal life, institutional stakes and the ongoing theorisation of adolescence. Along that path, three distinct threads lead toward what we now call the adolescence process:

1. On the personal level, Anna Freud's analysis by her father is infused with the tension, indeed the suffering, of adolescent conflict. Her case presentation before the Vienna Psychoanalytic Society in 1922 reads as a sort of perusal of this analysis in conjunction with the beginnings of a clinical theory of adolescence.
2. On the scientific level, Anna Freud's publications on adolescence paved a fundamental role for future specialists in this area.
3. The intersection of Anna Freud's own analysis with the construction of a theory of adolescence – in spite of, or thanks to, its counter-transferential activity – helped release adolescence from the psychoanalytic bedrock of infancy. The idea of relegating adolescence to infancy was particularly defended by Ernest Jones (1922) and many others after him, and is still heard today.

Figure 6.1 Anna Freud and Her Class, World War I.

Psycho-pedagogical study of the adolescent in Red Vienna

The Hietzing School was a psycho-pedagogical experiment which attested to the shared hope, among pedagogues and psychoanalysts alike, that one could think about children's education in a new way. There, the use of observation (which Anna Freud later developed as a work and research instrument) made possible the application of psychoanalytic ideas to a clinical contact. It was the first half of the 20th century, and the psychoanalytic ideal was then in full swing. As Rudolph Ekstein said, "Most of us hoped to contribute to the educational system and the future world through the knowledge of psychology, psychoanalysis and modern pedagogy, and lead to a renewed school system" (Ekstein and Motto, 1969, p. 10). Clearly, seeing Freud's ideas confirmed at Hietzing was a significant encouragement.

Anna Freud exemplified the alliance between psychoanalysis and pedagogy that ranged across a number of institutions. In 1916, when Oscar Pfister taught at the Swiss Pedagogy Society, he described psychoanalysis as a form of education and later coined the term "Pädaanalyse" to speak of pedagogical analysis (Ekstein and Motto, 1969). In 1919, Siegfried Bernfeld opened a home for orphaned children and adolescents of Jewish origin the following year. Bernfeld insisted that respect and unconditional love should supersede the teacher's inclination to exercise power over the child. In the same year,

Figure 6.2 Classtime at Oberhollabrunn.

Alfred Adler organised a network of free, school-based psycho-educational assessments for parents, children and teachers. But it was August Aichhorn who, more than anyone, introduced Anna Freud to Vienna's pioneering pedagogical and social services (Houssier and Marty, 2007). At his institution for troubled children and adolescents, Aichhorn rejected the idea of total liberation of the instincts; instead, he aimed for a clinical model where children in distress substitute their social symptoms with socially adjusted behaviors without sacrificing their wishes and ideals. (Figure 6.2)

In 1923, Anna Freud convened select Viennese analysts for an informal "Children's Seminar" aimed at training therapists to apply psychoanalytic principle to education. The group represented the first attempt to outline the methodological and clinical specifics of child and adolescent psychoanalysis. Aichhorn, Bernfeld and Wilhelm Hoffer met at the Freud apartment every Saturday afternoon, to discuss new cases of children and adolescents with Anna and, as Hoffer remembered, Sigmund Freud on occasion. Unfortunately, the group moved forward without Hermine von Hug-Hellmuth (murdered in 1924 by her 18-year-old nephew) and already rejected by establishment analysts. Historically, Hug-Hellmuth was the first analyst to take an active interest in adolescence.

The Hietzing School opened in 1927. That year, a second group of young psychoanalysts gathered around Anna Freud to create what would become the celebrated, though unofficial, *Kinderseminar* (Dyer, 1983). If one traces the evolution of psycho-pedagogical ideas from 1927 onward, we locate the origin of the Hietzing School in the first work on child psychoanalysis. In her inaugural presentation to the Vienna Institute of Psychoanalysis, Anna Freud asks specifically for a school organised according to the principles of psychoanalysis.

A training school for clinical work with children and adolescents

Anna Freud believed that the school environment of children in analysis should help them integrate their analytic work into daily social life while, at the same time, keep parents informed of their analytic progress. In order to facilitate this direction (and not to impede it), teachers should be trained in analysis as well. This model, still in use, takes into account the parents' fragile self-regard while protecting the space of the child's psychotherapy from potential parental intrusions. (Figures 6.3 and 6.4)

Like Anna Freud and their mentor August Aichhorn, Hietzing's two principal teachers, Peter Blos and Erik Erikson, came to psychoanalysis through pedagogy. The two young men adhered to John Dewey's "project method" of teaching: children need a personal stake in their learning. Erikson explained that a theme would be chosen, Eskimos for example, and all learning would revolve around Eskimo life: history and geography, but also mathematics, reading and writing. The teaching was interdisciplinary in

Figure 6.3 Anna Freud's Office at Berggasse 19, View 1.

Figure 6.4 Anna Freud's Office at Berggasse 19, View 2.

both the 7- to 10-year-old's class and the class for 11- to 14-year-olds. The children laughed a lot because their teachers believed that pleasure eases the learning process. The teachers proposed a combination of new play experiences, free discussions and lessons. At Christmas for example, a party was organised with games and other entertainment (songs, acrobats, dancers, boar head and mistletoe) around a meal to which Sigmund Freud was invited. Clearly, even without direct interpretation of the children's creative productions, their inner world was what intrigued Burlingham, Erikson and Blos as they become psychoanalysts.

In her own way, Anna Freud left the field open to teachers who, she knew, promised a future in psychoanalysis with adolescents. The two principals, however, were as deeply influenced by August Aichhorn as by Anna Freud from whose powerful presence they sought to extricate themselves. Aichhorn represented a guiding paternal figure. Indeed, one can hypothesise that Aichhorn took over the role held by Peter Blos' father during Erikson and Blos' teenage years in Karlsruhe. The men's friendship endured for the rest of their lives, and the theme of adolescence, the timing of their encounter, threaded their life work. (Figure 6.5)

For their supervision with Aichhorn, Blos and Erikson relied on the clinical material provided by Hietzing's young adolescent pupils. This contact

Figure 6.5 The School at Oberhollabrunn.

marked their first decisive step toward their later clinical work. Erikson describes how Aichhorn would offer individualised interpretations comparable to treatment. By 1933, once the Hietzing school closed and his analysis with Anna Freud was completed, Erikson was recognised by his Viennese peers as a psychoanalyst. For Peter Blos, though he did not become a psychoanalyst in Vienna (unlike Erikson) – which would explain his more "pedagogical" construal of the experience – he was profoundly affected by this period and adhered decisively to psychoanalysis after emigrating to the United States. After an early career centered on psycho-pedagogy, he worked with delinquent adolescents and pre-adolescents from the 1950s on. For instance, he later extended Margaret Mahler's concept of separation-individuation to include adolescence. Mahler too was inspired by Aichhorn.

Controlling violence and punishment

"In other schools, it would be funny to hang a paper on the professor's jacket. Here, it would not be funny," said a Hietzing pupil. Indeed, Erikson and Erikson (1980) later concluded that "we were too nice" with incidences of aggression between teacher and student. But in the beginning, the school is seen as a dream or a wonderful country, not only by students like Victor Rosenfeld and Ernst Halberstadt but also by the teachers for whom the founders "dreamed" the school (Friedman, 1999). (Figure 6.6)

How can one not be seduced by these open adults and choose pleasure (even the pleasure of learning) over the harsh laws of necessity? Within the pedagogical bond, seduction can lead to idealisation, itself a form of hide and seek in the teacher–student relationship (Houssier, 2011). The idealised love of adults, of which we find traces in the words of former Hietzing students, is a tense mirror of adult repression: the fundamentally ambivalent aspect of the parent–child bond is erased in favor of an illusion, that of a love

Figure 6.6 Eva Rosenfeld with Victor (Rosenfeld) Ross and Ernst Halberstadt (Freud).

without fault or disappointment. This idealisation questions the premise of an essentially "maternal" attitude which holds in whatever aggression is to be found in any relationship. Thus, Erik and Joan Erikson's "too nice" can be understood as students chiding their teachers, a hostile mode of relation centered on adult–child seduction where sublimation is the only possible result. Aggression is fully present, as evidenced by Erikson's observation of asocial behavior among "a dozen of our children aged between twelve and thirteen outside the school." Nevertheless, the anger of these young adolescents toward their teacher is seen as a universal phenomenon and not a shameful failing (Houssier, 2002). Erikson associates the adolescents' angry criticism of their teacher with a need for punishment. "They confessed openly that we do not respond enough to their need to be punished," said one student. "We are like balloons ready to explode and suddenly arrive in the void." Is this only the need for punishment, as identified by Sigmund Freud, or is it the fear that aggressive fantasies will not be tolerated in such a flexible context?

Is modern pedagogy, if it permits children to find themselves through creativity, less appropriate for adolescents and their drives awakened by incestuous and parricidal desires? As if it were a response to this exchange with his students, a fight broke out "the very next day" between two teenagers. Erikson interprets this as a rather positive direction. He advocates for a pedagogy which would not split the sexual and aggressive domains but, on the contrary, would link them and give the "omnipresence of disordered impulses" their due.

First steps toward a general theory

Anna Freud's most famous book *The Ego and the Mechanisms of Defense* (1936) is largely based on the analysis of the children and adolescents attending the Hietzing School. Like her father before her, her venture into child analysis concludes with chapters on adolescence. She highlights "asceticism" or "intellectualisation" as the defense mechanisms specific to adolescence, and thus opens the way to an understanding of the adolescent process in general instead of a series of pathologies (anorexia, psychosis, delinquency, etc.) occurring during the teen years. The Burlingham children, now adolescent themselves, are broadly represented in this work of her Viennese period. "This book was remarkable and was to exert great influence as the first psychoanalytic study of adolescence, the foundation of which appears in the first chapters devoted to the defenses of the ego and against the id and the superego," wrote Janet Sayers (1991, p. 238). As in Sigmund Freud's *Three Essays on the Theory of Sexuality*, the last part of Anna Freud's book is devoted to adolescence and sketches three original perspectives: (1) adolescence is not solely the continuation of infantile conflicts but poses specific problems related to the new intensity of sexual impulses in puberty; (2) adolescence brings out not so much the ego as the tension between the ego and the increased demands of puberty; and (3) the increased vitality of the instincts complicates psychic life, leading to a struggle between desire and fear of selfishly satisfying the instinctual drive (sexual desire vs asceticism).

As seen in the analyses of Bob Burlingham and Peter Heller (Heller 1992), Anna Freud bypasses the asocial tendencies, a recurrent term in her main work, to explain certain adolescent positions. She favors the idea of disengaging the object-libido allocated to the parental figures which causes an identificatory fragility, hence a weakening of the superego. The antisocial act is an integral part of what organises the adolescence process; this explains the frequency of the adolescent's transferential ruptures with the analyst.

Despite her interest in adolescent patients before World War II, Anna Freud stopped writing on the subject from the 1930s until about 1958. Prior to 1940, the troubled adolescent was commonly portrayed as a potential offender, always ready to act out in lieu of working. The prevailing idea of the "unanalyzable subject" also explains this lack of knowledge. But in 1957, a year before its publication, Anna Freud sent Donald Winnicott the text of what was originally a presentation to the British Psychoanalytic Society. She starts her 1958 article, titled "Adolescence," with an observation: the study of adolescence was dismal, and so few psychoanalysts treated adolescents that no general theory of could emerge. She would change that by transforming the idea of the "family romance" from a creation of latency to one of the potential traits of adolescence. Echoing her piece from 1922, Anna Freud repeats that the reveries of latency fade away to leave room for the terrifying fantastical scenarios of adolescence. (Figures 6.7 and 6.8)

Figure 6.7 Anna Freud ca. 1915.

Figure 6.8 Anna Freud, 1920s.

The 1958 text relies on the long-established and well-attended child and adolescent clinics, starting with the Hampstead Nurseries between 1940 and 1945, and later the Hampstead Child Therapy Clinic, both co-founded and directed with Dorothy Burlingham. Even if Anna Freud still thought of adolescence as a normal developmental weakness, her landmark 1958 text pushed analysts in a new direction and formed the basis of what appears today as a general psychoanalytic theory of adolescence.

In conclusion: Adolescent theory in practice today

Even if the Hietzing School, like other institutions, developed by trial and error, it created the possibility of delivering a novel psycho-pedagogical model. Apart from August Aichhorn's work, this type of experimental model is rare in psychoanalysis. Yet, coercion-free respectful education programs do exist though they may lack a theoretical foundation. These schools repeatedly welcome adolescents whose fractured and chaotic lives conflict with the today's prevailing rejection by institutions which, in fact, fear disruption under the guise of setting limits. This rejection guarantees the peace of those in charge of these adolescents, while largely actually making them into "untreatable" subjects. In the absence of any creativity, a simplistic ideology views sanction as the only approach. The psycho-pedagogical alliance seems to be, at the same time, repressed, forgotten and then reinvented, as if the audience it touches, children and adolescents, always show the opposite: in the absence of a generalisable model, creativity is the only possible way forward.

Some may seize on the (transformed) legacy of the Hietzing School, on its environment that interchanges treatment and family and on its lack of boundaries within the school's governance. On the other hand, one of the suggestions left by the school is the need for communication between the assessment (of both the fantasy and the real aspects of the child's life) and psychotherapy. Some of Anna Freud's ideals – one must individualise each child, she affirmed – always find resonance in the present. But Hietzing's greatest contribution by far was the demand for a specific assessment of each child or adolescent case, still performed in many of today's institutions.

The end of the 1950s marked a turning point in the elaboration of the theory of adolescence. Anna Freud initiated this movement with her 1958 article titled, like that of Jeanne Lampl-de Groot from 1960 and Peter Blos of 1962, "On adolescence." She upholds the need to define what adolescence is, beyond psychopathology or a developmental stage. The second and third generation of analysts could finally expand the metapsychological foundations of the adolescent process. Yet aside from Donald Winnicott, few authors outside Anna Freud's circle initiated new theory in adolescent psychoanalysis. Indeed, this first movement of theorisation came in the 1960s thanks to Pierre Mâle (1956) and Evelyne Kestemberg (1962) in France; Peter Blos, Erik Erikson and Kurt Eissler in the United States; and Moses Laufer (1964) in England. François Ladame (2011) recently specified that it was not so much his daughter whom Sigmund Freud failed to analyze, but her adolescence. Ladame goes on to suggest that Anna Freud's unconditional support of Laufer's work on adolescence stemmed from her own unresolved adolescent conflicts. Of course, Laufer will remember that one cannot be a psychoanalyst of adolescents without analyzing one's own adolescence. These words bring back the question of Sigmund Freud's adolescence and his self-analysis. Ernest Jones created an official story, according to which there was little to say about Freud's adolescence. In contrast, Alain De Mijolla argued that Freud's adolescence was not so quiet. Kurt Eissler essentially repeated the Jones version but came to a different conclusion. As for all creators, Eissler said, Freud's adolescence was not only conflicted but indeed tormented by a traumatic love deception. This would have led him to establish defenses by repressing his adolescent drive, not unlike his daughter's own psychic conflicts.

Fortunately, today we have the skills with which we can listen to and understand the adolescent, skills which we largely owe to the work and influence of Anna Freud. This has resulted in a range of new practices, the creativity of which responds to the polysemy of adolescent problems. It is no longer the adolescent who adapts to the treatment but the psychoanalysts who have varied their practice by taking into account the subject's shifts between normality and pathology. This range of clinical devices – from psychotherapy to bifocal or family therapies, psychodrama and psychopedagogy – corroborates the experience of Anna Freud and her theoretical-clinical point of view: the adolescent definitely occupies a noteworthy place in contemporary psychoanalytic theory and practice.

Illustrations

Figure 6.1 Anna Freud and her school class ca.1917, b/w photograph, David Prokross Collection, Boston Psychoanalytic Society and Institute Archives

Figure 6.2 Class at Oberhollabrunn, ca. 1919, photograph, Estate of August Aichhorn, Collection of Thomas Aichhorn

Figure 6.3 Edmund Engelman, Anna Freud's Consulting Room at Berggasse 19, 1938, album photograph, Estate of August Aichhorn, Collection of Thomas Aichhorn

Figure 6.4 Edmund Engelman, Anna Freud's Consulting Room at Berggasse 19, 1938, album photograph, Estate of August Aichhorn, Collection of Thomas Aichhorn

Figure 6.5 Eva Rosenfeld with Victor Ross and Ernst Halberstadt, b/w photograph, Eva Rosenfeld album, Sigmund Freud Museum, Sigmund Freud Privatstiftung, Vienna

Figure 6.6 The school at Oberhollabrunn ca. 1919, b/w photograph, Estate of August Aichhorn, Collection of Thomas Aichhorn

Figure 6.7 Anna Freud ca. 1918, b/w photograph, Freud Museum London

Figure 6.8 Anna Freud in the 1920s, b/w photograph, Freud Museum London

References

Blos, P. (1962) *On Adolescence: A Psychoanalytic Interpretation*. New York: The Free Press.

Dyer, R. (1983) *The Work of Anna Freud*. New York: Aronson.

Ekstein, R. and Motto, R. L. (1969) Psychoanalysis and Education: A historical account. In Ekstein, R. and Motto, R. L. (eds.). *From Learning for Love to Love of Learning*. New York: Brunner-Mazel, p. 10.

Erikson, E. H. and Erikson, J. (1980) Dorothy Burlingham's School in Vienna. In Schlein, S. (ed.). (1995) *Erik H. Erikson – A Way of Looking at Things*. New York: W.W. Norton.

Freud, A. (1922) Beating Fantasies and Daydreams. *International Journal of Psychoanalysis*. 4:89–102.

Freud, A. (1936/37) *The Ego and the Mechanisms of Defense*. Baines, C. (trans.). London: Hogarth.

Freud, A. (1958) Adolescence. *Psychoanalytic Study of the Child*. 13:255–278.

Friedman, L. J. (1999) *Identity's Architect: A Biography of Erik H. Erikson*. New York: Scribner.

Heller, P. (ed.). (1992) *Anna Freud's Letters to Eva Rosenfeld.* Madison, CT: International Universities Press.

Houssier, F. (2002) L'Hietzing School de Vienne (1927–1932). *Adolescence.* 20(2):405–416.

Houssier, F. (2007) August Aichhorn: Cliniques de la délinquance. In Marty F. (ed.). *Collection Recherches: Les troubles de l'enfance et de l'adolescence.* Paris: Champ Social Editions.

Houssier, F. (2010) Hypothèses sur les origines d'une filiation théorico-clinique. Quand S. Freud analyse sa fille. In Givre, P. and Tassel, A. (eds.). *Le Tourment Adolescent, Volume 2.* Paris: Presses Universitaires de France, pp. 29–49.

Houssier, F. (2011) Traumatisme et Perte d'Objet à l'Adolescence. *Carnet Psy.* 155:46–51.

Houssier, F. and Marty, F. (2007) *Eduquer l'adolescent?* Paris: Champ Social Editions.

Jones, E. (1922) Some Problems of Adolescence. *British Journal of Psychology.* 13:31–47.

Kestemberg, E. (1962) L'identité et l'identification chez les adolescents. In *L'Adolescence à Vif.* (1999) Paris: Presses Universitaires de France – PUF.

Ladame, F. (2011) Anna Freud et Moses Laufer, partenaires indissociables? *Topique.* # 115:121–125.

Lampl-de Groot, J. (1960) On Adolescence. *Psychoanalytic Study of the Child.* 15:95–103.

Laufer, M. (1964) Ego Ideal and Pseudo Ego Ideal. *Psychoanalytic Study of the Child.* 19:196–220.

Mâle, P. (1956) Etude Psychanalytique de l'Adolescence. In Nacht, S. (ed.). *La Psychanalyse aujourd'hui.* Paris: Presses Universitaires de France – PUF.

Sayers, J. (1991) *Mothers of Psychoanalysis: Helene Deutsch, Karen Horney, Anna Freud, Melanie Klein.* New York: W.W. Norton Company.

Chapter 7

The child in mind and body – the writing of Anna Freud and Dorothy Burlingham in *The Psychoanalytic Study of the Child*

Nellie L. Thompson and Hélène Keable

First published in 1945, *The Psychoanalytic Study of the Child* (*PSOC*) was founded by Ernst Kris, Heinz Hartmann and Anna Freud.[1] The work of two of the journal's leading contributors, Anna Freud and Dorothy Burlingham, include notable, and little discussed, pedagogical veins. Anna Freud's early profession and lifelong identity as a teacher is manifest in her psychoanalytic writings and reviews. Dorothy Burlingham re-imagined the education of blind children, one that met both their practical needs as well as gave them the means to express the reality and vicissitudes of their inner lives.

Anna Freud

Anna Freud was the *PSOC*'s foremost contributor during its first two decades. Her 16 papers fall into four distinct but related groups: child analysis and technique (1945, 1954a, 1959); developmental studies (1951, 1958, 1963); strictly theoretical papers (1946a, 1949, 1952a); and discussions of the work of colleagues (1952b, 1954b, 1960). These publications document how Anna Freud's vocation as a teacher from 1919 through 1924 (Young-Bruehl, 1988, pp. 64–102) found expression in her psychoanalytic activities. In the 1920s and 1930s, her teaching ranged from leading a seminar on child analysis at the Vienna Psychoanalytic Society to the Hietzing School; with Dorothy Burlingham, she led a pedagogical seminar for nursery school teachers and the short-lived Jackson Nursery. At the onset of World War II, the Hampstead War Nurseries in London continued the work of the Jackson Nursery. From 1952 on, the Hampstead Child Therapy Clinic (HCTC) and the Hampstead Child Training Therapy Course (HCTTC) enabled Anna Freud to bring together the psychoanalytic study of development with an immersive training program for child analysts and therapists.

The War Nurseries had rekindled theoretical and clinical issues first raised in the 1920s when child analysis was in a state of flux. Now these clinical issues and their theoretical standing were increasingly viewed within the prism of the impact of separation on young children and the influence of trauma on development. Consequently, Anna Freud increasingly systematised her thinking on the role of ego development and object relations in the young child's life and revised her technical approach to child analysis. These shifts in theory can be read in Anna Freud's 1945 "Indications for Child Analysis," her first paper on technique and child analysis since the 1926 lectures, "Introduction to the Technique of the Analysis of Children" (A. Freud, 1927a), presented before the Vienna Psychoanalytic Society, soon followed by "The Theory of Children's Analysis" (1927b). While the former was published in an American journal (Freud, 1929), the International Psycho-Analytical Library in London declined to publish it. After World War II "Indications for Child Analysis" was reprinted with Anna Freud's 1926 and 1927 papers in a slim book, *The Psycho-Analytical Treatment of Children*. She noted acerbically in the Preface: "It is not the author's fault that the early material contained in this publication is presented to the English reader at such a late date" (Freud, 1946b, pp. xi–xii). As if to defend the significance of the book's findings, she remarked that the knowledge gained from the study of normal child development in Vienna was germane to the education of children overall.

Anna Freud attributed the refusal of the International Library of Psychoanalysis to publish her early work to the influence of the London Kleinians. Coming at the *denouement* of the Controversial Discussions, the planning and creation of the *PSOC* in 1944/45 has frequently been viewed as a vehicle created to disseminate Anna Freud's thinking and work. This unfounded critique, however, ignores the declared aim of the journal's editors who envisioned the *PSOC* as a forum for dialogue among child and adult analysts, infant researchers, and those working in venues outside of psychoanalysis, in nursery schools, child guidance clinics and hospitals. In 1945 the status of child analysis itself was uncertain since many analysts did not consider it genuine psychoanalysis. However, the editors of the *PSOC* regarded the papers and reviews they published as salient evidence for the significance of child and infant studies for the future of psychoanalytic theory and practice, and thereby affirmed the role of child analysts and infant researchers in that future.

The *PSOC* was organised into different sections that covered a wide range of theoretical and clinical topics addressed from diverse analytic viewpoints. One of its aims was to publish papers based on both infant observation and the reconstruction of infantile development from adult analyses. Anna Freud, by contrast, was never truly comfortable in exploring the preverbal phase and in this instance her research aims did not coincide with those of the *PSOC*. Her bibliography was heavily weighted toward child development and the application of analytic principles to understand normal growth and pathological deviations.

Ernst Kris, however, urged Anna Freud to write a paper on object relations in the first year of life because he believed the Kleinians were claiming this topic as their own (Kris, 1945). Her 1946 paper "Psychoanalytic Study of Infantile Feeding Disturbances" did, in fact, explore the role of object relations in development. Despite the animosity between the Kleinians and Anna Freud and her circle, she cited Klein's writings in support of her own findings in two papers written in the early 1950s. In "The Role of Bodily Illness in the Mental Life of Children" (1952a), she described the response of children to surgery and how "the child's body may serve as a focal point" for fantasies of being attacked and overwhelmed (castrated):

> If, for example, the child's fantasies are concerned with his aggression against the mother projected onto her person, the operation is experienced as a retaliatory attack made by the mother on the inside of the child's body (Melanie Klein).
>
> (Freud, 1952a, p. 72)

In her review of James Robertson's *A Two-Year-Old Goes to the Hospital*, Anna Freud graphically imagined how a young child might respond to having stiches removed:

> [It] may well mean to Laura a terrifying experience, with grim, ghost-like figures advancing on her without warning, making a deliberate attack on her body to do her injury. Such events confirm children in their belief that their phantasies of being attacked, mutilated, annihilated are capable of coming true. According to the child's fixation to one particular set of unconscious imaginings the happening is understood by him as a retaliation for his own aggressive wishes (in Melanie Klein sense), as punishment for misdeeds, for death-wishes, as castration.
>
> (Freud, 1953, p. 285)

There is, however, a group of Anna Freud papers that have been undervalued for the light they cast on her as a responsive, engaged analyst in dialogue with colleagues whose theoretical and clinical writings on occasion differed significantly from her own. During the decade between 1951 and 1961, Anna Freud was the discussant of papers delivered at psychoanalytic meetings and congresses by prominent colleagues, a cohort that included Heinz Hartmann, Willi Hoffer, Phyllis Greenacre, Leo Stone, Edith Jacobson, John Bowlby and D. W. Winnicott (Thompson & Keable, 2016b, unpublished).

The proceedings of three of the five meetings were published in the *PSOC* (1952b, 1954b, 1960), while the *Journal of the American Psychoanalytic*

Association (1954c), and the *International Journal of Psychoanalysis* (1962), each published one of the meetings, thereby insuring their reach and influence on the postwar development of psychoanalytic theory and clinical practice. Anna Freud's role as the lead discussant on these occasions is intriguing. In some ways this role was a logical legacy of her background and her own contributions to the development of psychoanalysis; as the author of a seminal contribution to ego psychology, *The Ego and the Mechanisms of Defense* (1936); a leading exponent of one school of child analysis; and, as Freud's daughter, viewed (by herself and many analysts) as an arbitrator of the evolution of classical psychoanalysis in the postwar period.

At the 1951 International Psychoanalytical Congress in Amsterdam, Anna Freud discussed papers by Heinz Hartmann and Willi Hoffer on "The Mutual Influences in the Development of the Ego and Id" (Freud, 1952b). The aim of Hartmann's paper was to clarify the developmental relationship between ego and id against the emergence of different ego functions. He argued that essential to the study of this relationship is the direct observation of infants and young children, thus advocating for the role of child analysis in psychoanalysis (Hartmann, 1954). In responding to Hartmann's paper Anna Freud focused on the clinical implications of his theorising, emphasising that his thinking offers a pathway for understanding the factors that may impede or distort the young child's ego development. A unifying feature of Anna Freud's discussions of the work of colleagues is to highlight the clinical implications of the paper being discussed. Three years later, the New York Psychoanalytic Society sponsored the Arden House Meetings where Anna Freud discussed papers by Phyllis Greenacre, Heinz Hartmann, Leo Stone and Edith Jacobson. In responding to Greenacre's opening paper, "Infantile Neurosis" (Greenacre, 1954), she acknowledged her uneasiness about reconstructing the preverbal phase of infantile development. Nevertheless, she said, Greenacre's "thought-provoking" depiction of the role of rhythm in infantile development offered new insights into autoeroticism in infants and young children. Greenacre's position that all phases of libidinal development are present at birth – which Freud called a revolutionary revision – later takes its place in the developmental profile (Freud, 1954b, p. 16).

Anna Freud's exchanges with colleagues at the Arden House meetings contrast with the standard trope of Anna Freud as Melanie Klein's rival and the forceful exponent of her own vision of child analysis and development. In response to Ernst Kris' description of the planning for the Arden House meetings, she described herself as excited by this "whole adventure" (Kris, 1954; Freud, 1954c). The adventure she welcomed was the chance to engage freely with friends and colleagues without having to write a formal discussion. These exchanges are a reminder of how vital collaborative work was to Anna Freud throughout her life beginning with the Vienna child analysis seminar, the Hietzing School, the Jackson Nursery, the War

Nurseries and the HCTTC. The collaborative foundation and aims of these endeavors fostered Anna Freud's identity as a teacher, her first professional role, across a range of activities: writing, clinical seminars and the development of the curriculum for the HCTTC. In the last years of her professional life, she educated lawyers, judges and doctors about the vital importance of giving foremost considerations to the psychological well-being of children with whom they came into contact. Her *PSOC* papers explored the developmental challenges of childhood and adolescence; their clarity of thought articulated a clinical pathway for acting in the "best interest of the child."

Finally, the freedom of thought Anna Freud found in the role of discussant, notably illustrated at the Arden House Meetings, was replicated at the Hampstead Child Therapy Training Course when she presided over the Wednesday meetings when the entire clinic gathered to listen to and discuss a clinical case presentation. Ava Bry Penman, who trained at Hampstead in the late 1960s and early 1970s, has vividly described Anna Freud's discussions at these meetings.

> I know I am not alone in remembering above all Anna Freud's discussions at Wednesday meetings. They were powerful cameos of her psychoanalytic thinking... It was as if she were inhaling the entire presentation, as well as some suddenly appearing memories of similar cases, related theoretical points, and now, new ideas for explorations. She would then begin to speak with a great storyteller's comfort and command and all this with a girlish enthusiasm and perhaps surprise at the new cluster of thoughts she was about to share most confidently. It was stunning the way she could invariably and with seeming ease find in any presentation something of great interest. So, she might say something like this. 'What we have heard here today is the story of a child who' – and then she might summarize, integrate and invigorate in a few sentences what she had just heard. She would continue ... 'and this story is similar to a clinic patient of some years ago and raises interesting issues which have the following history in our field, starting with comments by my father.' Finally, she would say, 'Of course, there remains the questions of X and Y, which are open for further discussion now among us here today.'
>
> (Penman, 2017, p. 30)

This passage, a riveting account, captures how Anna Freud's discussion of clinical material rested on a pedagogical approach that drew on her ability to organise her thoughts and impressions about the clinical material into a narrative that was itself a teaching tool for a fuller grasp of the familiar clinical and analytic issues presented by the case as well as those unique to the child patient.

Dorothy Tiffany Burlingham

Dorothy Burlingham's writings and clinical work with two distinct groups of children, twins and blind children, established an accomplished, if unacknowledged, psychoanalytic identity distinct from Anna Freud's. Her *PSOC* papers explored how the object relations and ego development of these children were complicated by their special circumstances – tracing how their psychic development both mirrored and diverged from that of children unburdened by the absence of vision or having two early objects.

Burlingham's psychoanalytic thinking and clinical work developed from her absorption with the nature and consequences of the earliest mother–child bond. In "Empathy Between Infant and Mother" (1935), she characterised the mother–child relationship as suffused with empathy, a "specific bond" affecting "the child's functioning, and capacity for adaptation throughout his development" (Kennedy, 1980, p. 78).

> It is my contention that young children have a greater capacity for observation than had been thought previously; that they observe the direct expression of affect as well as the efforts to deny emotion; that they are especially receptive to indications of those repressed impulses on which the mother's character is based, are seduced by them and use them in turn to seduce the mother; and that these capacities are lost as the child matures, develops and adapts to the environment. In short, empathy between infant and mother, mysterious and almost uncanny as it used to appear formerly, is here shown as lodged to a large degree in the acuteness of the child's perception.
>
> (Burlingham, 1967, p. 779 [1935])

Retrospectively, this evocation of the complexities of the mother–infant affective relationship is prescient with its emphasis on the infant's early psychic development as a milieu, a relationship, within which the infant is completely dependent upon the mother. Although these papers were published before the *PSOC* was founded, their depiction of the role of the conscious and unconscious affective relationship between mother and child remained the foundation of Burlingham's psychoanalytic thinking and clinical practice.

Twin studies

In Dorothy Burlingham's first three papers for the *PSOC*, she reports on her studies of twins (1945, 1946, 1949). A detailed monograph comparing three sets of twins (Burlingham, 1952) followed in 1952. Her family history undoubtedly contributed to Burlingham's interest: the siblings who preceded her were twin girls. Michael Burlingham's fine biography of his grandmother characterised the enduring bond between Dorothy and Anna Freud as "ultimately like a twinship based on mutual identification; each infused the other in positive ways" (Burlingham, 1991, p. 618). Nonetheless, chance also played a determining role in facilitating her studies of twins. The War Nurseries sheltered three sets of identical twins and gave Burlingham an unusual opportunity to observe how their psychic development differed from the usual mother–baby dyad. Among the questions Burlingham's papers considered were: the consequences for twins when their first object relationship encompasses both the mother and the twin sibling; the effect of this triadic relationship on the bond with the mother; and the impact on the mother of nurturing babies who are identical in appearance. Mothers of twins acknowledged, on occasion, that they could not love both twins until they found each child's individual uniqueness (Burlingham, 1946, p. 68).

Blind children

Beyond the twin studies, Burlingham's investigations of blind children represent her most important and lasting contribution to psychoanalysis. "Entirely on her own," Anna Freud recalled in her memorial eulogy for Dorothy Burlingham, "she opened contact with the headmaster of a large Jewish residential home for blind children, observed their educational methods, and accepted her first blind child patient into analysis" (Freud, 1980, p. xii). Burlingham had visited the *Israelitisches Blindinstitut* (Israeli Institute for Blind Children), established in 1872 and located on the Hohe Warte in Vienna's 19th District. Siegfried Altmann, then the Director of the Institute, however, offered a different account of Burlingham's first visit. (Figures 7.1–7.3)

Figure 7.1 Portrait of Siegfried Altmann.

Figure 7.2 Israelitisches Blindeninstitut.

Figure 7.3 1945 bombed garden of the Institute.

In a 1956 interview with Kurt Eissler for the Sigmund Freud Archives, Altmann recalled that on this occasion Burlingham was accompanied by the psychoanalyst Felix Deutsch.

> … Mrs. Burlingham, a particularly outstanding person, came once … with Felix Deutsch… [he] asked me, if she could observe, conduct studies with us at the Institute. And how would I prefer to have it, which times and so on. I told her she could come anytime, day or night, whenever she wishes, that the institute is completely open to her, she does not need ask about anything she wants to do. She should do as she pleases. She was with us for a couple of years, she observed pupils and I sent pupils to [her] flat.
>
> (Altmann, 1956, p. 21)

Neither Anna Freud nor Altmann specifies the date of this visit. A February 1936 letter from Burlingham to Deutsch, after his emigration to America in January, suggests that it occurred in 1935.

> Dear Dr. Deutsch, I am afraid you may not think very much of my work at the Blind Institute since you left. Most everything we saw in the first weeks somehow seems different now, less pronounced, less definite… Dr. Altmann is anxious to do all he can for me… It is. certainly a wonderful opportunity that you have given me. Lets (*sic*) hope I can make something of it.
>
> (Burlingham, 1936)[2]

Burlingham's 1935 decision to visit to the Blind Institute with Felix Deutsch followed upon the publication, earlier that year of "Empathy between mother and child." The psychic and emotional development of infants and young children, Burlingham concluded, is inexorably influenced by their sensitive reading of the mother's facial expressions as well as of her conscious and unconscious feelings that may be incompatible with her actual facial expression. What are the consequences for the mother–infant dyad and the child's development when the visual link is missing – when the infant is blind? This question alone was sufficient to inspire Burlingham's decision to study and treat blind children. There is, however, another consideration whose admittedly uncertain role must be nonetheless weighed. Her analyst, Freud, was a member of the Board of Trustees of the Institute.

To step back for a moment, Dorothy Burlingham and Felix Deutsch were not the first psychoanalysts that Siegfried Altmann had met. In 1918 he was briefly introduced to Freud by Paul Federn. In 1921, Altmann organised an educational conference on the blind and invited Siegfried Bernfeld to speak about the relation between psychoanalysis and pedagogy; Bernfeld's talk was "sensational" (Altmann, 1956, p. 7). Altmann clearly intrigued Eissler when he mentioned that he had had "lively communications" with Josef Breuer, for many years the President of the Pribram'schen Home for Blind Girls in Hütteldorf, advising him on questions related to the blind (ibid, pp. 1–2).

In a 1924 phone conversation, Altmann invited Freud to join the Institute's Board of Trustees with no obligation to attend Board meetings. Nor did he fail to mention that Arthur Schnitzler and Richard Beer-Hoffmann were already members of the Board. Yet Freud, who rented a neighboring villa in the Hohe Warte for the summer, seems not to have called on the Institute until August 1933 when he made two visits within days of one another on August 8 and 10. (Figure 7.4)

Freud was accompanied on August 8 by Ernst Kris, the art historian and psychoanalyst, who was interested in the sculptures made by blind children. (Figures 7.5–7.7)[3]

Freud returned two days later informing Altmann that he wanted to visit the Institute's facilities and that he had "not yet processed what [he] saw the day before yesterday. But it is most interesting" (ibid, p. 11). Altmann recounts that he escorted Freud into the garden where they sat under a maple tree while nearby some blind children were playing, orphans living at the Institute during the summer holidays. (Figures 7.8 and 7.9)

One young girl presented Freud with a bouquet of flowers, describing them as "fragrant white tea roses." The flowers prompted Freud to ask Altmann about the language of the blind. "If it is the language of the sighted

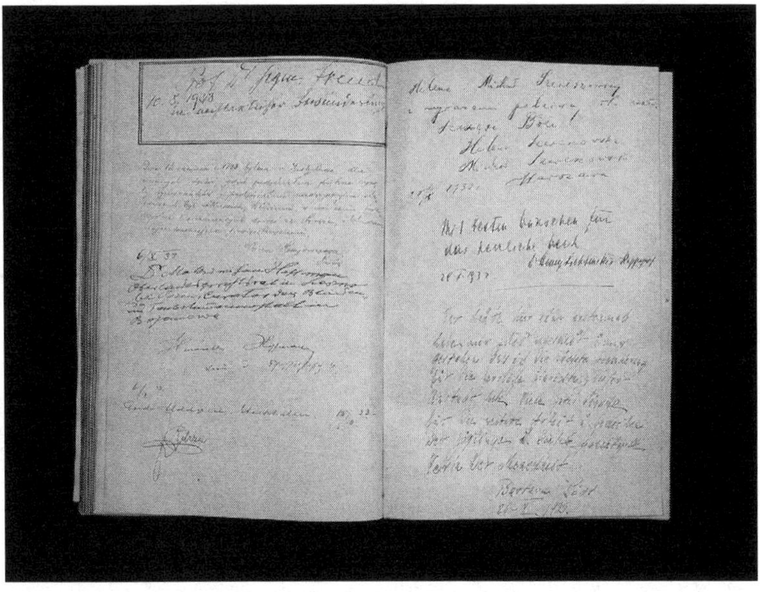

Figure 7.4 Freud added "in neighborly admiration" to his signature in the Institute guestbook.

Figure 7.5 Children modeling clay.

Figure 7.6 Children's sculptures.

Figure 7.7 Children's sculptures.

Figure 7.8 Orientation exercise: examining fruit.

Figure 7.9 Girl and garden plants.

or different in some way—white and tea-rose, that is the language of the sighted, after all the blind cannot recognize color" (ibid, p. 12). Other questions followed: What do we know of their dreams? Do blind people try to undo their loss, acquiesce or disavow it? What games do blind children and adults play? Is visual pleasure replaced by tactile pleasure?

Dorothy Burlingham had been in analysis with Freud since 1927. As an intimate of the Freud household, she would have been aware of Freud's connection to the Institute. Surely they discussed and analyzed her ambition to study the psychic development of blind children. Freud's curiosity about the language of blind children and their psychological response to sightlessness are taken up in Burlingham's *PSOC* papers. On the one hand, these questions arise naturally when thinking about the plight of blind infants and children. On the other hand, this does not negate the likelihood that Burlingham's determination to pursue her inquiries was immeasurably strengthened by the knowledge that Freud shared her interest in understanding the psychic experiences and responses of these children to their blindness.

Burlingham's first paper on blind children, "Psychoanalytische Beobachtungen an blinden Kindern" (1940, 1972), sympathetically and realistically described the endless challenges faced by blind children in a sighted world. She illustrated these challenges by turning a critical eye on how blind children are educated, an approach that is an extension of her role in establishing the Hietzing School, the Jackson Nursery and, with Anna Freud, a psychoanalytic seminar for nursery school teachers. Before taking her first blind child, Jakob, into analysis Burlingham first wanted to observe him in his school setting. In a letter to Felix Deutsch she confessed that she had:

> never realized so clearly the difference between a child who had never seen at all, and those who had seen or who had a light shimmer – *the amount a blind child has to learn is simply appalling.* It was clearest to see in his arithmetic lesson where rows (?) meant nothing to him – *where our vocabulary did not mean anything to him.* It isn't that he is slow at learning he is exceptionally clever.
>
> (Burlingham, 1936, italics added)

Burlingham pointedly underscored that "the education of the blind has at all times had the same goal; to prepare him as far as possible to share the life of the seeing world." In other words, the aim was to prevent the blind child from appearing different (Burlingham, 1940, 1972, pp. 276–277). In effect the education of blind children encouraged, even required, denial of their sightless state. This critique speaks to Freud's question as to whether blind children disavow their blindness – beyond any natural wish to see blind children are educated to behave and talk as if they can see. Burlingham further observes that the conscious psychic life of blind children is formed on the basis of "misconceptions and misinterpretations" of what they experience. The energies of blind children are continually consumed by a dual psychic life rooted in the fact that their constant contacts with the sighted world conflict with their own experiences, interfering with their capacity to adapt to life on the basis of their own abilities and limitations. Two special characteristics of blind children, nonetheless, facilitate their efforts to adapt to the sighted world: the rapidity of their speech development and the richness of their fantasy world. Yet the blind child "learns [the] language of a world to which his access is largely barred by his inability to perceive it. Although there is no doubt that the blind child can acquire language," Burlingham voiced considerable doubt that this vocabulary accurately conveys the blind child's inner life (ibid, p. 278).

Burlingham offered her own prescriptions for the education of blind children. It should begin in a kindergarten adapted to their needs, especially insofar as the training of their senses is concerned. Special primary schools should give equal weight to manual work and intellectual stimulation. Learning to write (the expression of thought) should take precedence over learning to read (the intake of new concepts). These guidelines would contravene the harm caused by an education that failed to nurture the blind child's inner life. Burlingham advocated for a pedagogy designed to preclude the development of adverse character traits such as vagueness, submissiveness and insincerity – the "unavoidable by-products of our present-day education of the blind" (ibid. p. 279). Blindness leaves these children at the "mercy of the seeing," that in turn induces a fear of being abandoned, left to confront fantasised dangers alone. "Consequently, a fear of aggression is instilled in blind children that inhibits its spontaneous expression and contributes to relationships to the sighted comprised of fear, envy, dependency, submission and admiration" (1940; 1972, p. 279).

In 1952 Burlingham had a nursery for blind toddlers built in the garden of the Hampstead Course building, not unlike the Hietzing School in Eva Rosenfeld's garden in Vienna. "The school was located in a special little cabin, designed by Ernst Freud to be safe and convenient for the sightless, in the back garden of 21 Maresfield Gardens" (Young-Bruehl, 1988, p. 337). The nursery accommodated six young blind children overseen by at least two adult supervisors and served a research project, directed by Burlingham, on the psychic development of blind children. The nursery school closed in 1976 "when too few normal children were available to form a group." Work continued, however, with individual blind children (Wills, 1980, p. 85).

The resulting eight papers on blind children that Burlingham published are characterised by her keen appreciation for the ways in which these children compensate for their loss of vision. Yet in "Hearing and Its Role in the Development of the Blind" (1964), Burlingham points out how the blind child's concentrated attention when listening is often mistaken for withdrawal when its underlying purpose is to establish a connection to the external world through the child's focused attention on their internal world; the blind child's exploitation of their hearing is negatively interpreted. To apprehend the blind child's concentrated listening as withdrawal is to fail to grasp how these children orient themselves in the world by drawing on past experiences and memories. In this, and in so many other ways, the sighted world fails to appreciate or understand the accomplishments of blind children.

In "Some Problems of Ego Development in Blind Children" (1965), Burlingham is adamant that when the development of sighted and blind children is compared,

> "the nature and range of their achievements tend to be underrated … [the] ingenuity the blind child actually expends at every stage" of development and the problem solving that is a constant in their lives is ignored.
>
> (Burlingham, 1965, p. 194)

In order to acquire language and speech the blind child must vanquish cognitive challenges unknown to the sighted child.

> While speech comes naturally to the sighted child, in contact, communication, and identification with his first love objects, for blind children

> learning the language of the sighted is an intellectual feat, comparable in its formidableness to the other tasks of adaptation to a sighted world such as motor self-control, orientation in space, object recognition.
>
> (ibid, p. 202)

The crux of the problem is that while blind children, imitating the sighted, speak fluently when they enter nursery school, many of the words they use are meaningless to them – a predicament whose consequences for the blind child Burlingham first addressed twenty-five years earlier. The blind child has "to build their image of the world without visual impressions, from tactile perceptions of the nearest objects and acoustic perceptions of those that are further removed" (ibid, pp. 203–204). This visual void may be countered by the blind child's attentiveness to their bodily sensations, yet this adaptation is often seen as "withdrawal" and an over-involvement with their own bodies. It is

> more correct to say that the blind child makes use of his own body and its experiences to compensate for his lack of experience in the external world. A child whose attention is turned in this direction cannot help but register the stirring of impulses, the changing sensations derived from affects, long before they are conceptualized psychologically. Such physical representations of what will later be called love, hate, sexual desire, etc. are stored away somewhere in the memory of all children, but are more vivid, more important, and probably more accessible in the blind than in the sighted.
>
> (ibid, p. 204)

For this reason, blind children "are oriented toward their own inner world and their minds are constantly preoccupied with going over past experiences."

Toys and activities that integrate the body, its senses and sensual or physical experiences gratify and stimulate children generally, and this is especially true for the blind child. In "Occupations and Toys for Blind Children" (1965), Burlingham explores the challenge of finding such toys. The developmental arc of blind and sighted children is closest in infancy "when all children have the mother's body as their first plaything" (Burlingham, 1968, p. 477). A pathway for the body's libidinalisation is paved when the mother strokes, touches and plays with her infant who, in turn, enjoys having their body played with. The pathway diverges, however, because the sighted child eventually adopts a transitional object in place of the mother's body, whereas the blind child remains attached to her body far longer. Burlingham counters the concern that the mother's extended play with her blind infant's body may be too stimulating; she argues that "the well-known blindisms, i.e. the rhythmical rocking, swaying and eye-rubbing are the result of too little stimulation through mutual body-play in infancy" (ibid, p. 478).

The mother's voice takes the place of vision in maintaining contact with her blind baby who, in turn, often plays at producing sounds. This play may widen to include a pleasure in music and "may well lead on to the playing of real instruments." (Figure 7.10)

Burlingham observes that

> It is not difficult to illustrate with examples that this meets a real and deep need in the child and seems to be the nearest substitute for vision that can be found as far as emotional expression and involvement are concerned.
>
> (ibid, p. 479)

In Burlingham's 1940 paper she decried the lack of concern for nurturing the inner life of blind children exemplified when they are taught language whose words are often meaningless to them. Musical sounds, whether instrumental or vocal, are a pathway whereby the blind child can identify and express, in the language of music, emotions, feelings and aesthetic experiences that give voice to their inner lives.

Figure 7.10 The piano lesson.

Conclusion

As psychoanalysts, Anna Freud and Dorothy Tiffany Burlingham both integrated pedagogy into their writings and psychoanalytic activities, but it takes a distinctive form in each. Anna Freud's original vocation as a teacher informed both her theoretical and clinical writings on child development. From the Hietzing School in 1920s Vienna to the creation, in 1952, of the Hampstead Child Therapy Clinic and the Hampstead Child Training Therapy Course in London, collaborative and pedagogical projects are integral to her identity as a psychoanalyst. Her role as a discussant of the contributions of both prominent colleagues and trainees at the HCTTC has been emphasised as an under-appreciated commitment to dialogue as a pedagogical tool where participants are both teachers and learners.

Once she arrived in Vienna, Dorothy Tiffany Burlingham focused on psychoanalysis and pedagogy, and joined Anna Freud in a range of thriving education projects starting with the Hietzing School. Like the Course for Educators and later, the War Nurseries of the early 1940s, many of these projects revealed as much about her sensitivity to children as they did about new possibilities in pedagogy. Her psychoanalytic writing on blind children is unusual in that they critiqued traditional education of blind children while, at the same time, presenting new insights into the children's affective being. As blind children learn and orient themselves in the sighted world, they are frequently misunderstood and their often remarkable capacities are disregarded. The development and richness of the blind child's inner life is forfeited when their language mimics the sighted world, Burlingham said, especially when the purpose of their education is to erase signs of their difference from others. Because the absence of vision may, and often does, distort the child's ego and character development, new forms of education are necessary. When she resumed writing about the psychic development of blind children in the early 1960s, Burlingham's thinking was enriched by the psychoanalytic literature on infant development that flourished in the late 1930s, 1940s and 1950s. New research on the blind infant's sense of self as separate from the mother reinforced the centrality of the infant's physical relationship with the mother and experience of its own maturing body. Burlingham added in her own research from her specialised nursery school; she wrote about the heightened role of bodily experiences, sensations and senses in the psychic development of blind children as they navigated the sighted world. Her papers are replete with psychological observations that reflect both a sensitive understanding of the challenges these children face and a deep appreciation of their ingenuity, capacious memory and problem-solving capacities.

Acknowledgments

We would like to acknowledge and thank Robin Verner and Ulike May for their assistance in translating Siegfried Altmann's interview with Kurt Eissler. We would also like to express our gratitude to Michael Simonson, Curator, Leo Baeck Institute, New York, for his assistance in granting permission to reproduce photographs from Siegfried Altmann papers.

Illustrations

Figure 7.1 Portrait of Siegfried Altmann, photograph, Siegfried Altmann Papers, Leo Baeck Institute, New York
Figure 7.2 *Israelitisches Blindeninstitut*, photograph, Siegfried Altmann Papers, Leo Baeck Institute, New York
Figure 7.3 Bombed garden of the Institute, photograph, Siegfried Altmann Papers, Leo Baeck Institute, New York
Figure 7.4 Sigmund Freud's signature in the guestbook of the *Blindinstitut*, 1933, Siegfried Altmann Papers, Leo Baeck Institute, New York
Figure 7.5 Children modeling clay, photograph, Siegfried Altmann Papers, Leo Baeck Institute, New York
Figure 7.6 Children's sculptures, photograph, Siegfried Altmann Papers, Leo Baeck Institute, New York
Figure 7.7 Children's sculptures, photograph, Siegfried Altmann Papers, Leo Baeck Institute, New York
Figure 7.8 Orientation exercise: examining fruit, photograph, Siegfried Altmann Papers, Leo Baeck Institute, New York
Figure 7.9 Girl and garden plants, photograph, Siegfried Altmann Papers, Leo Baeck Institute, New York
Figure 7.10 The Piano Lesson, photograph, Siegfried Altmann Papers, Leo Baeck Institute, New York

Notes

1 The origins, aims and leading contributors of the journal during its first two decades were the subject of an earlier paper *The Psychoanalytic Study of the Child: A Narrative of Postwar Psychoanalysis* (Thompson and Keable, 2016a).
2 After Felix Deutsch immigrated to the United States, he published "The Sense of Reality in Persons Born Blind" (1940). His interest in blindness appears to have followed from research on the psychic consequences of losing an organ. In a footnote he reports that his investigations were undertaken at the Perkins Institute for the blind in Watertown, Massachusetts. There is no mention of the Israeli Institute for the Blind in Vienna.
3 Altmann invited an art historian, Dr Munz, to be present at these modeling sessions, who with Viktor Löwenfeld co-authored *Plastische Arbeiten Blinder* (Munz & Lowenfeld, 1934). Altmann later gave an inscribed copy to Freud (Molnar, 1992, p. 291). Ernst Kris was interested in the relationship between the

artist's image of the body, their own bodily experiences and how this influenced their portrayal of human subjects, hence his interest in the sculptures made by the blind. In "Approaches to Art," Kris references Munz & Loewenfeld's book, noting "The influence of the image of the body on artistic productions is most dramatically illustrated by the highly impressive sculptural creations of the blind child" (Kris, 1952, p. 56).

References

Altmann, S. (1956). Interview with Kurt R. Eissler, April 6th, Sigmund Freud Papers, Manuscript Division, U.S. Library of Congress, Washington, D.C.

Burlingham, D. (1932). Kinder analyse und Mutter. *Zeitschrift für Psychoanalytische Pädagogik 6*:269–289. [Child analysis and the Mother] *Psychoanalytic Quarterly 4*:69–92, 1935. In *Psychoanalytic Studies of the Sighted and Blind* (1972) (pp. 3–28). New York: International Universities Press.

Burlingham, D. (1935). Die einfühlung des kleinkindes. *Imago 21*:429–444. Empathy between infant and mother. *Journal of the American Psychoanalytic Association 15*:764–780. In: *Psychoanalytic Studies of the Sighted and Blind* (1972) (pp. 52–70). New York: International Universities Press.

Burlingham, D. (1936). Letter to Felix Deutsch, 3 February. Papers of Felix Deutsch, Hanns Sachs Library, Boston Psychoanalytic Society and Institute.

Burlingham, D. (1940). Psychoanalytische Beobachtungen an blinden kindern, *Internationale Zeitschrift für Psychoanalyse & Imago 25*:297–335. Psychoanalytic observations of blind children. In: *Psychoanalytic Studies of the Sighted and Blind* (1972) (pp. 227–279). New York: International Universities Press.

Burlingham, D. (1945). The fantasy of having a twin. *Psychoanalytic Study of the Child 1*:205–210. In: *Twins. A study of three pairs of identical twins.*

Burlingham, D. (1946). Twins: Observation of environmental influences on their development. *Psychoanalytic Study of the Child 2*:61–73.

Burlingham, D. (1949). The relationship of twins to each other. *Psychoanalytic Study of the Child 3/4*:57–72.

Burlingham, D. (1952). *Twins: A Study of Three Pairs of Identical Twins with 30 Charts.* New York: International Universities Press.

Burlingham, D. (1964). Hearing and its role in the development of the blind. *Psychoanalytic Study of the Child 19*:95–112.

Burlingham, D. (1965). Some problems of ego development in blind children. *Psychoanalytic Study of the Child 20*:194–208.

Burlingham, D. (1972). *Psychoanalytic Studies of the Sighted and the Blind.* New York: International Universities Press.

Burlingham, M. (1991). The relationship of Anna Freud and Dorothy Burlingham. *Journal of The American Academy of Psychoanalysis 19*:612–619.

Deutsch, F. (1940). The sense of reality in persons born blind. *The Journal of Psychology 10*:121–140.

Freud, A. (1927a). Introduction to the technique of child analysis. In: *The Writings of Anna Freud, Vol.* I (pp. 3–62). New York: International Universities Press, 1968.

Freud, A. (1927b). The theory of child analysis. In: *The Writings of Anna Freud, Vol.* I (pp. 162–175). New York: International Universities Press, 1968.

Freud, A. (1936). *The ego and the mechanisms of defense. The writings of Anna Freud, Vol. II.* New York: International Universities Press, 1966.
Freud, A. (1945). Indications for child analysis. *Psychoanalytic Study of the Child 1*:127–149.
Freud, A. (1946a). The psychoanalytic study of infantile feeding disturbances. *Psychoanalytic Study of the Child 2*:119–132.
Freud, A. (1946b). *The psycho-analytical treatment of children: Technical lectures and essays.* New York: International Universities Press.
Freud, A. (1949). Aggression in relation to emotional development: Normal and pathological. *Psychoanalytic Study of the Child 3/4*:37–48.
Freud, A. (1951). Observations on child development. *Psychoanalytic Study of the Child 6*:18–30.
Freud, A. (1952a). The role of bodily illness in the mental life of children. *Psychoanalytic Study of the Child 7*:69–81.
Freud, A. (1952b). The mutual influences in the development of ego and id: Introduction to the discussion. *Psychoanalytic Study of the Child 7*:42–50.
Freud, A. (1953). Review. A Two-year old goes to hospital—Scientific film by James Robertson. *International Journal of Psychoanalysis 34*:284–287.
Freud, A. (1954a). Psychoanalysis and education. *Psychoanalytic Study of the Child 9*:9–15.
Freud, A. (1954b). Problems of infantile neurosis: A discussion. *Psychoanalytic Study of the Child 9*:16–71.
Freud, A. (1954c). Letter to Ernst Kris, 15 February 1954, Papers of Anna Freud, Manuscript Division, U.S. Library of Congress, Washington, D.C.
Freud, A. (1958). Child observation and prediction of development: A memorial lecture in honor of Ernst Kris. *Psychoanalytic Study of the Child 13*:92–124.
Freud. A. (1959). Clinical studies in psychoanalysis: Research project of the Hampstead Child Therapy Clinic. *Psychoanalytic Study of the Child 14*:122–131.
Freud, A. (1960). Discussion of Dr. John Bowlby's paper. *Psychoanalytic Study of the Child 15*:53–62.
Freud, A. (1963). The concept of Developmental Lines. *Psychoanalytic Study of the Child 18*:246–265.
Freud, A. (1980). In Memoriam Dorothy Burlingham 1891–1979. *Psychoanalytic Study of the Child 35*:x–xiv.
Greenacre, P. (1954). Problems of infantile neurosis: *Psychoanalytic Study of the Child 9*:16–91.
Hartmann, H. & Hoffer, W. (1952). The mutual influences in the development of ego and id. *Psychoanalytic Study of the Child 7*:9–30.
Kennedy, H. (1980). Dorothy Burlingham Memorial Issue. *The Bulletin of the Hampstead Clinic 3*:78–79.
Kris, E. (1945). Letter to Anna Freud, 20 June 1945. Papers of Anna Freud, Box 57, Manuscript Division, U.S. Library of Congress, Washington, DC.
Kris, E. (1952). *Psychoanalytic Explorations in Art.* New York: International Universities Press.
Kris, E. (1954). Letter to Anna Freud, 10 February 1954. Papers of Anna Freud, Box 41, Manuscript Division, U.S. Library of Congress, Washington, DC.

Molnar, M. (1992). *The Diary of Sigmund Freud 1929–1939. A Record of a Final Decade.* New York: Charles Scribner's Sons.

Munz, L. & Loewenfeld, V. (1934). *Plastische Arbeiten Blinder.* Brünn: Rudolf M. Rohrer.

Penman, A. (2017). Unpublished. The Hampstead Clinic: Memories of a Psychoanalytic Education. Oral History Workshop #79, *Anna Freud Revisited.* American Psychoanalytic Association Meetings, January 19. 2017. Archives & Special Collections, A.A. Brill Library, New York Psychoanalytic Society and Institute.

Thompson, N. & Keable, H. (2016a). The Psychoanalytic Study of the Child: A narrative of postwar psychoanalysis. *American Imago 73*:343–365.

Thompson, N. & Keable, H. (2016b). Unpublished. "Anna Freud as a Discussant." Oral History Workshop #79, *Anna Freud Revisited.* American Psychoanalytic Association Meetings, January 19, 2017.

Wills, D. (1980). Contributions read during the memorial meeting at the Hampstead Clinic. *The Bulletin of the Hampstead Clinic 3*:85–89.

Young-Bruehl, E. (1988). *Anna Freud: A biography.* New York: Summit Books.

Chapter 8

Young Dorothy Burlingham

Paul Werner

Pourquoi chercher à le connaître
Sans soulager vos maux?

–Rameau, *Les Boréades.* [1763]

The story could have come out of a Henry James novel, a tale of America's suspicion of, and attraction to, the Old World. A well-to-do American has moved to Europe; back home the family, concerned that their relative has been estranged and possibly corrupted, sends an emissary to assess the situation and, if possible, bring back the errant lamb.

In this case, however, the protagonists are real. And the struggles between the two families are telling, not only of American culture but of the differences between American and European readings and misreadings of psychoanalysis. They are revealing, ultimately, of the history of psychoanalysis, of psychoanalysts and psychoanalysis itself.

The patriarch of the European family, pacing the garden "so afraid, so terrified for Dorothy" while awaiting the Americans, is Sigmund Freud (Eva Rosenfeld in Burlingham, 1989, p. 199). "Dorothy" is Dorothy Tiffany Burlingham, daughter of the Art Nouveau designer Louis Comfort Tiffany. Born into the influential elites of New York in 1891, Dorothy grew up in the shadow of a renowned father whose household she escaped in 1914 to marry a physician of her own social class, Robert Burlingham. Eleven years later Dorothy took her four children to Vienna. In short order she started analysis with Freud, became a member of his household and entered into a long-lasting partnership with Freud's daughter Anna, a woman with her own experience of a powerful father. Soon Dorothy and Anna set up the Hietzing School, a magnet for faculty and students either born or educated in America, many of whom would return or move to the US. But the psychoanalytic and educational theories and practices they took back from Vienna were, in fact, not unlike those movements of resistance that first attracted Dorothy to Freudianism.

Eager to reclaim custody of the children, Robert Burlingham visited Vienna in 1929 accompanied by a lawyer. Dorothy and her new-found family were "down on America and American things" according to Judy de Forest Taves, a cousin who would later take her analytic training back to Boston (Burlingham, 1989, p. 199). On August 26, Robert privately confronted Freud over Dorothy's physical and emotional needs – an uneven match. From Robert's surviving notes it is evident, as in the novelistic version, that while the American was playing checkers, the European was playing three-dimensional chess:

> R.B.: Do you consider psychoanalysis a barrier between us?
> S.F.: No, but your attitude toward psychoanalysis Dorothy may well consider a barrier.
> [...]
>
> (Burlingham, 1989, p. 203)

Robert's straightforward concerns fit poorly with Freud's complex views which, according to Freud, were Dorothy's as well. Freud saw American culture itself as deeply contrary to psychoanalytic theory, and presumably he and Dorothy shared or discussed this. Conversely, Americans had, and still have, a complex relationship with Freud: from the outset "America welcomed psychoanalysis more warmly than any other country" (Hale, 1971, p. 4), while another, dominant sector of American culture developed a resentment of psychoanalysis that has lasted to this day.

In his luminous elegy of 1939, *In Memory of Sigmund Freud*, H. W. Auden (1940, p. 57) described Freud as:

> a whole climate of opinion
> Under whom we conduct our differing lives;
> Like weather he can only hinder or help ...

Auden's adulatory view matches that of Freud's American detractors; only the valuations differ. Psychoanalysis, according to one of Freud's American critics, provides "a theory, a technique, an organization, an ethos, an ethic, a climate" or again a "dominant idiom for the discussion of human personality and of human relations" (Gellner, in Capshew, 2014, pp. 164–165). Even before Freud's 1909 visit to America, psychoanalysis offered a counter-narrative, a check to the worldview of a culturally and politically dominant section of society, a resistance against the regulative structures it imposed on key aspects of life: the familial, the sexual, the cultural, the economic. Freud challenged the American "climate" with a rival climate of opinion. To Americans like Dorothy Burlingham who found themselves at odds with the dominant *mentalité*, psychoanalysis offered a profoundly new alternative. With her flight to Vienna she adopted this alternative, actively rejecting those aspects of her worldview that clashed with Freudian psychoanalysis. Her life story contains *in nuce* all that separates the two perspectives.

American social and cultural historians have long pointed to the religious doctrine of Arminianism as a driving force in American culture (Howe, 1991a, pp. 56–59; Schmiesing, 2017, pp. 61–64). Formulated by the Dutch preacher Arminius in 1610, transferred to the American colonies in the mid-18th century, Arminianism effectively challenged the dominant Calvinist doctrines in religious and social discourse. Arminianism was key to the development of a national American culture: independent, self-consciously democratic, focused on the individual at the expense of community. The new doctrine offered small-town citizens of the emerging republic the belief that Salvation could be achieved by the individual's choice to be saved without divine (or Government) intervention. That outlandish expression, "Have you found Jesus?" is the purest distillation of Arminianism in America today. The will in itself is sufficient; but the sinner has to want to change.

By the middle of the 19th century, the message of Arminianism – individual initiative, independent will and selective optimism – had been integrated into "the general drive to establish a proper moral framework for laissez faire" (Williams, 1988, p. 254). "The religious advocates of free will soon reduced Calvin's social morality to a code of personal righteousness that paralleled and reinforced the individualism of Locke" (op. cit., p. 250). Meanwhile, the end of the Civil War saw the rise of a new social class with its own priorities and mentalité. In New York City, the Republican Party rose to power as the party of the Anglo-Saxon elites, in opposition to the Democrats, the party of immigrants and white workers. Massive urban poverty and marginalised immigrant populations forcefully challenged the myths of can-do willpower and social egalitarianism that were the foundation of American political and economic life (Foner, 1971, pp. 23ff.). The new elites striving to dominate the political, cultural and moral leadership of New York City turned Arminianism to their advantage. The promotion of "individual choice" (or "personal responsibility," as it is now called) over social determinism provided self-justification for those who stood to profit from a widening income disparity. American's "lively faith in human perfectibility" (de Tocqueville, in Foner, 1971, p. 38) was best understood as a lively faith in one's own perfectibility and that of the institutions one upheld, not the faith of others. In other words, "the trouble was bad men, not institutions" (Williams, 1988, p. 254). As every reader of Uncle Tom's Cabin recognised, the answer to slavery, wage-driven or other, was not to abolish wage slavery or slavery itself, but to bring out one's inner Good Master.

In the decades leading up to the Civil War the second Arminianist "Awakening" targeted small-scale semi-rural employers and their employees (Carwardine, 1996, p. 294). By the mid-1860s, however, the modes of production and consumption had changed, radically altering relations among producers and consumers and the manner in which those relations were articulated. Mercantile elites of the major urban centers developed their own particular ethos. The new *mentalité* bore many traces of the old evangelical ethos but was adapted to the elite's position within the system of production, a technique of the self-appropriate to their place in the new social order. To solidify its status within a rigidifying hierarchical system, this new, economically dominant class merged self-control and social control as two distinct aspects of a single self: Arminianism retained the Calvinist notion of Predestination and rejected its emphasis on social justice. The Saved could not save the Damned, whose fate had been determined. As a result, the Saved and well-off (the two being indistinguishable) did good works that signaled their own salvation and their determination "to act justly within an unjust world" (Saxton, 2003, p. 47). (Figure 8.1)

Thomas Eakins' 1875 painting, The Gross Clinic, conveys the entrenchment of Arminianist attitudes among the elites of the Eastern Seaboard. According to one narrative, the painting celebrates the emergence of amputation as a curative science, the triumphant evolution from its status as a

Figure 8.1 Thomas Eakins. Portrait of Dr Samuel D. Gross (The Gross Clinic), 1875.

mere mechanical procedure. Had that been the artist's intention, one would expect the scene and actors to convey a quality of empathy suggested in the admiration of the observers and the gratitude of the sufferer. Instead, Eakins presents Doctor Gross as a model of muscular self-reliance in the image of the "ethical athleticism" of American divines (Carwardine, 1996, p. 282), with Divine Inspiration shining over the doctor's forehead as a Light from Above. However, contemporary viewers were repelled by Eakins' painting and the doctor's total detachment from the pain he inflicts on another. Is Doctor Gross mastering himself or others? He is actually doing both at once. The fact that the patient is a charity case underlines the moral and empathic distance between doctor and patient, as if following that Methodist preacher who found certain people "irredeemably flawed since 'they despised no man for his sins'" (Carwardine, 1996, p. 300). Doctor Gross' brand of athleticism lies, like the preacher's, precisely in his resistance to empathy, in contrast to Freud's painful realisation, thirty years later, that empathy was a non-negotiable aspect of the therapeutic relationship (Freud, 1905). In this light Michael Fried's well-known argument (Fried, 1998) that The Gross Clinic presents a narrative of castration anxiety is not so much incorrect as incomplete: as in most of his work, Eakins' underlying narrative is resistance to the transference.

Dorothy's Burlingham's paternal grandfather, Charles Lewis Tiffany, was not only a beneficiary of the new mercantile ethic: as a prominent member and leader of his generation of entrepreneurs, he was an architect of this system of social control. Emerging from a small-town merchant background, by mid-century the elder Tiffany had established one of the wealthiest families in New York and an immensely successful business in the luxury trade, Tiffany and Co. He was an original member of the Union League Club, founded in 1863 to unite the moneyed movers within the Republican Party. Though the Union Club hosted energetic and often divisive debates over the moral and practical direction of American institutions, all agreed that "the class who have the largest pecuniary stake in the good order of the city and who also command its moral forces" (Burrows and Wallace, 1999, p. 928) should run the city's institutions, public or private. Haswell Green, a League member who almost singlehandedly developed the concept of public–private partnerships (Hammack, 1988) pioneered a range of modern municipal services and was involved in founding both the Metropolitan Museum of Art and Central Park.

Charles Lewis Tiffany, the studiously respectable purveyor of luxury goods, had such a close affinity with his contemporary P. T. Barnum, the down-in-the-gutter huckster, that he borrowed some of Barnum's public relations techniques. Both men came from pre-industrial Connecticut, an area still known as the Nutmeg State for its tradition of carving fake nutmegs out of wood and hawking them to gullible buyers. C. L. and P. T. capitalised on 19th-century America's troubled awareness of the asymmetry of social transactions in general, and economic transactions in particular.

Just as Barnum's Circus gave urban populations the satisfying myth of the country bumpkin hoodwinked on a trip to New York, so too, Tiffany and Co. sustained the upper-class fantasy that costly purchases vindicated their taste. Expensive taste was proof of moral fitness and, simultaneously, the Tiffany firm's own integrity. In the new world of consumerism, authority belonged to those who could define the fitness of the customer to the product and vice versa (Bauman, 2007, p. 157). The discipline of consumption replaced the discipline of the workshop.

Parallel with this shift in the focus of virtuous activities, the urban elites disagreed about the feasibility of improving conditions for the working class. Many of the reformist ideals from the turn of the 20th century had originated in the Arminian Second Awakening of the 1840s: education should be universal so that the near-Damned could use what little agency God had left them to improve themselves; women were to be emancipated from their enslavement, sexual and otherwise, to allow their innate feminine goodness to blossom (Howe, 2007, p. 846). A sizeable group of Union League Republicans rejected the idea that the Unwealthy were eternally damned. Instead of committing to improved factory conditions, they aimed for larger "moral" and "aesthetic" progress: virtue in consumption, not in production. From the outset, the founding missions for Central Park and the Metropolitan Museum of Art caused fierce conflict. In one opinion, Central Park could offer all classes "an elevating vision of nourishment and civility" (Homberger, 1994, p. 274); in another, the park might give the poor a chance at fresh air; to which a third posited that adding windows to the fetid slum tenements might better answer that need (Homberger, 1994, p. 249). The question was resolved by a proposal from the aesthetic entrepreneur Donald G. Mitchell, a mentor to Charles' son Louis Comfort and a relation by marriage:

> To those living in cities whose rear windows look upon neglected or dingy areas or courts ... the equipment of a window with rich designs would be a perpetual delight
>
> (Burlingham, 1989, p. 57)

Taste, as Oscar Wilde would point out (1891), is the great unequaliser. By the time Louis Comfort Tiffany launched his career the Aesthetic Movement was promoting the aestheticisation of social relations. The information asymmetry that had so empowered P. T. Barnum and Charles Tiffany was transferred to the level of Culture.

By the mid-1870s in England, William Morris was clamoring for art and culture to provide the working classes with the means of reclaiming non-alienated labor. His call was heard in America or perhaps misinterpreted. In 1877 the legendary interior decorator Candace Wheeler founded the New York Society of Decorative Artists whose goal, she later explained, was "work for the army of helpless women of N.Y. who were ashamed to beg & untrained to work" (Koplos & Metcalf, 2010, p. 17). Louis Comfort Tiffany, who had joined the Society but quit soon after to form his own group, wrote to Wheeler:

> You had better join us. It is the real thing, you know; a business, not a philanthropy or any amateur educational scheme. We are going after the money there is in art, but art is there after all.
>
> (Burlingham, 1989, p. 59)

There could be no question on which side of the window Louis stood.

Charles had practiced the luxury trade at the front of the store so that his son could take over the Aesthetic part of the business. Louis would produce luxury objects and expand the mercantile mentality into other spheres. Charles' trusteeship at the Metropolitan Museum of Art and his position at the Union League ensured Louis' access to wealthy patrons. Meanwhile, and in response to the growing radicalisation of the American working class, the League's purportedly charitable principles led to a resurgence of church building, this time with a new goal: spirituality was more effective than social engagement. As one preacher put it, "Rich men became necessary to us" (Carwardine, 1996, p. 286). Louis Comfort was afforded a comfortable supply of commissions for stained-glass windows. His main rival, John Lafarge, was marginalised and effectively cast out by Charles' capital and connections.

Glass, the material upon which Louis Comfort Tiffany built his fame, functioned within the cultural context of Gilded Age America as an efficient, multifaceted metonymy, incorporating spheres of human experience that at first glance would seem vastly divergent. In their religious settings, Tiffany's stained-glass windows refer to Medieval concepts of Faith – or, more accurately, 19th-century fantasies about the power of Faith to answer moral and epistemological doubts in a corrupt century. The transparency of glass stood as a metaphor for the Protestant affirmation of the Visibility of Grace: the ability to track the stock market ratified one's material salvation in the same way one's ability to see Truth and Beauty was the mark of spiritual salvation. Building churches and endowing museums made both competencies visible.

A palpable sense of epistemological righteousness, coupled with an underlying discomfort, permeates the cultural productions of late-19th-century America. In their awkward way the stained-glass windows of Louis attempt to bridge the conflicting claims of realistic representation with the organisation of the textures and colors of glass. In the fiction and art criticism of Henry James it's the sense of epistemological righteousness that predominates as the protagonist or viewer is challenged to confirm his or her moral rectitude through his or her an intuitive grasp of an artwork or an individual – sometimes of both at once. Likewise, by the end of the 19th century, photography abandoned its earlier Romantic affirmation of the mutability of vision in favor of an empirical approach, the guarantor of epistemological correctness. Photography in the Age of Empire objectivised relationships of domination and subservience as natural. Tiffany's secular experiments with glass as a decorative art follow a similar dynamic, absorbing foreign or "exotic" elements into a vision that implicitly transcends the epistemological and moral limitations of his sources. In this way he followed his father's path from mercantile importer of precious exotica to creative overseer of their production.

Dorothy Trimble Tiffany bore the full brunt of her father's visual autocracy. She held vivid memories of her otherwise emotionally distant father avidly photographing her as a child. Even late in life, reporting to her grandson, she remained disturbed that Louis hid his interest in her behind the supposedly objective lens of a camera. Louis insisted on equating Dorothy and her sisters with the flowers he loved to raise (Burlingham, 1988, pp. 94ff.). The equivalence between young female children and flowers is a commonplace in Gilded Age culture, both in literature and in the visual arts. Claims of empirical objectivity helped the viewer confirm to himself that little girls could be seen without lust in one's heart, keeping at bay a hovering fear of incest. To quote a common French proverb of the time, "The first man who compared a woman to a flower was a genius; the second was a fool." The question whether Tiffany was a genius or a fool haunted Dorothy throughout her life.

On May 15, 1914, a grand feast was held at Laurelton Hall, the Tiffany estate. Louis invited 150 "men of genius" to "inspect the flowers" among which his own daughters were paraded in flowing robes (Frelinghuysen, 2006, pp. 196–198). (Figure 8.2)

Figure 8.2 Dorothy Trimble Tiffany, age 22.

As late as 1978 Dorothy "shuddered to recall" these festivities (Burlingham, 1988, p. 131). Four months afterwards she married Robert Burlingham in a modest ceremony:

> White asters and purple clematis entered largely into the color scheme … a bower of clematis had been erected … Pink asters and orchids etc. covered the walls of the court.
>
> (*New York Times*, 1914)

Dorothy's process of identity formation had suffered a blow with the death of her mother Louise in 1904, when Dorothy was twelve. After that her father's increasingly erratic behavior had made her development even more difficult. It was no easier after marriage, as her husband's behavior soon showed symptoms of bipolar disorders. But Dorothy could rely for support on her network of cousins from the de Forest family, one of the most prominent reformist families in America. Much of her resistance to the paternal *mentalité* came from them; so too did ways of thinking that eventually turned her toward psychoanalysis and Freud.

The patriarch of the family was Robert Weeks de Forest. A lawyer born to wealth and married into wealthier, Robert's life as a "full-time philanthropist" (Hijiya, 1980, p. 407) led him to promote or initiate a broad range of charitable and cultural organisations from the Metropolitan Museum of Art to the Charity Organization Society (COS) of New York. As President of the Metropolitan Museum of Art from 1913 until his death in 1931, de Forest replaced the self-serving policies of his upper-class predecessors with programs encouraging openness and accessibility. Under his stewardship the Met reached out to primary schools because, as de Forest would later explain, art is "useful for influencing our ideals and moulding the lives of our children" (Hijiya, 1980, p. 409). One thinks of the prominent place given to art in the curriculum and the artists among the faculty at the Hietzing School.

Weeks' influence on American social policy reached further, and with greater effect, than his cultural leadership, though both came from a similar ideological stance, the elite *mentalité* he shared with Charles Lewis Tiffany. As President of the COS from 1881 to 1931 Robert rarely diverged from the guiding philosophy of its founders and their belief that public affairs should be directed by "the class who have the largest pecuniary stake in the good order of the city and who also command its moral forces" (Burrows and Wallace, 1999, p. 928). The imperative that the moneyed classes should step in wherever Government was unable or unwilling to help may have influenced Dorothy Burlingham and Anna Freud's decision to found a school in Vienna in 1927; the Austrian Government had, that same year, scuttled the school reforms of the progressive Minister of Education, Otto Glöckel, and there were similarities in management style between the newly empowered Christian Socials in Austria and the old elites of Gilded Age New York (Boyer, 1995, pp. 240–241).

According to de Forest, efforts to reduce poverty did more for the soul of the giver than for the well-being of the receiver:

> [A man] must accomplish with all his heart and soul whatever task is before him in the hope that at the end of a full life he will have done one thing or said one word or written one line which, added to the small winnowed garnering the world possesses, may a hundred thousand years hence complete some harvest of perfection.
>
> (Hijiya, 1980, p. 408)

This Arminian statement of faith would later find its counterpoint in Freud's own, in the last pages of *Civilization and its Discontents*:

> I have endeavored to guard myself against the enthusiastic prejudice which holds that our civilization is the most precious thing that we possess or could acquire and that its path will necessarily lead to heights of unimagined perfection ... The fateful question for the human species seems to me to be whether and to what extent their cultural development will succeed in mastering the disturbance of their communal life by the human instinct of aggression and self-destruction.
>
> (Freud (1930), 1961, p. 111)

One major difference between de Forest and Freud is the latter's conscious refusal to adopt the position of a transcendent authority, reiterating on the last page of his book what he stated on the first. The second difference is that Freud saw change (good or bad) occurring (or not) through the interplay of social forces and individual psyches. In contrast, de Forest, in the spirit of "Christian Capitalism," denied that souls could be changed and that the social environment held any role in effectuating or delaying change – an attitude that William Appleman Williams finds contrary to the teachings of Christ, Marx and Freud (Williams, 1988, pp. 472ff.). (Figure 8.3)

"The trouble was bad men, not institutions" (Williams, 1988, p. 254). Anders Zorn's portrait of de Forest, painted in 1901, departs from the Swedish painter's usual vibrant palette to depict Robert as another version of Doctor Gross: coolly scientific, emotionally removed, more interested in the efficient organisation of distribution to the "worthy" than in improving their condition. The attitude shared by de Forest and Dr Gross reappeared in the early 20th century, when a bitter struggle for legitimacy broke out within American health care. Ostensibly in the name of scientism, the struggle was little more than the same old-time religion under a different name.

Figure 8.3 Robert W. de Forest, 1901, Anders Zorn.

It was that same struggle that affected Dorothy Burlingham's development through adolescence and young adulthood.

According to Ferdinand Alquié, one of Immanuel Kant's most trusted editors, the German philosopher's mature thinking was first expressed in the suggestion that one must carefully control one's impulse to help indigent people. Even better, the impulse should be curbed until Reason can implement a higher, objective form of Justice (Alquié, 1980, p. 441; Kant, 1764, p. 463). In that sense Robert Weeks de Forest was a devoted Kantian. He forbade his children to give money to beggars, but when the *New York Times* instituted its "Neediest Cases" column in 1911, Robert handed a list to his grandchildren along with ten dollars and instructions to think over the list carefully (Hijiya, 1980, p. 411). Charity was a thing of the mind, not the heart.

However, de Forest was not alone. By the last decades of the 19th century, the more scientifically rationalising members of Europe and America's dominant classes had found in Kant what Kant himself had attempted to implement all along: an alignment of metaphysical truths with the material interests of the Bourgeoisie. American religious movements were merely a reflection of this idea. The demand for social justice need no longer be swept under the prayer rug; it could be reasoned away. "Science" and "rational organisation" became the buzzwords of the efficient dispensation of virtue. In this spirit, de Forest founded the first American graduate school of social work in 1904. The new, scientific approach to social work would organise the distribution of charity and disregard the actual environmental and political conditions of the recipients while paying special attention to their moral "worthiness." The fantasy that the two areas of investigation, the individual and the environmental, are mutually exclusive persists today among some (but not all) groups of social workers and their critics (Danto, 2009, p. 67). "Individual agency and historical or cultural determinism are once more brought onto the wrestling mat for the diversion of the public," to quote the British sociologist Anthony Giddens (1979, p. 45).

Within months of the school's opening, however, the social workers in training found that their real-life, hands-on experience in the field confirmed the exact opposite. Theoretical barriers between the somatic and the environmental, the individual approach and the social, had little actual bearing in their practice with clients burdened with all the overdetermined complexities of individual trauma, environmental pressures, racism, poverty, sexism and divergent cultural values (Hale, 1971, p. 140). American social workers were to become some of the most consistent followers of Freud's work – a trend virtually ignored in the literature on Freud's early reception in America. Freudian theory validated the social workers' use of casework precisely because it grounded human development in an ongoing process of individual and environmental integration. Nevertheless, social work and psychoanalysis were targeted, each on their own, by a range of ideologies founded on induction, especially the type of moralising induction favored under the name of Science. Today still, the most prestigious proponents of American Scientism argue that Freudian psychoanalytic theory contains "untestable epistemological claims" (Capshew, 2014, p. 165) – a case of the kettle needing to check its privilege.

Kantian thought and its derivatives are based primarily on analogies to Vision as the organising principle of phenomenal perception. This holds true for the American metaphysical/scientific tradition, indebted as it is to theological questions about the visibility of Divine Grace. What was originally demanded of COS social workers was the ability to discover the presence of Divine Grace in their clients. This provoked a crisis of authority in the new field since, according to Kantian reasoning, the ability to divine the Truth (that is, to make objectively verifiable epistemological claims) is itself a sign of an ego that has transcended its own subjectivity. In 1915, in a contorted piece of philosophical mealy mindedness, Abraham Flexner's speech to the National Conference of Charities and Correction claimed that Social Work could not be called a profession because it lacked the noumenal dimension that would grant it authority: there was only one universal value sphere, that of Reason, and social workers – who of course were mostly women – had no claim to it (Flexner, 1915). Shortly thereafter the American Psychoanalytic Association solved the problem of its own legitimacy by excluding all but MDs from its ranks. Consequently, American psychoanalysts legitimised the therapist's power in the clinic. Freud had already complained in 1923 that preserving the transcendental authority of the therapist most likely reinforced the patient's narcissistic tendencies (Freud, 1923, p. 49). In Arminianism, the patient need only "find Freud" as one "finds Jesus" – the surest indicator of potential failure. Conversely, the disavowal of this claim to authority attracted those who had most to lose from the system of legitimation and deligitimation in American culture. Inabel Burns Lindsay, an early graduate of de Forest's school, an African American and the first Dean of the Howard University School of Social Work, said that psychoanalysis gave her the very tool that allowed her to "be aware of the projection onto factors outside oneself" (Danto, 2009, p. 74). Counter-transference begins at home.

This, then, is the context that shaped Dorothy Tiffany's earliest intellectual and emotional development. It countered the dominant narrative she inherited both from her father, Louis Comfort Tiffany, and from Robert Weeks de Forest. Strict gender roles were important to the upper-class mission of spiritual reform in late 19th-century America, though less so to immigrant and lower-class populations still involved in pre-capitalist social relations (Rydell & Kroes, 2005, n. 53, p. 45). As a rule, the "feeling" role was assigned to the wife, and the public role of ruthless mercantile calculation to the husband. In retrospect Dorothy found little emotional solace in her mother, whom she described as "rather stern ... but very lovely too" (Burlingham, 1989, p. 96). Her challenge as a young woman was to define herself as thinking rather than feeling in a situation where the feeling role was monopolised, first by her father and then by her husband.

According to Michael Burlingham, however (p. 117), "the greatest influence on Dorothy in the aftermath of her mother's death" was Julia de Brasher Forest, Dorothy's "Aunt Julia" and sister of Robert Weeks de Forest. Julia had been a close friend of and intellectual companion of Louise Tiffany: Dorothy's older sister was named after her. Julia and Louise were trustees of the New York Infirmary for Women and Children, founded by Robert. After Louise died in 1904 "Aunt Julia" and her relatives provided a counterweight to Louis Comfort Tiffany's incremental instability and later to Robert Burlingham's deteriorating emotional state. After Julia's death in 1910 the younger de Forests took on the same role: it was Julia's nephew, Alfred V. de Forest, son of her brother Lockwood, who convinced Dorothy to go to Vienna for analysis (Burlingham, 1989, p. 146). Decades later, Dorothy remembered sitting beside her mother while Aunt Julia read from, and translated, Freud's *Interpretation of Dreams*. Dorothy would have been twelve years old at most; the book would have been published just four years earlier (Burlingham, 1989, p. 118). Julia's copy probably came from her life partner Eleanor Kilham, who had a doctorate in Medicine from the Woman's College attached to the New York Infirmary and who had pursued advanced medical studies in Zurich and Vienna where, presumably, she bought the book. The relationship between Eleanor and Julia may have served as a model for the later relationship of Dorothy and Anna Freud.

As Dorothy matured intellectually, she followed Eleanor Kilham and the younger branch of the de Forest family's interest in legitimising non-European cultures. This was not unusual in the decades straddling 1900, when reformist movements in anthropology, museology, art, literature and of course the health sciences, attempted to challenge cultural and moral absolutism within the dominant ethos. A distant relative, the painter George de Forest Brush, built a career by portraying Native American people in a positive light. Kilham herself collected Native American basketry. Julia herself was a photographer and author of an oft-reprinted *Short History of Art* (de Forest, 1881). Julia's brother Lockwood de Forest, the former associate of Louis Comfort, sponsored the development of craft workshops in India, quite unlike Louis' practice of incorporating foreign elements into a superior vision – his own. Alfred V. de Forest's attraction to Freud may have started with his father Lockwood's interest in the Indian "Unconscious" (Burlingham, 1989, p. 149).

Later in life Dorothy would recall happier days, away from her demanding family, spent discussing foreign cultures with de Forests. They subscribed to the belief that individuals are fundamentally good, but the institutions to which individuals must adapt are far more problematic. This same belief undergirded progressive anthropology in the US well into the first half of the 20th century (Benedict, 1946, pp. 10ff.). It must have resonated with the influential anthropologist Franz Boas as he listened to Freud lecturing at Clark University in 1909: field work is field work, whether sociological, anthropological or charitable. The awareness of the subjectivity of other cultures raised the same possibilities that Inabel Burns Lindsay would later find liberating: it decentered the controlling authority of a *sujet supposé savoir* or Transcendental Ego, be it therapist, father or other.

Ultimately, were one to collect into a single construct the disparate pieces that composed the American mentalité that Dorothy Burlingham resisted and to select those pieces most relevant to psychoanalysis, that construct would be visuality. Dorothy confronted the concept of Vision in different forms throughout her life. From her father to her extended family, all were intensely involved with visuality. On a metaphoric level, "Vision" stood for the revelation of moral worth, from Charles Lewis Tiffany's vision of the honest merchant to the vision his artist son offered the viewer. Conversely, Vision, according to Robert Weeks de Forest or even Louis Comfort Tiffany, was the ability to see and by seeing to reveal one's moral worth to self and others:

> I once was lost, but now am found
> Was blind but now I see …
>
> (Newton, 1779)

Under such conditions psychoanalytic work in America could only be understood by patient and therapist alike as discovery, not change – as it still is. A commentator from *The New Yorker* recently explained, "The goal of therapy is to bring those things to light" (Menand, 2017).

Because Vision provides a model for Perception in all its forms, the metaphor of vision can be made to offer a model for all epistemologies: in standard medical thinking all symptoms are etiological. For Freud, however, there may be no apparent connection between the appearance and the underlying cause – a principle introduced in that most epistemological of Freud's writings, *Interpretation of Dreams*. Dorothy's motive for moving to Vienna, she would later claim, was that her eldest son Robert Jr had suffered from asthma from childhood, and she decided a medical treatment of physical symptoms alone was useless without addressing the deeper causes. *Interpretation of Dreams* performed the same role for a generation of health professionals and activists: it undermined the hegemonic belief that the study of otherness is simply a performance to benefit artists and anthropologists.

Finally, there is Dorothy's major achievement as a psychoanalyst, her writings on childhood blindness, discussed elsewhere in this volume. Questioning how blind people perceive the world has been a staple of epistemological inquiry since Diderot's *Lettre sur les aveugles à l'usage de ceux qui voient* (1749), a classic examination of the relationship between innate and environmentally determined perception. In Dorothy's hands the investigation turns into a powerful criticism of vision as a defining structure in culture, akin to Benjamin Whorf's anthropological work on language.

Paul Ricoeur (1977, pp. 33ff.) put it accurately. Freud's method of investigation, along with Nietzsche's and Marx's, is a system of interpretation based not on clarifying, but on unmasking: a hermeneutics of suspicion radically at odds with a hermeneutics of revelation. That suspicion and its opposite were fully displayed in Vienna, the day when Robert Burlingham resumed his discussions with Freud, accompanied by his lawyer (Burlingham, 1989, p. 204):

> You consider us gentlemen, do you not?
> —Dr. Burlingham is a gentleman, but you are a lawyer.

Illustrations

Figure 8.1 Thomas Eakins. *Portrait of Dr. Samuel D. Gross (The Gross Clinic).* Oil on canvas, 1875. Philadelphia Museum of Art, Gift of the Alumni Association to Jefferson Medical College in 1878 and purchased by the Pennsylvania Academy of the Fine Arts and the Philadelphia Museum of Art in 2007 with the generous support of more than 3,600 donors, 2007-1-1

Figure 8.2 *Dorothy Trimble Tiffany, age twenty-two.* b/w photo (artist unknown), May 15, 1914. Collection of Michael J. Burlingham

Figure 8.3 Anders Zorn. *Robert W. de Forest.* Oil on canvas, 1901. Museum of the City of New York

References

Alquié, F. (1980) "Introduction aux *Observations sur le sentiment du beau et du sublime,*" in *Oeuvres philosophiques* I. *Des premiers écrits à la Critique de la* raison pure, ed. Emmanuel Kant (Paris: Gallimard-Pléiade).

Auden, W. H. (1940) "In Memory of Sigmund Freud." *Selected Poetry.* New York: Modern Library (1958) pp. 54–58.

Bauman, Z. (2007) *Consuming Life.* Cambridge, MA: Polity Press.

Benedict, R. (1946) *The Chrysanthemum and the Sword – Patterns of Japanese Culture.* Boston, MA: Houghton Mifflin Co.

Burlingham, M. J. (1989) *The Last Tiffany: A Biography of Dorothy Tiffany Burlingham.* New York: Atheneum.

Boyer, J. W. (1995) *Culture and Political Crisis in Vienna. Christian Socialism in Power, 1897–1918.* Chicago: University of Chicago Press.

Burrows, E. and Wallace, M. (1999) *Gotham – A History of New York City to 1898.* New York: Oxford University Press.

Capshew, J. H. (2014) "History of Psychology, since 1945. A North American Review," in *A Historiography of the Modern Social Sciences*, ed. R. E. Backhouse and P. Fontaine (Cambridge: Cambridge University Press), pp. 144–183.

Carwardine, R. (1996) "'Antinomians' and 'Arminians': Methodists and the Market Revolution," in *The Market Revolution in America: Social, Political, and Religious Expressions, 1800–1880*, ed. Melvyn Stokes and Stephen Conway (Charlottesville: University Press of Virginia).

Danto, E. A. (2009) "A New Sort of 'Salvation Army': Historical Perspectives on the Confluence of Psychoanalysis and Social Work." *Journal of Clinical Social Work* 37, pp. 67–76.

de Forest, J. B. (1881) *A Short History of Art.* New York: Phillips & Hunt; Cincinnati and Chicago: Walden & Stowe.

Flexner, A. "Is Social Work a Profession?" *General Session Presentation on May 17 at the Forty-Second Annual Session of The National Conference of Charities and Correction*: Baltimore, Maryland May 12–19, 1915.

Frelinghuysen, A. C. and Hutchinson, E. (2006) *Louis Comfort Tiffany and Laurelton Hall: an Artist's Country Estate.* New York: Metropolitan Museum of Art and New Haven: Yale University Press.

Foner, E. (1971) *Free Soil, Free Labor, Free Men: The Ideology of the Republican Party before the Civil War.* London and New York: Oxford University Press.

Freud, S. (1905) *Fragments of an Analysis of a Case of Hysteria. The Standard Edition of the Complete Psychological Works of Sigmund Freud*, Volume VII (1901–1905), pp. 1–122.

Freud, S. (1923) *The Ego and the Id. The Standard Edition of the Complete Psychological Works of Sigmund Freud*, Volume XIX (1923–1925), pp. 1–66.

Freud, S. (1930) *Civilization and its Discontents.* Translated and edited by James Strachey. New York: W. W. Norton & Company, 1961.

Fried, M. (1998) Realism, *Writing, and Disfiguration: On Thomas Eakins and Stephen Crane.* Chicago: University of Chicago Press.

Giddens, A. (1979) *Central Problems in Social Theory: Action, Structure, and Contradiction in Social Analysis.* Berkeley: University of California Press.

Hale, N. G., Jr. (1971) *Freud and the Americans – The Beginnings of Psychoanalysis in the United States, 1876–1917*, New York: Oxford University Press.

Hammack, D. (1988) "Comprehensive Planning before the Comprehensive Plan: A New Look at the Nineteenth-Century American City," in *Two Centuries of American Planning*, ed. Daniel Schaffer (Baltimore: Johns Hopkins University Press), pp. 139–65.

Hijiya, J. A. (1980) "Four Ways of Looking at a Philanthropist: A Study of Robert Weeks de Forest." *Proceedings of the American Philosophical Society*, 124/6 (December 17), pp. 404–418.

Homberger, E. (1994) *Scenes from the Life of a City. Corruption and Conscience in Old New York*. New Haven: Yale University Press.

Howe, D. W. (2007) *What hath God Wrought: The Transformation of America, 1815–1848*. New York: Oxford University Press.

Howe, D. W. (1991) "Charles Sellers, the Market Revolution, and the Shaping of Identity in Whig-Jacksonian America." Review of Charles Sellers, *The Market Revolution: Jacksonian America, 1815–1846* (New York: Oxford University Press, 1991), in Noll, M. A., ed. (2001) *God and Mammon: Protestants, Money, and the Market, 1790–1860*. Oxford University Press: pp. 54–74.

Kant, E. (1764) *Observations sur le sentiment du beau et du sublime*. in *Oeuvres philosophiques* I. *Des premiers écrits à la Critique de la raison pure*, Ferdinand Alquié, ed. (Paris: Gallimard-Pléiade 1980), pp. 449–509.

Koplos, J. and Metcalf, B. (2010) *Makers: A History of American Studio Craft*. University of North Carolina Press.

Menand, L. (2017) "Why Freud survives." *New Yorker Magazine*, August 28, 2017.

New York Times (1914) "MISS TIFFANY, BRIDE OF DR. BURLINGHAM; Youngest Daughter of L. C. Tiffany Weds House Surgeon of Roosevelt Hospital IN LONG ISLAND CHURCH Simple Country Wedding with Breakfast at Laurelton Hall, Oyster Bay - Autumnal Decorations." *New York Times* (September 25, 1914), p. 11.

Newton, J. (1779) "Amazing Grace." *Olney Hymns*, Olney, Buckinhamshire, pp. 53–54.

Rameau, J-P. with de Cahusac, L. (?) (1763), *Abaris ou les Boréades*. Opera (unpublished).

Ricoeur, P. (1977) *Freud and Philosophy: An Essay on Interpretation*. Savage, D. (trans.) New Haven: Yale University Press.

Rydell, R. W. and Kroes, R. (2005) *Buffalo Bill in Bologna: The Americanization of the World, 1869–1922*. Chicago: University of Chicago Press.

Saxton, A. (2003) *The Rise and Fall of the White Republic: Class Politics and Mass Culture in Nineteenth-Century America*. London: Verso Books.

Schmiesing, K. (2017) *Merchants and Ministers: A History of Businesspeople and Clergy in the United States*. Lanham: Kensington Books.

Wheeler, C. (1918) *Yesterdays in a Busy Life*. New York, Harper and Brothers.

Wilde, O. (1891) "The Soul of Man under Socialism." *The Artist as Critic. Critical Writings of Oscar Wilde*, ed. Richard Ellmann (Chicago: University of Chicago Press, 1982), pp. 255–289.

Williams, W. A. (1988) *The Contours of American History*. New York: W.W. Norton.

Chapter 9

Step by step

Vienna between the Wars: an Overview

Alexandra Steiner-Strauss

> Our only wish is for peace and tranquility.
> But the reality right now is not very keen on fulfilling our wishes.
> Anna Freud to Ernest Jones, February 23, 1934

"The breakdown of the Austrian Empire and the aftermath of the First World War, the famine, the hunger riots in Vienna and the runaway inflation have often been described. They destroyed the world in which I had grown up; and there began a period of cold and hot civil war, which ended with Hitler's invasion of Austria, and which led to the Second World War." In these words of witness, Karl Popper (2002, p. 31) captures the historical slide of Austria *entre guerres*. The difficulty with describing the years between 1918 and 1939, however, is made even more difficult because of Austria's unique juxtaposition of two images: one portrays the ravages and ultimate triumph of a populist, militaristic core; the other portrays one of the most accomplished upswings of political progressivism in modern history. A reading of some of Sigmund and Anna Freud's most important books – *Mass Psychology and the Analysis of the Ego, Civilization and Its Discontents* (1930), *Moses and Monotheism* (1939) or *Introduction to Child Analysis* (1927) and *The Ego and the Mechanisms of Defense* (1936) – should be centered within this interwar chronology. With dizzying rapidity, the Freud family saw the Austro-Hungarian monarchy end along with World War I, the republic of German Austria proclaimed, the rise of a red, modern Vienna, civil wars between the parties of the left and the right, the shift to an authoritarian, Christian-social state under Chancellor Engelbert Dollfuss, his assassination during the Nazi "July Coup" of 1934, the seizure of power by Kurt Schuschnigg until his Berchtesgaden meeting with Adolf Hitler on February 12, 1938, and the ascent of the National Socialist Arthur Seyss-Inquart to Minister of the Interior. When Schuschnigg's referendum to prevent the Nazis from seizing power in Austria failed, National Socialist troops invaded Vienna on March 13, 1938, unopposed. The Freuds left for their London exile three months later. A recent transnational analysis of interwar Vienna is revealing. Interpreting these years as "a lesson in the process of authoritarian transformation of societies," Wenninger and Dreidemy (2013, p. 7) posit that

> the genesis of the dictatorship under Engelbert Dollfuss and Kurt Schuschnigg offers itself as a convenient microcosm to study processes that played out, along similar lines, during the interwar period in many other countries. More than that: since numerous European conflicts grew out of the Austrian situation, it is by no means exaggerated to say that in the early 1930s, Austria's ideological, organizational and military fields should be investigated and understood as a center of the European struggle between democracy and fascism.

The title of this essay is taken from a speech by Engelbert Dollfuss, who in 1933 announced he would "do everything step by step to force the Marxists to their knees" (Lewis, 1990, p. 111). And Dolfuss did this exactly – step by step, the systematic diffusion of fascism transformed the young republic into an authoritarian state with a united party (the Patriotic Front) and a new constitution. Democratic suffrage was banned along with Social Democracy and its institutions. Interestingly, the Nazi Party was banned as well. To date, the assessment of this period between 1934 and 1938 remains the subject of intense controversy between historians and politicians: "For more than sixty years, scholarly inquiry into the Dollfuss/Schuschnigg era has suffered from divisiveness and politicization perhaps best reflected in the use of the charged terms *Ständestaat* (corporate state) versus Austrofascism. … While those on the Right have tended to portray the Dollfuss/Schuschnigg governments strictly as a defensive bastion against Nazi Germany, those on the Left have indicted these governments as decisive contributors to the successful *Anschluss* through their rejection of parliamentary democracy" (Lassner and Bischof, 2003, p. 1). The contrasting narratives endure and the two chancellors, Engelbert Dollfuss and Kurt Schuschnigg, are rated very differently depending on the political affiliation of the narrator.

Austria was never exempt from the political upheavals and uncertainties of World War I, nor the war's virtually incalculable impact on European society and governments. But unlike other countries, postwar Austria assumed an entirely new state and civic identity. As Eli Zaretsky (2006, pp. 151ff.) writes

> During the war, Western civilization perished and were reborn. No one could deny the wild hate of those murderous years: ten million people killed or maimed during four and a half years of fighting meant two million deaths each year of the war, six thousand every day. The

> four-month battle on the Somme alone claimed half a million lives in 1916; the battle of Verdun killed seven hundred thousand in ten months.

Zaretsky continues: "contemporaries were completely oblivious to the extent of destruction and destruction. ... The war not only shook the liberal worldview of the nineteenth century, it also profoundly changed the identity of the survivors." For Austria, World War I ended the Habsburg monarchy while the proclamation of the Republic of German Austria created a new geographical and political state. Catastrophe descended on the new country. Because Hungary, Bohemia, Moravia, Silesia and Galicia had supplied the Austrian part of the former monarchy with food (especially grain and meat), their loss resulted in the famines of 1918 through 1921. At the same time, the Spanish flu and tuberculosis killed off large swaths of the population. Otto Wagner, Koloman Moser, Gustav Klimt, Victor Adler, and Sophie and Heinrich Freud, all died in these epidemics. Fuel and paper shortages decreased productivity; war-related inflation made savings worthless. Changed political structures saw civil servants and military dismissed from their stable government positions, decimating the once-prosperous middle class. Out of this chaos, what eventually formed was a starkly divided Austrian identity: the conservative Catholic bourgeoisie formed the electorate for the Christian-Social Party, while the working class and the liberal bourgeoisie were represented mainly by the Social Democratic Party. A third force was formed by the Pan Germans who saw a small Austria as unworkable and promulgated the country's absorption into Germany. In any case, unification with Germany was banned by the Versailles peace treaties in 1919 (Figure 9.1).

Within this bourgeoisie, the Freud family found itself relying on donations from friends and foreign patrons to survive the war. Freud was relieved that his sons Martin, Ernst and Oliver all returned home safely, whereas 1,000,000 soldiers of the k.u.k. Monarchy (*kaiserlich und königlich,* or Imperial and Royal) had died at the front. Speaking to the social and economic disparities made starkly visible by World War I, a changed Freud gave his famous lecture at the Budapest Psychoanalytic Congress in September 1918 and focused on two new themes: the state should join the analysts in making therapy widely available and the need for consistency in psychoanalytic training.

World War I had, in some sense, benefited the field of psychoanalysis. Among the analysts, Sándor Ferenczi, Ernst Simmel and Karl Abraham treated large numbers of traumatised soldiers suffering from war neurosis (or shell shock), and though some argued that it allowed the military to send soldiers back into combat, Freud saw it as genuine progress (Danto, 2016). In fact, psychoanalysis gained a completely new sociopolitical significance. The value of psychoanalysis for the treatment of mental problems

Figure 9.1 Postcard promoting the *Anschluss* with Germany, 1918.

was recognised; the word "trauma" took on a completely new meaning; and pan-European institutions were created to handle the mental health needs of the general population, children and adolescents included. Anna Freud took a note. Along with Alfred Adler, August Aichhorn and Siegfried Bernfeld, she developed some of the first psychoanalytically oriented facilities for Viennese youth. As Helene Deutsch told the 12th International Psychoanalytic Congress in 1931, in Wiesbaden,

> Much of this attraction of the Viennese Training Institute is due to the particularly successful work of Anna Freud and August Aichhorn. The latter's courses for welfare workers and educators are extraordinarily popular and have already assumed the character of a regular training course.
>
> (Mühlleitner & Reichmayr, 1995, p. 109)

Siegfried Bernfeld was connected to the Vienna Circle with Moritz Schlick and Ernst Mach, and also to Karl and Charlotte Bühler's Psychological

Institute at the University. The young republic welcomed social scientists, among them Paul Lazarsfeld, Marie Jahoda, Egon Brunswik and Otto Neurath.

> Back in Vienna we were all full of energy and excitement. It was like exploring a whole new continent, and we were the explorers and had a chance to change things. (...). Even in the darkest years after 1930, much of that hope and expectation remained in the midst of all the doubt all skepticism,

recalled Anna Freud (Coles, 1991, p. 9). Against a backdrop of postwar shortages and economic crises, this sweep of progressivism would influence Anna Freud all her life. With the support of Otto Bauer's influential journalism for *Arbeiter-Zeitung*, Jakob Reumann was elected Vienna's first Social Democratic mayor when his party, whose successful campaign promoted a sociopolitical model of a "new" human being, won the Vienna municipal elections on May 4, 1919. In the first years of the grand coalition (1919–1920), a groundswell of new federal legislation fundamentally improved the lives of many Austrians: social security laws and tenant protection, labor law innovations such as paid holidays and the eight-hour working day, health and social insurance, and the introduction of workers' councils. Reumann kept to the vision of a socially just city and society. Social Democracy built its own culture, with a network of child and youth organisations, workers' training centers with lectures and lending libraries, its own art center, sports clubs and political associations. Workers' housing, such as the community apartment cluster in Ottakring which was considered exemplary throughout Europe, combined library, residence, lecture halls and even laboratories. Designed for family life at an affordable rent and under decent conditions (though some critics say that the apartments were largely used by the liberal middle class), the buildings were adorned with the well-known symbol of Red Vienna. The Karl Marx-Hof in Vienna's 19th District or the Reumann-Hof in the Margareten neighborhood are among the best-known examples. Reforming Vienna's housing policy was Hugo Breitner's priority. A brilliant city councilor, Breitner's financial policy included a range of "luxury taxes" which financed municipal projects while bringing postwar hyperinflation under control. In broadly parallel strokes, Julius Tandler made enormous progress in modern social and health care, while Otto Glöckel transformed the school system (Figure 9.2).

The *Arbeiter-Zeitung* became one of the most important daily newspapers in Austria. In the natural and social sciences, members of the "Vienna Circle" pioneered new epistemologies from logical positivism to theoretical physics. The research tradition of the famous University of Vienna Medical School continued, especially once young republic's scientists won a string of Nobel Prizes: Fritz Pregl (1923), Richard Zsigmondy (1925),

Figure 9.2 Kinderübernahmestelle Vienna IX, Day Nursery 1929.

Julius Wagner-Jauregg (1927), Karl Landsteiner (1930), Erwin Schrödinger (1933), Victor Franz Hess (1936) and Otto Loewi (1936).

In the cultural sphere, productions of international significance were staged despite the city's financial constraints. In 1919 the Vienna State Opera showcased the world premiere of Richard Strauss' *Die Frau ohne Schatten* based on a libretto by Hugo von Hofmannsthal. In 1920, Max Reinhardt, Richard Strauss, Hugo von Hofmannsthal and Alfred Roller launched the Salzburg Festival, which was planned as an Austrian counterpart to Bayreuth. David Josef Bach, the head of the Social Democratic Art Center, organised major music and theater festivals in Vienna in 1920 and 1924. With the appointment of Richard Strauss as director of the Vienna State Opera, the city could pride itself on hosting one of the most important modern composers and a musician of world renown (if politically conservative). Erich Korngold's *Die Tote Stadt*, Hans Pfitzner's *Palestrina*, Alban Berg's *Wozzeck*, Ernst Krenek's *Jonny spielt auf* and Brecht and Weill's *Three Penny Opera* all premiered in Vienna as well. Artists like Oskar Kokoschka, Richard Gerstl, Anton Hanak and the architects of the new objectivity (Josef Frank's international *Werkbundsiedlung* exhibit in 1932, for example) conveyed innovative mergers of art and everyday reality (Figure 9.3).

Figure 9.3 Oskar Kokoschka, Overview of the Kinderheim Wilhelminenberg, 1931.

From the perspective of the performing, fine and applied arts, Vienna sustained an equal, if not greater, rise to the "second modernity" of the 1920s seen in Berlin, Paris, London or Moscow.

The end came suddenly, though not without warning. On January 30, 1933, Adolf Hitler became German Chancellor; the *Nationalsozialistische Deutsche Arbeiterpartei* (NSDAP) gained a legitimising majority in the German elections of March 5, 1933. Anti-Semitic riots and Nazi terrorism intensified. The German Nationals, initially represented in Vienna mainly by the corps of academic fraternities, increased in numbers, strength and violence from the 1920s onward. Although Jews had been granted legal equality in 1867 during the monarchy (a measure resented by Karl Lueger and the pan-German nationalist Georg Schönerer), Jewish students and professors at the University were singled out for virulent physical attacks and beaten unprotected by the police. The Christian Social Party and the pan-German nationalists, alarmed by the large number of Jews among the Austromarxists, distributed conservative pamphlets and election posters demanding the removal of Julius Tandler, Hugo Breitner and Otto Bauer. Reaction to the assassination of Moritz Schlick (who was not Jewish but a philosopher) on the steps of the main building in 1936 showed the strength of academic anti-Semitism (Figure 9.4).

Figure 9.4 University of Vienna, Moritz Schlick commemorative site.

The National Socialist students and professors enacted a particularly violent enmity against Jews and Social Democrats at the medical faculty. Muriel Gardiner, an American psychoanalyst in training, remembered the scenes vividly:

> "Anti-Semitism was nothing new in Vienna, and even before I entered medical school, perhaps long before, it was known that of the two anatomical sections in the two wings of the Anatomy Building, a tract of Jews and Socialists were frequented and the other of Christian-Social and anti-Semites. Now it became clear that in the latter tract many were Nazis. Often they tried to attack the socialists and sometimes became violent. I can remember my first experience of this kind: I was sitting at a long dissecting table with several other American Jewish students when one of them shouted in English, 'Come, the Nazis are coming! Keep the knives ready!' Somehow there was no bloody battle back then, but worse things happened in other cases (when I was not there) when Jewish students were injured and even toppled out of windows.
>
> (Gardiner, 1989, pp. 45ff.)

Like many other psychoanalysts – among them Wilhelm Reich, Otto Fenichel, and Grete and Eduard Bibring – who took medical degrees at the University of Vienna, Muriel Gardiner studied at the First Anatomy Institute headed by Julius Tandler, a Jew and a Socialist (Ferdinand Hochstetter, a known advocate of Nazi racial hygiene theory, directed the Second Institute). Pan-German National, openly anti-Semitic deans and departmental directors (Wenzel Gleispach, Wolfgang Abel), kept Jews away from important university posts and positions. Despite their advanced academic credentials, they were compelled to teach outside the University system and relegated to "private professorships" (Hanak-Lettner, 2015; Taschwer 2015). Among the Jewish students, membership in the Emunah community, a student union to which Martin Freud belonged, provided a measure of unity (M. Freud, 1957, p. 164). Sigmund Freud became an honorary member of the Emunah in his later years.

With paramilitary groups like the *Heimwehren* on the Right, and the Republican Defense Alliance led by Julius Deutsch on the Left, both parties were primed for combat. Even during the 1920s, as the Austrian National Socialists sought to emulate Germany's rising NSDAP, the local Christian Socials clashed repeatedly with the Social Democrats. The aggressive use of new media such as posters, leaflets, photographs and films, as well as a strong emotionalising language, intensified the ideological contrast between red and black, between city and country. The first big clash – and the start of the formative events of the 1930s – were the "Schattendorf shots" on January 30, 1927, and the fire of the Palace of Justice on July 15. The January 30th meeting of the *Frontkämpfervereinigung*, in the Burgenland village of Schattendorf, had resulted in an armed dispute with the Republican Defense League, and a *Schutzbündler* and a schoolchild killed. In the newspapers, the campaign for the federal elections of April 1927 focused on nothing else.

On April 20, 1927, the *Arbeiter Zeitung* published the *Kundgebung des geistigen Wien* [Announcement of Intellectual Vienna] which responded to the growing political tensions.

> In view of the political struggle in this city, we feel obliged to our conscience, to make the following statement: The essence of Spirit [Geist] is above all Freedom, which is now endangered and we feel obligated to protect it. The struggle for a higher humanity and the battle against inertia and desolation will always be ready for us. We are ready now.

In addition to Sigmund Freud, this statement was signed by the range of cultural and political leaders who made Red Vienna great: Alfred Adler, Karl Bühler, Hans Kelsen, Robert Musil, Franz Werfel, Alma Mahler, Oskar Strnad, Anton Webern, Egon Wellesz, Franz Cizek and many other supporters. And yet, or as some say surprisingly, the Christian Social Party won with Ignaz Seipel as Chancellor. It was a great blow to social democracy. The trials of the Schattendorf's shooters started in June 1927 and ended the following month with their virtual acquittal. Tensions erupted on July 15. A general strike of the municipal electrical

Figure 9.5 Fire at the Palace of Justice, Vienna 1927.

workers was called. The trams stopped. Protesting workers marched first to the university, then around the Ringstrasse to the Palace of Justice which was set on fire. Police and military intervention resulted in 94 dead and talk of civil war spread like the fire itself (Figure 9.5).

Images of the Palace of Justice fire burned deeply into Austria's literary memory. Started in the 1930s, published in 1956, Heimito von Doderer's 1400-page novel *The Demons* was dedicated to the events of 1927. Elias Canetti (1982, p. 253) described the great fire in his autobiography *The Torch in My Ear*.

> Fifty-three years have passed and the agitation of that day is still in my bones. It was the closest thing to a revolution that I have physically experienced. Since then, I have known quite precisely that I would not have to read a single word about the storming of the Bastille. I became a part of the crowd, I fully dissolved in it, I did not feel the slightest resistance to what the crowd was doing.

Some of the most important works on group phenomena were written by Austrians who, in their youth, had witnessed the burning of the Palace of Justice and the power of an enraged mass. Wilhelm Reich wrote, *The Mass Psychology of Fascism* in 1933; in 1960 Canetti wrote *Crowds and Power*. The writer Hermann Broch, who had been analyzed by Freud, dealt with the "mass mania" and designed a "mass brain theory" in the novel *The Enchantment*. He even founded a Research Institute for Mass Hysteria before his emigration in 1938. In 1921 Sigmund Freud, still recovering from

World War I and anticipating the events of the 1920s and 1930s, wrote the essay *Mass Psychology and the Analysis of the Ego* in which he referred, inquiringly, to the studies of Gustave Le Bon's *Psychology of the Masses*, Ludwig Kraskovic's *The Psychology of Collectivities* (1915), Wilfred Trotter's *Instincts of the Herd in Peace and War* (1916) and William McDougall's *The Group Mind* (1920). The experience of the masses and mass movements in World War I had greatly increased and changed the understanding of the crowd as a factor in political and cultural discourse. In the 1920s and 1930s, masses, or crowds, took on political significance, and also – as in the case of the Palace of Justice – the sense of threat:

> One could also say that the phenomenon of modern violent masses is one of the most significantly irritating experiences for traditional humanism as classical enlightenment – because when they are organized in masses, human beings are able to deny humanistic behavior and the capacity for self-responsibility,

explains the Viennese cultural historian Wolfgang Müller-Funk (2012, S. 177). All the major parties, the National Socialists included, tried to mobilise, politicise and manipulate the masses. In 1931, for example, the *Heimatschützer* staged a "March on Vienna" based on Mussolini's "March on Rome" (*Pfrimer-Putsch*). Outlawed National Socialists regularly organised "walks" across the Ring and the Social Democrats organised mass parades and festivals celebrating, for example, May 1st (Figure 9.6).

Figure 9.6 May 1st Parade, Vienna 1931.

The Christian Social Chancellor Engelbert Dollfuss, in office since 1932 and a declared opponent of Austria's *Anschluss* to Germany, made the unfortunate decision of responding to the NSDAP seizure of power in Germany by banning both the NSDAP and the Social Democratic *Schutzbund*. On March 4, 1933, Dollfuss abolished the Parliament. In his speech at the Vienna Trabrennplatz on September 11, 1933, during the first general appeal of the Fatherland Front in the context of Catholic Day, he set out new guidelines for the authoritarian state based on Christian values:

"We reject *Gleichschaltung* and terror. We demand an elevated Christian, German Austrian state under strong, authoritarian leadership! Authority does not mean arbitrariness; authority is ordered power; it is the leadership of responsible, selfless, dedicated men." And after the abolishment of the Parliament came the new "Constitution of the Federal State of Austria of April 24/ May 1, 1934: In the name of God, the Almighty, from which all right emanates, the Austrian people receive their Christian, German state" (Preisner & Löhning, 2018, p. 334) (Figure 9.7).

This "acceptance" quickly led the way to its opposite, the stream of forced exile. Otto Bauer was banished immediately and wrote this interesting critique from Prague:

> We had already made a mistake. By filing a motion in Parliament, we sought to prevent the Dollfuß-Fey government from responding to a two-hour protest strike by the railroaders on March 4th. Since the government had a majority of only one vote, every vote counted. But

Figure 9.7 Engelbert Dollfuss, February 1934.

we lost a voice in that Renner presided as President of the National Council and therefore could not vote. (…) That's why Renner resigned from my presidency – because of a conflict with the Christian Socials. The Christian Social and the Greater German Vice President had resigned. In the following days, Hitler won his big election victory. But in Austria, in our eagerness to protect the threatened railroaders, we had not considered the direct influence that the revolution in Germany could exert on our country. Thus, it was Renner's resignation from the Dollfuss government that in advertently provided the pretext for eliminating Parliament.

(Bauer, 1934, p. 24)

In this way, Dollfuss wanted to prevent the NSDAP (which was gaining more and more votes in Austria) from coming to power "democratically" and at the same time eliminate the working-class struggle and the *Schutzbund*. Proximity to Mussolini's Italy promised – for the time being – military protection against Hitler's Germany.

In February 1934, the Republican *Schutzbund* rose up against the Dolfuss government and failed. Today, the bullet holes remain carved into the *Gemeindebauten* walls, echoing Julius Deutsch's description of the attacks (Figure 9.8):

Figure 9.8 Bullet holes in the Karl Marx-Hof, 1934.

> The fight for the Karl Marx-Hof was one of the heroic acts of the February conflicts. The army had enclosed it with an iron ring. Their infantry used rifles and machine-guns to shoot up the front of the building. On the Hohe Warte, protected from the *Schutzbund* open fire, the artillery showered the Karl Marx-Hof with a hail of heavy shells, although there were hundreds of women and children in the apartments.
>
> (Deutsch, 1947, p. 13)

Deutsch quotes a worker who had participated in the *Schutzbund* battles: "We thought of ourselves as the legal defenders of the Austrian constitution, which the Federal Chancellor had dispensed with in March 1933.... We were all very tired; we felt we had lost a battle, but not the war." This optimism would not be fulfilled, of course; for Austrian Social Democracy, the war was lost for eleven years after February 1934. Any ongoing signs of social democracy were hidden and illegal (Maimann & Mattl, 1984). When Deutsch's book was republished in 1947, this narrative is introduced with the following explanatory text: "The following report on the heroic struggle of the Republican *Schutzbund* is taken from his book *The Civil War in Austria*, of which only a few hundred copies could be smuggled across the border to Austria. The few who owned it treasured it as a precious and at the same time dangerous treasure, because its possession meant prison and a detention camp."

Muriel Gardiner also remembered the attack. "When the shots started on Monday, February 12, 1934," she wrote (1989, p. 11)

> I was in my analytic session with Ruth Mack Brunswick, in her apartment in the Hasenauerstraße in Vienna's 18th district. Army units and police of the fascist Dollfuss government had begun the attack on the large residential buildings, where they suspected gatherings of armed members of the Socialist Defense Association. (...) Already in many places police and soldiers were standing with machine guns, military vehicles drove on the streets. The trams had actually been stopped and cleared; only a few civilians or civilian vehicles were seen. I remember the day as dark and cold – but perhaps that was because of the scary atmosphere of impending disaster, like the onset of a solar eclipse.

Dollfuss took the uprising as an occasion to ban all parties except for the Fatherland Front. The rights to vote, assemble and demonstrate were abolished; newspapers were censored; and the trade unions and broadcasting companies put under state control. Social-democratic culture and its innovations were systematically decimated: almost all the workers' libraries and art centers were closed; social-democratic and Marxist literature was removed from the general libraries; the workers' newspaper was banned and, though printed in Prague, could be brought into Austria illegally at the risk of prison or detention camp. In 1934, the camp Wöllersdorf was set up, to which the National Socialists and the leaders of the Social Democrats were taken.

Both Dollfuss and Schuschnigg not only built their states on the power of the executive (police, army and administration), but also benefited from the active support of major industrialists, the Catholic Church and the monarchists. Interestingly, some of Vienna's Jews (most of whom were Social Democrats) could be found to favor Dollfuss and later Schuschnigg, in the hope that these regimes would ward off the terror of German National Socialism. Martin Freud explains his interpretation of the Freud family's paradoxical position:

> The second civil war occurred in the summer of 1934. Hitler had but recently assumed power in Germany and the Nazis now tried to get Austria into their grip. Because Austria's army and police force had not yet been seriously undermined by Nazi conspiracy and intrigue, they failed this first time and the failure gave father and his family another four years of freedom in our native land. The Freud family were anything but neutral during this second civil war; our sympathies were with the Chancellor Dolfuss and his successor, Schuschnigg" (M. Freud, 1957, p. 62). Martin's sister offered another view. "Our only wish is for peace and tranquility," Anna Freud wrote to Ernest Jones on February 23, 1934. "But the reality right now is not very keen on fulfilling our wishes."

For Austrians raised since February 1934, the date has had a profound impact on the nation's collective memory. The civil war-like state and the ensuing wave of arrests and releases of NSDAP members, and then of Social Democrats, made for a native anxiety. Karl Seitz, Hugo Breitner, Robert Danneberg, Julius Deutsch, Otto Glöckel and many other significant Social Democrats and Communists were dismissed from their posts, arrested and often imprisoned. Otto Bauer and Julius Deutsch fled to Brno and Prague. The first wave of what is politely called emigration but is actually forced exile from Vienna started after July 1934, with Social Democrats, Marxist and Jewish politicians, scientists, writers and artists: Otto Neurath (1934 Prague), Josef Frank (1934 Sweden), Helene and Felix Deutsch (1935 USA), Stefan Zweig (1934 London), Alfred Adler (Scotland then USA, 1937), Marie Jahoda (1937), Paul Lazarsfeld (1935 USA), Hilde Spiel (1936 London), Karl Popper (1937 New Zealand) and Ernst Gombrich (1936 London) (Städtler, 1993; Warren, 2009).

In 1936, Kurt Schuschnigg signed the "July Agreement," which obliged Austria to coordinate with Germany on foreign policy and lift the ban on the NSDAP (Figure 9.9).

Figure 9.9 Kurt Schuschnigg, Vienna, September 1934.

Freud analyzed the event. "Our political situation seems to become more and more gloomy," he wrote to Ernest Jones on March 2, 1937. "The invasion of the Nazis can probably not be checked; the consequences are disastrous for analysis as well. The only hope remaining is that one will not live to see it oneself. The situation is similar to that of 1683, when the Turks were outside Vienna. At that time military reinforcements came over the Kahlenberg – today nothing like that is to be expected. ... If our city falls, then the Prussian barbarians will swamp Europe. Unfortunately, the power that has hitherto protected us – Mussolini – now seems to be giving Germany a free hand. I should like to live in England like Ernst, and travel to Rome, like you" (Paskauskas, 1993, p. 757). Between 1936 and 1938 National Socialists moved into public office. On February 12, Adolf Hitler demanded that Schuschnigg promote Arthur Seyss Inquart, the National Socialist, to Minister of the Interior and also cancel the referendum on a possible *Anschluss* with Germany. One month later, Schuschnigg resigned and Seyss-Inquart was appointed Chancellor. On March 13, 1938, the annexation of Austria to Germany was completed. The Nazis erased all traces of the Dollfuss-Schuschnigg years, just as Dollfuss and Schuschnigg had removed signs of social democracy from public spaces. The 1928 monument of the Republic of German Austria, for example, (already contentious because it showed only the social-democratic politicians Victor Adler, Jakob Reumann and Ferdinand Hanusch) was removed in 1934 and not replaced until 1948.

By then, most of psychoanalysts from Vienna and Berlin had already fled abroad, often first to Great Britain and from there to the USA. Asked why the Freud's departure was so late, Anna Freud answered soberly:

> Some knew it immediately and left Germany as early as 1933. But we lived in a neutral country and yet had to recognize what the whole world began to recognize: that Hitler and his murderous troops would invade one country after another. The death camps, the conquest – that came later. Sure, Nazi anti-Semitism was the worst thing. But even then, you must remember that in the shadow of one's entire life we are rather appalled to hear only five percent of what we have become accustomed to here and now. That would alert you. We, too, of course, were alarmed, but we had already survived decades of such behavior.
>
> (Coles, 1991, p. 44)

Anna Freud did return to Vienna but not until 1971 – and for short stays at that. Today, the city of Vienna commemorates her pioneering work in the field of practical child analysis at the "Anna Freud Kindergarten" and maintains the same building on Rudolfsplatz where Maria Montessori's progressive education methods for a "Haus des Kindes" were fulfilled and Anna Freud and Dorothy Burlingham set up the Jackson Nursery for toddlers.

In Conclusion

After the 1918 collapse of the old European state systems, Europeans themselves were confronted with a completely different attitude to life, social, political and personal. Walter Gropius (Gropius, 1919, p. 11) aptly put it in 1919: "Today's artist lives in an era of dissolution without guidance. He stands alone. The old forms are in ruins, the old human spirit is invalidated and in flux toward a new form." Tragically crystallized as the 'New Order' in Austria and Germany under Hitler's Nazi regime, and Stalin's equivalent in the Soviet Union, we ask whether Gropius' 'new form' ended with World War II. A new kind of identity, unforeseeable until 1918, was required. This effort to reshape civic society, arguably still emerging from the shattering of national ego in 1918, began with Austria's First Republic.

As the social historian Jill Lewis (1990, p. 98) views it, the interwar Republic developed in three political phases: the democratic republic (1918–1933), the dictatorship (1933–1934) and the Austrofascist corporate state. Contemporary historians of psychoanalysis like Eli Zaretsky recognise the impact of this sequence on the field. It was despite – or precisely because of – he says, the political turbulence of those twenty years, that Sigmund and Anna Freud created works of lasting effect. From the compelling mechanism of political developments in the years between 1918 and 1938, as this essay has outlined, the struggle for a new Austrian identity emerged.

Illustrations

Figure 9.1 Color postcard, 1918; Front: image of Austria's *Anschluss* with Germany. Back, printed poem: "They wanted to haunt us to pieces / hit us to the marrow / Now we want to build the bridge / Because eternity makes strong!" (Ella Triebnigg). Private Collection

Figure 9.2 Children's Day Nursery, Vienna's 9th District, 1929. Associated Press b/w photograph, Private Collection

Figure 9.3 Oskar Kokoschka, View of the Kinderheim Wilhelminenberg, 1931, Wienmuseum, © Fondation Oskar Kokoschka, Vevey/2018, Bildrecht

Figure 9.4 Moritz Schlick commemorative site on the Philosophy Staircase, University of Vienna, "Moritz Schlick, Protagonist des Wiener Kreises, wurde am 22. Juni 1936 an dieser Stelle ermordet. Ein durch Rassismus und Intoleranz vergiftetes geistiges Klima hat zur Tat beigetragen" ["Moritz Schlick, leader of the Vienna Circle, was murdered here on 22 June 1936. The fascism and intolerance that had poisoned the general climate underpinned the deed."] Photo: A. Steiner-Strauss

Figure 9.5 Fire at the Palace of Justice, Associated Press b/w photograph date stamped July 28, 1927, Private Collection

Figure 9.6 May Day in Vienna, Associated Press b/w photo date stamped May 5, 1931. Original text (pasted to the back of the photo) "General View of the May Day Celebration in Vienna, with Parade Marching through the Rathausplat(sic). Disturbances were reported in many of the European Capitals." Private Collection

Figure 9.7 Dr Engelbert Dollfuss, Associated Press b/w photo date stamped February 18, 1934. Original text (pasted to the back of the photo) "Dr. Engelbert Dollfuss, Austria's Chancellor, photographed as he spoke to a large gathering of the Christian Socialist Union of Freedom at the Starchand Siedlung in Vienna recently. Left to right: Deputy Kunschak, Friedrich Stockinger, the new Minister of Commerce, and the Chancellor during the speech." Private Collection

Figure 9.8 Bullets in the walls of the Karl Marx-Hof, 1934, b/w postcard, Private Collection

Figure 9.9 Dr Kurt Schuschnigg, Associated Press b/w photo date stamped September 19, 1934. Original text (pasted to the back of the photo) "National Memorial Day Celebrated in Vienna. Dr. Kurt Schuschnigg, the Austrian Chancellor, shown speak during Memorial Day Services at the Burgtor – the great Archimperial Palace. The Burgtor was consecrated as a memorial to Austrians who fell and fought for their country through three centuries from 1618 to 1918." Private Collection

References

Bauer, O. (1934) *Der Aufstand der österreichischen Arbeiter. Seine Ursachen und seine Wirkungen.* (Sozialistische Hefte Folge 20) [The Uprising of the Austrian Workers. Its Causes and Its Effects (Volume 20 of *Sozialistische Hefte*)] Prague: Verlag der Deutschen sozialdemokratischen Arbeiterpartei.

Canetti, E. (1982) *The Torch in my Ear. Memoirs 1921–1931.* Joachim Neugroschel (tr.) New York: Farrar, Straus and Giroux.

Coles, R. (1991) *Anna Freud oder der Traum von der Psychoanalyse.* Frankfurt: Fischer Verlag 1955.

Danto, E. A. (2016) Trauma and the State with Sigmund Freud as Witness. *International Journal of Law and Psychiatry* 48:50–56.

Deutsch, J. (1947) *Der Kampf im Karl-Marx-Hof.* In: *Die Wahrheit über den Februar 1934.* (Sozialistische Hefte Folge 12) [The fight in Karl Marx Hof. In: *The Truth about February 1934.* (Volume 12 of *Sozialistische Hefte*)] Vienna: Sozialistischer Verlag.

Freud, A. to Ernest Jones, Letter of February 23, 1934. In Young-Bruehl, E. (ed.) (2008) *Anna Freud: A Biography*, 2nd edition. New Haven: Yale University Press, p. 290.

Freud, M. (1957) *Glory Reflected. Sigmund Freud – Man and Father.* London: Angus & Robertson.

Gardiner, M. (1983) *Code Name "Mary": Memoirs of an American Woman in the Austrian Underground.* New Haven: Yale University Press.

Gropius, W. (1919) Ja! Stimmen des Arbeitsrates für Kunst in Berlin [Yes! Votes for the World's Council for Art in Berlin], Berlin 1919. In Wilk, Ch. (ed.) (2006) *Modernism. Designing a New World 1914–1939.* London: V&A Publication.

Hanak-Lettner, W. (2015) *Die Universität. Eine Kampfzone* [The University. A Battleground] Vienna: Picus Verlag.

Kundgebung des geistigen Wien [Announcement of Intellectual Vienna], April 20, 1927, Vienna: *Arbeiter Zeitung.*

Lassner, A. and Bischof, G. (2003) Introduction. In Pelinka, A. (2003) *The Dollfuss/Schuschnigg Era in Austria. A Reassessment* (Contemporary Austrian Studies, Vol. 11) New Brunswick, London: Routledge.

Lewis, J. (1990) Conservatives and fascists in Austria 1918–1934. In Blinkhorn, M. (ed.) *Fascists and Conservatives. The Radical Right and the Establishment in Twentieth-Century Europe.* London/Boston/Sydney/Wellington: Unwin Hyman.

Mühlleitner, E. and Reichmayr, J. (1995) The Exodus of Psychoanalysts from Vienna. In Weibel, P. and Stadler, F. (eds.) *Vertreibung der Vernunft -The Cultural Exodus from Austria.* Vienna: Springer Verlag.

Maimann, H. and Mattl, S. (1984) *Die Kälte des Februar. Österreich 1933–1938.* [The February Freeze: Austria 1933–1938] Vienna: Junius Verlag.

Müller-Funk, W. (2012) *The Architecture of Modern Culture: Towards a Narrative Cultural Theory.* Berlin/Boston: Walter de Gruyter & Co.

Paskauskas, R. A. (1993) *The Complete Correspondence of Sigmund Freud und Ernest Jones 1908–1939.* Cambridge: Harvard University Press.

Popper, K. (2002) *Unended Quest. An intellectual Autobiography.* London/New York: Routledge Classics.

Preisner, M. and Löhnig, M. (eds.) (2018): *Quellen zur deutschen Verfassungsgeschichte der Moderne.* Regensburg Edition Rechtskultur.

Stadler, F. (1993) (ed.): *Vertriebene Vernunft I und II. Emigration und Exil österreichischer Wissenschaft 1930–1940* [The Cultural Exodus from Austria]. Vienna and Munich: LitVerlag.

Taschwer, K. (2015) *Hochburg des Antisemitismus. Der Niedergang der Universität Wien im 20. Jahrhundert.* [Stronghold of anti-Semitism. The decline of the University of Vienna in the 20th century] Vienna: Czernin Verlag.

Warren, J. (2009) "*Weiße Strümpfe oder neue Kutten*" [White Stockings or New Cowls. Cultural Decline in Vienna in the 1930s] pp. 32–55. In Holmes, D. and Silverman, L. (2009) *Interwar Vienna. Culture between Tradition and Modernity.* Rochester, NY: Camden House.

Wenninger, F. and Dreidemy, L. eds., (2013) *Das Dollfuss/ Schuschnigg-Regime 1933–1938. Vermessung eines Forschungsfeldes* [The Dollfuss / Schuschnigg regime 1933–1938. A Survey of the Research] Wien-Köln-Weimar: Böhlau Verlag.

Young-Bruehl, E. (2008) *Anna Freud: A Biography*, 2nd edition. New Haven: Yale University Press.

Zaretsky, E. (2006) *Freuds Jahrhundert. Die Geschichte der Psychoanalyse.* [Freud's Century. The history of psychoanalysis] Vienna: Paul Zsolnay Verlag.

Zaretsky, E. (2015) *Political Freud. A History.* New York: Columbia University Press.

Index